To my parents

Acknowledgments

This book is a more or less chronological account of my medical career and background starting in 1967 when I entered college. Most major events are corroborated by official contracts, legal correspondence, department minutes and memos, letters and newspaper articles. The timing of some cases and events over thirty years ago, however, are only estimates and are indicated as such. Several medical textbooks and clinical or scientific studies are quoted and cited within the text.

For information and stories concerning Cannon Mills and the town of Kannapolis, I have drawn heavily from *Cannon Mills and Kannapolis* by Timothy W. Vanderburg; 2013, University of Tennessee Press. I am grateful for this book as it has greatly complemented and added interest to my memoirs. Vignettes concerning my parents and my childhood are largely based on their wonderful autobiographical book *An American Family in the Twentieth Century* (Jeannette M. and William B. Cottrell; 1987, self-published.) Likewise, I am grateful for the textbook *Anesthesia and Neurosurgery* by Cottrell and Turndorf; 1986, C. V. Mosby Company. James E. Cottrell, MD (no immediate relationship to myself); is the former chairman and distinguished professor of the Department of Anesthesia at SUNY in Brooklyn, New York.

My wife, Becky, deserves much credit for allowing me the time away to accomplish the pleasant but time-consuming task of writing.

A special thanks to my good friend, Gerry Dionne, for his intensive review and suggestions, which helped make my story more readable. Also to Lucy Hill for her advice and interest in the writing process.

I am grateful to my beta readers, Angela McConnell, CRNA, Rebecca McCall, CRNA, and Russell Suda, MD, for their interest and suggestions. I thank Bill Swan, MD, for his interest and willingness to discuss and corroborate the early history of the Department of Anesthesia at Cabarrus Memorial Hospital. I am also greatly indebted to Don Smith of CME Computers Made Easy. Without his assistance this project would have been impossible.

Preface

‌

There are several motivators behind this documentation of my career in medicine, and in anesthesiology, as it approaches its conclusion. The primary motive is catharsis; a self-administered psychotherapy reviewing a career full of stressful cases, ego confrontations, financial and political turmoil in the medical community, plus personal challenges involving marriage, divorce, and the problems of raising children in environments of variable stability.

A second reason for this overview is to add to the history of the Cottrell family that my father, William B. Cottrell, successfully initiated with *An American Family in the Twentieth Century* in 1987, and *Descendants of Nicholas Cottrell of Rhode Island* in 1988. Although mine is more autobiographical than these earlier works, I believe it's an appropriate means to a similar end.

A further motivator for the book would be to serve any interested party a means for appreciating the challenges of a medical career from the inside, and to witness how the philosophy and practice of medicine has evolved over the past four decades. Although the first two objectives dominate the content and organization of my story, I would be delighted if it happened to be of interest to readers beyond the family.

I have no political agenda in writing this book. I have found much to like in each phase of my medical career, and at least a little to dislike. Likewise, I do not seek to defend all the decisions and actions I took during my career. My intent is merely to show what it was like to be in the middle of an evolving medical practice. My mistakes are genuinely my own property. No one can take them from me—not that I presume anyone would want to.

Contents

—◦◦◦—

College and Medical School

Sometime in the summer of 1976 in the drab cafeteria of Shands Hospital in Gainesville, Florida, I wolfed down my lunch while commiserating with several other residents about the punishing hours and insane demands of our residency training. At one point an orthopedic resident confessed to me that, while he realized anesthesia played an important role in the outcome of surgery, he didn't understand why anybody would actually choose it as a specialty. He shared this opinion straight-faced, without condescension or vitriol. Apparently, he really believed what he said. Whether intentional or innocent, this challenge to my reason for living triggered a cascade of rebuttal in my mind. Should I explain how the basic skills of airway management and circulatory support inherent in our specialty are universally essential to the survival of critically ill patients? Or should I merely remind him that the biochemical and metabolic activities at the cellular level are essential for health and life itself? No! Such an answer would be ill-received and appear defensive. So I merely smiled at him and said, "I used to feel the same way until I actually did a preceptorship in anesthesia in medical school."

In the forty years since that conversation, I've had ample time to reflect on my career choice and its consequences, not so much in a rueful or judgmental manner, but as an objective means to appreciate how the decision has affected my life. I'd like people to see that the practice of anesthesia is so ingrained in my mindset and so inter-twined with my daily rituals that I sometimes have difficulty distin-guishing my professional self from the rest of my life. I feel like a sled dog on a long cross-country trek. I am always glad to discover when I stop to rest that the harness is not actually part of my body, and that I have a real existence outside of the mission.

So if my life and career as an anesthesiologist are viewed as a cross-country journey, the obstacles and side excursions on that jour-ney were far more varied and menacing than one could imagine. Yet somehow I reached my destination in good shape. The details of how that happened intrigue me even now. To explain them I must go back to 1967. That's when it all began.

Unlike many physicians, I didn't spend my early years dream-ing of becoming a medical doctor. I gravitated toward some field of science, but a career as an astrophysicist or a research chemist seemed to demand greater cerebral chutzpah. Therefore, when I entered the University of Tennessee in September of 1967, I chose to pursue a BS in chemistry as opposed to a premed or engineering curriculum, the other popular fields of study for males with a strong bent toward math and science. Thus I chose a path less traveled not knowing where it would lead.

As it turned out, I did indeed graduate from UT in June 1971 with a BS in chemistry with high honors. Courses in physical and analyt-ical chemistry and advanced math brought out the best in me. For better or worse, I was a full-fledged science nerd, before science nerds were cool.

My social life was another matter. Except for a brief fling with a girl in my calculus class, my social calendar was a blank on the weekends. This was serious; something had to save me from extreme nerdom. My involvement with the AFS (American Field Service) Returnee Club on campus was one escape hatch. UT students who, as high schoolers, had been in an AFS foreign exchange program sponsored a college weekend for all European AFS students then attending high school in Tennessee. I was privileged to chair that planning committee my sophomore year, and served as president of the club my junior year.

A second escape route from the darkest corners of nerdsville was my obsession with exercise and physical fitness. I don't know if it was out of vanity, insecurity, or just an uncomplicated desire to better myself and become a healthy role model, but I was dedicated to staying fit. This meant almost daily workouts including pull-ups, bench presses, squats, running and swimming, all in a carefully planned rotation to avoid injury or burnout. Unencumbered by any conspicuous athletic gifts such as size, speed or quickness, all-round fitness was important to me. During my freshman year I came in third in the mile run with a time of five minutes flat and an hour or so later placed second in the 880-yard run with a time of two minutes and 13.9 seconds in the campus-wide intramural track meet held on the Tom Black Track in April 1968. By my senior year I could do ten reps with 215 pounds on the bench and twenty-five full squats with 185 pounds on my back on a good day. I weighed about 168 pounds at that time.

Fortunately for me I had, and still have, a third stream of interest, a love of folk music and soft rock, especially if it involved the acoustic guitar. This guitar infatuation ignited in the summer of 1966. Returning from Norway on the *Seven Seas* I met several students who could play well enough to bring out my latent guitar lust. Songs by Peter Paul and Mary, Pete Seeger, Bob Dylan, and others were all the craze. I was hooked for life. With the remaining thirty-five dollars from my "Norway cash," I bought my first guitar as soon as I got home. I now own a 1985 Alvarez, a 1990 jumbo Taylor, and a 2012 OM Martin. But that's a story for later.

By the end of my third year at UT (Spring 1970), choices concerning career direction began to monopolize my attention. Yes, I had a solid academic lock on chemistry, but did I really want to be a research chemist? There was a kaleidoscope of doubt. About this time I read an article in *Reader's Digest*, of all places, predicting a shortage of doctors, and there were other pieces in periodicals predicting an excess of certain types of science-oriented graduates. My brother-in-law suggested I apply to medical school. Seems like a no-brainer now, but it was a major shift in thinking at the time. My father was a nuclear physicist, his father a teacher and principal. On my mother's side were a dentist and a chemistry professor at MIT. Plenty of intellectual horsepower in the family tree, but no MDs. So I thought, why not?

I began the process by signing up to take the MEDCAT later in the year and writing to medical schools. I was a curious mix of insecurity and enthusiasm. The job market had nudged me in a specific direction, and I accepted the challenge.

I elected to keep my goal of a BS in chemistry, as an undergraduate degree, even though it meant several senior courses in physical chemistry and quantitative analysis that had little direct relevance to a medical career. This was because I felt an obligation to complete a pre-existing goal. Had I changed my major to a standard premed curriculum, I may have had a slightly easier last year, and possibly been a little better prepared for medical school.

I felt resolved but a little embarrassed when I informed Dr. Shirley, chairman of the Chemistry Department at UT, that I was not going on in chemistry but applying to medical school. To his everlasting credit, and my immediate relief, he responded that he liked the idea that there would be at least a few doctors out in the world with a good solid chemistry background. This cleared the way for me. I completed the BS in chemistry, and without looking back, firmed up the decision to enter medicine.

I applied to five, count them, five medical schools: Emory, Duke, Vanderbilt, UT, and Cornell. Accepted outright at Emory, UT, and Vanderbilt, I was an alternate at both Duke and Cornell. Admittedly, Emory was more expensive than UT, but I needed a change. Somehow I knew a shift in venue would be good for me. My father favored UT, but agreed to support me wherever I went. I feel a deep and abiding gratitude for my parents, who paid my tuition and other major expenses at Emory. I finished medical school debt free, an advantage I didn't fully appreciate at the time. However, I was sufficiently self-aware to know that the least I could do was live frugally.

Apparently, I didn't know the right people because I spent the summer before medical school working at EMCO Williams, a company that made bathroom sinks and countertops, in Sevierville Tennessee. It was a forty-minute drive from my parents' home in what is now Farragut in Knox County. I accepted this job only after unsuccessfully applying at five area hospitals for a summer job as an orderly. I know making countertops was only a summer job, but it was not my idea of career advancement.

The work entailed mixing a limestone compound with resin and a catalyst in a big vat, and pouring the mixture in a timely manner into a mold to harden into the finished product. I tried to pay attention, but on one occasion I forgot to add the catalyst to the mixture. It didn't harden properly. My coworkers helped me dump the gooey mess in a field behind the shop so the boss man wouldn't find out. Each day I came home from work with T-shirts covered with resin and limestone. Surprisingly, some of the shirts survived through medical school as mementos of that summer.

I initially earned $1.80 per hour. This increased to two dollars after a trial period. Unfortunately, the speeding ticket I received driving home on Chapman Highway more than wiped out that day's pay. It's worth noting that I gained a deepened respect for the blue collar workers of east Tennessee. Working shoulder to shoulder keeps you in touch with humanity. When the truck brought a load of fifty-pound bags of limestone, I hefted two bags at a time to keep up with the more macho employees. They treated me as one of the gang, despite knowing that I would soon be entering medical school.

I bought my first car that summer of 1971, a '65 Ford Custom 500 for $350. This was an obvious necessity since I would be going to school in Atlanta. The odometer was stuck on 72,000 miles, I presume because someone had broken it when trying to reset it. When I traded it in six years later it still read 72,000. The only major mechanical problem was a fuel pump that gave up the ghost on I-75 near Hahira, Georgia, a few years after I bought it. The manual gear shift also had a minor idiosyncrasy. Occasionally the gears would lock, requiring me to open the hood and jiggle the gear mechanism to unlock it. Fortunately, this never happened in the middle of a busy street.

Finally I entered Emory Medical School in Atlanta in September 1971 with a strong background in basic science, but essentially no experience or specialized knowledge of medicine. The first year included basic courses in anatomy, biochemistry, and microbiology, all requiring a good bit of reading and memorization. I studied and struggled for mediocre grades. Not only was the subject matter all new to me, but the competition for grades was an order of magnitude higher now. I was in the big leagues now. It was telling that a nursing student with whom I became friendly was astonished that I was unfamiliar with many basic medical terms such as hematocrit. But being a little behind the curve only made me more determined.

In the summer of 1972 I landed a job with the American Red Cross Blood Bank on Monroe Drive in Atlanta. In this job I functioned as an RN. On some days I would obtain vital personal information and do brief exams to assure the volunteer donor was a suitable candidate to give blood. On other days I functioned as a venipuncturist, actually removing blood from the donors. Some days we would collect blood at the main center on Monroe, and other days take the bloodmobile to surrounding towns and businesses for a full day's outing. An adequate supply of safe donor blood is a necessity for many surgical procedures and should not be taken for granted. So this was good experience and highly relevant to my ultimate career in anesthesiology.

Things improved somewhat my second year of medical school. For one thing, the study of physiology that year was more to my liking. This is the study of the body's basic functions from a physics and chemistry point of view. For once I felt I had a slight experiential edge over many students. Also by this time I had moved out of the tiny room in the graduate dorm into a garage apartment off Ridgewood

Avenue, about a half mile from campus. The cost was ninety dollars per month; split two ways, forty-five dollars per month for me. My roommate claimed the better room. My bedroom was actually a screened-in porch that opened into the main living area. Big oak trees kept the room shaded and pleasant in summer, but in the winter the room temperature would get down into the forties, requiring multiple blankets to keep warm.

Sometime in the spring of 1973, an anesthesiologist on the Emory staff announced to the class that there were summer preceptorships in anesthesia available in many hospitals throughout the country, sponsored by the ASA (American Society of Anesthesiologists). After class I told her I would be interested in applying for one of the positions. Unable to leave it there, I added that it was not a likely specialty for me because it seemed to be a boring one. She almost choked when I said that, and quickly corrected my misconception.

That summer of 1973 found me at the Baptist Medical Centers in Birmingham, Alabama. Four weeks were at the hospital on Montvale and the other four weeks were at the older site on Princeton. I admit I was dazzled with the glamour and sophistication of the modern operating room, and likewise impressed by the important roles played by the anesthesiologist and nurse anesthetist. But at that point I had no skills to offer in an operating room. I tried to act like I knew the ropes, but I was more like a puppy exploring an expensively laid dinner table. Already having been chastised for bumping into a sterile table, the chief of anesthesia handed me a spinal needle. Time for some hands-on learning. Of course, I dropped the needle on the floor, contaminating it and delaying the case. Nevertheless, the experience opened my eyes to the importance and excitement of the operating room. It was a worthwhile summer in Birmingham.

Back in Atlanta in September I began my first clinical rotations of medical school. This is when students get their first official exposure to real patients in a real hospital. After a month of psychiatry at the Georgia Mental Health Center on Briarcliff Road, I started my medicine rotation at Grady Hospital in downtown Atlanta. As third-year medical students we made rounds with interns, residents, and attending physicians, and functioned as "junior" doctors. We learned how to write orders, draw blood for lab work, and participate in the major decisions in the care of the mostly indigent patients. We were on call every third night, spent those nights in the hospital, and generally worked at least part of the next day post-call.

Making the important transition from academia to the practical world of medicine was the big challenge of this rotation. It was time to interact with the patients, garner useful information, and make practical recommendations for the treatment of discovered problems. It isn't unusual to find that some students who are strong academically have trouble with this transition. Of course, the converse is also true; some students who are mediocre academically perform very well in the clinical setting. I fell in the latter category.

Grady Hospital is a historical landmark in downtown Atlanta, not far from Georgia State University and Underground Atlanta. Emory uses it as a primary teaching hospital for medical students and many residency programs. The first Grady opened in 1892 with a donation from Henry Grady, an advocate for the "New South" and later editor of the *Atlanta Constitution*. The current building was opened in 1958 at 77 Butler Street. It has twenty-one stories, 953 beds, and is one of the largest public hospitals in the country. Before the days of integration, it was sometimes referred to as the Gradys (plural) because there were distinct wings, some for "colored people" and some for whites only; in effect two hospitals in one. Even after integration in the 1960s, some still refer to it in the plural. It is known as a center of medical training, as a very busy trauma center, and for its chief of neurosurgery, Sanjay Gupta.

I spent many nights in this dreary-looking building, intimidated by the demanding medical and surgery residents. While on call doing a urine analysis on the medical floor at 4 a.m., I looked out on I-75 near the junction of I-20 from the small lab on the fifth floor; it was a bleak vision of my existence in concrete, steel, and endless traffic. I felt like a prisoner doing time. In a few hours I would present my new patients on morning rounds and experience the usual grilling. The days when I was at the top of my class in physical chemistry and advanced differential equations at UT seemed lost in a distant past. What in the dickens had I gotten myself into? A modicum of relief would occur when I got off the next afternoon and could go back to my apartment and crash.

Many students who complete their medicine rotation at Grady consider it a turning point in becoming a doctor. Many go through periods of depression, fatigue, and sleep deprivation, but they usually emerge with a sense of accomplishment and even elation knowing they survived the test: a realization of what medicine is all about.

Medicine was followed by rotations in surgery, OB-GYN, pediatrics, and a brief exposure to anesthesia. By the end of the academic year (May 1974) I had a broadly-based exposure to medicine. I was surviving reasonably well, but had no clear idea which specialty I would pursue. Had I been forced to state a likely candidate, I may have suggested some subspecialty in medicine such as nephrology or pulmonology. Thus far, however, no specialty was calling my name.

Yet there was a bright spot. I was elected by my classmates to represent Emory at the four-day Southern Medical Association's annual meeting in November 1973 in San Antonio at the Hotel Palacio de Rio. It was an honor, but my role was purely passive, attending informational meetings on Medicare and political issues of the times. The highlight was a musical performance at the final dinner by Roger Williams. I received a nice plaque and several years of SMA journals, but I never became active in the society. It all seemed like a dream after being feted in high style at the meeting, I immediately had to return to my stressful medicine rotation at Grady for several more weeks.

At the beginning of the summer of 1974 I qualified to do a clerkship in a military hospital. I requested Walter Reed Medical Center in Bethesda, Maryland, for a rotation in internal medicine. When I reported for duty at Walter Reed in June, however, I found there had been a bureaucratic snafu. No position was available for me in medicine. They seemed a little embarrassed and asked me what other specialty I might prefer. Remembering my interesting experience in Birmingham the previous summer, I said I would be happy to do the clerkship in anesthesia if a spot was open. A quick phone call to the Department of Anesthesia, and I was officially accepted in that department. Fate had directed me toward a specialty that would be my lifetime career. Sometimes things just fall into place.

The chief of anesthesia at that time at Walter Reed was Colonel "Dutch" Lichtman, a gentle giant of a man with a love of anesthesia. Under his aegis I worked alongside the army anesthesia residents, attending their conferences and performing many of the same duties that they did. The patients were veterans. During this time I developed some skills starting IVs, intubating, and doing spinal blocks. Because many of the vets were of World War I vintage, I felt I was working with living history.

Attendings at Walter Reed were experienced, well-trained physicians who were usually there to repay the army for assistance with their medical education. Understandably, there was a high turnover among attendings. I was lucky in that one such physician on staff took a special interest in my education and well-being. He saw that I was a little insecure as a medical student working with residents who were at least two years ahead of me in training. The man, with the distinctive name, Roy Cucchiara, made a difference for me. He made my summer clerkship both enjoyable and an excellent learning experience. In later years I noticed Dr. Cucchiara's name on a number of medical research articles emanating from the Mayo Clinic, arguably the most prestigious medical center in this country. Years later I noted that he became the chairman of the Department of Anesthesia at Mayo Clinic, a major distinction. Later still, he served as chairman of the Department of Anesthesia at the University of Florida Teaching

Hospitals. I always hoped that I might run into him at a national meeting so I could thank him for his encouragement and support. Since it never happened, I'll do it here: thank you, Dr. Cucchiara.

On August 8, nearing the end of the summer clerkship, Dr. Lichtman invited all the residents and myself to his house for a cookout. After we enjoyed our hamburgers and sides we gathered around the TV and watched in amazed silence as President Richard Nixon resigned. It felt strangely coincidental to be in the vicinity of the capital during this historic event. It was not a happy occasion, but I was glad our country was getting this phase of its history over with.

This was the time my career came into focus. Before the summer of 1974 I had been an average medical student without direction. After my clerkship at Walter Reed, however, I had a decisive game plan: specialize in anesthesiology. It all came together. My background in math, chemistry, and physics gave me a depth of understanding of the physiology and pharmacology related to administering anesthesia. My summer experiences in Birmingham and at Walter Reed gave me a jumpstart in experience. The realization of my calling was a very satisfying moment.

My senior year at Emory, 1974–1975, consisted mostly of electives, and was generally less stressful and more enjoyable than the preceding years. Unfortunately, our landlord raised the rent on the garage apartment from $90 per month to $110 per month. That may not sound like much, but for me it was a budget-buster. For a while I shared a house on Briarcliff with three other medical students. The month of March saw me house-sitting for an anesthesia secretary who was visiting her home in South Africa. In all, I had five different addresses my senior year.

Besides frequently changing my addresses, I worked for extra money at Piedmont Hospital as an extern every sixth night during my senior year. I would spend the night there doing scut work: starting IVs and doing EKGs on private patients. This made life easier for the private practice MD and gave me a small source of income. It also served as a great motivator to become proficient at starting IVs in the middle of the night since I was committed to a full day of regular school the next morning.

After graduating from medical school in May 1975, I had a few weeks off before starting my residency July 1 with the University of Florida Teaching Hospitals in Gainesville. This allowed some time for reflection. I had entered medical school fairly clueless about how the system worked, but emerged with a clear focus and confidence that I was pursuing a great specialty. At twenty-six I was still single with no immediate prospects, but I had dated several nurses and was confident that a permanent relationship was going to happen soon.

The world had changed since 1971. We had seen the Watergate scandal, the resignation of a president, and the fall of Saigon. Top hits in 1975 were "Love Will Keep Us Together" by Captain and Tennille and "One of These Nights" by the Eagles. Top movies were *One Flew Over the Cuckoo's Nest*, and *Jaws*. The country was struggling to feel better about itself, and I was determined to show the world that I could play a useful role in the field of medicine.

Residency

My first choice in the matching process for internship and residency was the University of Florida Teaching Hospitals in Gainesville, Florida, and that's exactly what I got. To build a safety net I had also interviewed at Case Western Reserve in Cleveland, Ohio; Mayo Clinic in Rochester, Minnesota; and the University of Miami, Miami, Florida. I found the move to Florida less intimidating than the move to Atlanta had been. For one thing I was older and at least a little more savvy. Gainesville is much smaller and user-friendly than Atlanta. But I think the biggest confidence booster was that I knew I was on a great career path.

The move to Gainesville was not without its challenges, however. All my belongings were easily packed in my '65 Ford except for my desk. It was an old wooden flat-top style with two deep side drawers and one large shallow drawer in the middle. It had belonged to my grandfather, so I was determined to take it. Too big to fit well in the trunk, I had no other choice but to place it there with the end sticking out the back; I did secure the trunk lid over it with a strong rope. I couldn't shake the theme from *Beverly Hillbillies* from my mind as I drove along.

I headed south, not on I-75 to Gainesville, but southwest to Columbus, Georgia, so I could call a nurse I had met during a family practice rotation at the Medical Center in Columbus. I thought we could have lunch, then I would be on my way to Florida. I stopped at the first phone booth I found in Columbus and called the number I had scribbled on a scrap of paper in my billfold. No answer. Why had I not called ahead to prearrange for this potential lunch outing? I have no explanation, except that which plagues all young men when dealing with women, an underdeveloped prefrontal cortex. I was largely operating on impulse.

All I had to do now was head southeast across southern Georgia about sixty miles and hook back up with I-75. This route took me past Plains, Georgia, Jimmy Carter's hometown, and then through the small city of Americus. A few miles past Americus I noticed some dark, ominous clouds that had appeared out of nowhere. In a few more minutes, there was a heavy downpour the likes of which I hadn't seen in years. I have lived and traveled in many states in this country. They all have idiosyncratic and freak weather patterns at times. But nobody can do a sudden cloudburst like south Georgia.

I could barely see the road. Some cars pulled over. I continued very slowly and cautiously. The rain was unrelenting. Deep puddles of water developed and assured my car got a good soaking underneath as well as on all sides. And then I noticed it: a chugging sound from the engine. I continued driving. The chugging got worse. I remembered that once before when the car got a good soaking it made a similar sound. Something in the electrical system was getting damp causing a short. I tried to rev the engine in neutral to prevent it from stalling. Not successful. It chugged to a complete stop. I was able to steer it off the road with its dying chug.

I sat and waited. In about twenty minutes the rain vanished as quickly as it had appeared. I turned the key in the ignition hoping for a miracle. I am not a mechanic, but I know from years of experience which sounds are promising and which are not. This time the sound said, "No way, Jose."

So I was stranded. I weighed my options. I estimated it was only five or six miles to the next town where hopefully a mechanic was on duty. On the one hand I was a good runner; it was not out of the question to go for help on foot. Otherwise, I could sit, wait, and try to flag down a passing vehicle, if there were any. Then I noticed an old white farmhouse about a hundred yards off the road. It was the old Federal style with a tin roof. Behind the house were several dilapidated outbuildings and an overgrown field with occasional pine trees that gradually merged into a pine forest. No brainer. I slowly approached the house looking for signs of life. I saw none except for a few chickens. I climbed the stairs to the front porch; the door was wide open. I knocked. "Hello," I called out. No answer.

I could have entered and used the phone or done anything I wanted; clearly no one was home. The wind was gently blowing the curtains through the open door. It was like a scene from *The Twilight Zone*. Was this some kind of trap? I was a little freaked, so I decided to move on. The vision of this deserted house has haunted me ever since.

Returning to my car, I tried to wave someone down. I could see them avert their glance at the last second to avoid my desperate plea. Naturally, the 1969 movie *Easy Rider* with Peter Fonda and Dennis Hopper came to mind. At the end of the film, riding their motorcycles through south Georgia (or was it north Florida?) a redneck in a pickup truck didn't like their long hair and motorcycles. He did them in with his shotgun.

I was a little shaggy in those days. I wore wire-rim glasses and had on a well-worn Henley shirt that day. Though I wasn't riding a motorcycle and my hair wasn't all that long, maybe I would encounter the wrong person. Or maybe nobody would stop to give me a ride. Suddenly I saw a man in a beat-up pickup truck pull off the road in front of my stalled Ford. He was a little grungy and was missing a tooth or three but had cheerful eyes. Thankfully he offered to give me a lift into town. I climbed in the truck bed and rode alongside several bushel baskets of Georgia peaches.

The peach farmer took me to a large gas station in town that had a mechanic on duty. The mechanic was a clean-cut, somewhat oversized man in his middle thirties. He seemed eager to help. I hopped in his late model pickup truck and he drove me and his ten-year-old son back to my stranded car. Knowing just what to do, he opened the hood and removed the distributor cap. He wiped it clean and then sprayed something on it. We then jump-started the car. It ran beautifully. I was afraid he was going to give me an outrageous bill, like fifteen or twenty dollars. I couldn't believe it when he said, "That's okay, no charge." I began to think I had misjudged south Georgians. I sheepishly offered him a five dollar bill, which was all I could afford, and he immediately handed it to his son. He was a good man.

My grandfather's desk survived the ordeal just fine except for the part that had been exposed to the rain. The desk is in my basement now. I plan to get it refinished someday.

When I arrived in Gainesville, I had barely enough money to pay my first month's rent and buy food until I received my first paycheck. I recall I had to get an attending physician in the department to sign for me so I could open a bank account. I was too proud to ask my parents for money, though I'm sure they would have obliged. When I got my first biweekly paycheck, based on an annual salary of $11,500, I was very happy. I was used to living off about $2000 per year in medical school, excluding tuition and books, etc. Though not much, it had been sufficient.

Many doctors do a year of general internship before starting a specialized residency. At Florida, the internship year was integrated into the residency. Instead of doing a one-year internship followed by a two-year residency, I did a three-year residency that included the internship. Shortly after I finished training in 1978, the requirements increased to a three-year residency in addition to internship—four years in all—in order to be eligible for board certification. Furthermore, some physicians do an extra elective year of training to subspecialize; e.g., cardiac or pediatric anesthesia, making a total of five years of training. Hopefully this helps clarify a confusing topic.

Consequently, following a few weeks off, I went straight from medical school into the anesthesia service at the Gainesville VA Hospital on July 1, 1975. The VA was part of the University of Florida Teaching Hospitals and was directly across Archer Road from Shands, the primary hospital. The chief of anesthesia at the VA during that period was Dr. Haven Perkins, or "Perk," as he was known to everyone at the VA. Perk was well-respected both by surgeons and the anesthesia staff.

Perk had completed a residency in cardiovascular surgery and was in private practice for several years before he did his residency in anesthesia. When asked why he switched specialties, he would say, with a big grin, that he was allergic to the surgery gloves. He was legendary if only because of a verifiable story that he scrubbed in on an open heart surgery case to help the surgery resident sew up a hole in the heart of a VA patient who was crashing. Besides all that he was a good anesthesiologist. I don't know anyone who didn't hold him in high esteem.

I was slightly more advanced than the average beginning anesthesia resident in experience, but still pretty much of a novice in the overall scheme of things. Nevertheless, after about four weeks at the VA, they decided to let me give a general anesthetic by myself; i.e., with no other anesthesia personnel, MD, or nurse anesthetist in the room. It was the rough equivalent of a first solo flight in an airplane. You know the theory behind what you are doing. You have the technical skills to perform the needed tasks. You also know how to think critically and to respond to changing conditions of the flight (anesthetized patient), but you have never put it all together without someone with more experience by your side to assist and reassure you. You are confident, but you also realize that placing a breathing tube incorrectly, just like incorrectly adjusting the ailerons on a plane, could cause the patient to crash and burn.

With my first solo case, I carefully prepared the patient by placing the electrocardiogram (ECG) leads and blood pressure cuff (BPC) on the patient. I checked out the breathing circuit to make sure there were no significant leaks, and then gave the patient oxygen to breathe via the anesthesia mask. I properly positioned the head. I made sure the suction was available. I made sure that the appropriate drugs were available, and that a working laryngoscope, several endotracheal tubes with stylets, and oral airways were available.

I gave the patient 20 ml. of sodium pentothal. After assuring myself that I could ventilate the patient via the mask by squeezing the anesthesia bag and observing his chest rise, I gave him 100 mg. of succinylcholine, also called anectine or sux. Then I carefully opened his mouth with the scissor maneuver (placing my thumb on the lower teeth and my middle finger on the upper teeth and then twisting). I slowly but deliberately slid the laryngoscope blade (a MAC 4, I believe) down the right side of the mouth, being careful to avoid any injury to the teeth or soft tissue, to help sweep the tongue to the left side of the mouth. This was to help me have an unobstructed view of the epiglottis first, and then the glottis, the opening between the vocal cords that leads to the trachea.

I tried to work rapidly so that I could place the endotracheal tube in the trachea and begin to manually ventilate his lungs before he became hypoxic. But I also made an effort to avoid frantic or jerky motions.

My view of the larynx could have been better; mucosal tissue and oral secretions made it difficult to see. After about twenty seconds of adjusting the depth and angle of my laryngoscope blade, I finally had a good view of the vocal cords. I grabbed the endotracheal tube with my right hand, keeping my left hand securely around the laryngoscope handle. I attempted to insert the tip of the endotracheal tube through the glottis, but I couldn't make the tip of the tube go through the cords. It kept slipping off the arytenoid cartilage at the last moment. Finally, I lifted up a little more with the laryngoscope handle and was able to make the tip of the tube enter the trachea. The patient bucked slightly. His oxygen level dropped at least a little, but this was 1975, ten years before the oximeter was available, so I'll never know how low his oxygen saturation actually went. But I felt I was okay. All I had to do now was to turn on the anesthetic gas to keep him asleep and begin to ventilate him via the endotracheal tube.

But then I began to feel a little fretful. The patient seemed to be doing fine, but what would have happened if I had not been able to put the endotracheal tube in the trachea? He had not been easy to ventilate by mask before I gave the anectine. After poking around the glottis with the tube, he could have easily developed a laryngospasm (closure of the glottis by the cords) or a bronchospasm, either of which could make ventilation by mask almost impossible. Every new resident is taught that patients can and have died from failure to ventilate. I noticed sweat on my forehead and I felt a little queasy. I began to worry. Maybe it was a mistake to choose this residency program. If they trusted me to do a case by myself this early in my training, they might not know what they are doing.

Then through the OR door's window, I saw Perk looking in. He had been watching the whole time and had a big grin on his face. I felt like a child who had just learned to ride a bike and gained his parent's approval. A little wobbly at first, I felt more confident as I rolled down the driveway and was then off to more adventures.

When the VA patient awoke, he said he had a little soreness in his throat, but felt good overall. He further told me that it was the best anesthetic he had ever had. Whether he really meant it or just wanted to make me feel good, I wasn't really sure. Nevertheless, this experience confirmed what I had been told by older residents: "VA patients are the easiest to please and among the most grateful that you will ever meet." I found that attitude of appreciation to be, with few exceptions, a hallmark of our veterans.

I was able to gain valuable clinical experience at the VA. As I gained the confidence of Perk and other attending anesthesiologists, I was allowed to do more and more on my own. As with many professions that have a slow learning curve, I was continuously alternating between insecurity and overconfidence. One memorable case in those early weeks served to humble me a bit. I had put the patient to sleep in the usual manner, and without anyone assisting. The induction went smoothly and I performed the intubation easily without trauma or incident.

The patient was to have a cystoscopy and some bladder surgery by the urologist. After induction I secured the endotracheal tube with tape and began to ventilate the lungs. The OR tech then put the patient's legs into the stirrups and the urologist introduced his scope into the urethra. This can be a very stimulating procedure. (I found that out years later when I had one done in the urologist office.) Unknown to me, the induction dose of sodium pentothal had mostly worn off, and the maintenance gas, ethrane, had failed to achieve an adequate level of anesthesia, or anesthetic depth. In anesthesia jargon he was "light." When the urologist introduced the scope into the urethra, the patient reacted by wrapping his legs around the urologist head and farting. I quickly increased the anesthetic depth by giving more sodium pentothal and increasing the concentration of ethrane being delivered. From that point the case proceeded uneventfully, and the patient had no recall of the events. The "art" of anesthesia is highly dependent on a sense of timing of the various anesthetic drugs and gases as well as the technical procedures being performed.

A question frequently asked among anesthesia residents: "Who would you rather have giving your family member an anesthetic? Doctor A, who is academically brilliant, but mediocre clinically, or Doctor B, who is mediocre academically, but technically brilliant?" Residents I know choose Doctor B every time.

After a two-month rotation at the VA hospital, I was sent across the street to Shands, the primary teaching hospital of the residency program and also the largest. The chairman of the Department of Anesthesia was Dr. Jerome (Jerry) Modell. He was widely regarded as a brilliant administrator as well as a world expert on treating near drowning victims. A hallmark of the residency program was a series of daily lectures and case presentations at 6 a.m., provided by various faculty members and occasionally by residents. In addition, several times a year we would have VIP guests visit and give talks at these early morning sessions. I remember such distinguished guest as Dr. Robert Stoelting, Dr. Sol Schnider, and Dr. Robert Kirby. This didactic part of the program helped place it a step above most residency programs.

I did a couple of months in the surgical ICU under Dr. Elmer (Bud) Klein. Bud was an excellent teacher and inspired a number of residents to become "intensivists." An intensivist is a doctor who spends his workday solely in the ICU attending to the unique problems of critically ill patients. Learning the cardio-respiratory physiology necessary to understand and treat the problems of the ICU patients was a highlight of my residency. I considered becoming an intensivist, but ultimately chose the more traditional role for anesthesiologists, specific to the operating room. Subsequently, I did a rotation in general surgery and then cardiovascular surgery, functioning as a surgery intern. Those rotations helped me gain the perspective of a surgeon who was dependent on anesthesia services.

Eventually I made it to the main ORs at Shands as a traditional anesthesia resident. Dr. Connie de Padua was the coordinator for anesthesia services in the main ORs, but most of the faculty served time there. The OR suite at Shands was bigger, busier, and more diverse than the OR suite at the VA. In addition, in-house call was intense, frequently involving all night cases. There was a good mix of neurosurgery, vascular, thoracic, general, orthopedic, ENT, GYN, urology, and of course trauma cases. If the VA had been a good place to learn the ropes and get my feet wet in anesthesia, Shands was a full immersion.

We learned how to place all the usual invasive monitors; i.e., arterial lines, central lines (CVP), and Swan-Ganz catheters in patients of all sizes and ages. We also learned special needs of specific surgeries such as fluid and blood requirements, special positioning challenges for individual surgeries, and special postop needs such as postop ventilation and pain control options.

We learned a wide variety of anesthetic techniques, but all of them fell into one of three major categories: 1) General anesthesia, the classic form of anesthesia in which the patient is rendered totally unconscious during the surgery and generally requires control or assistance of ventilation, usually with an airway device inserted via the mouth. 2) Regional anesthetic techniques in which a part of the patient's body is numb due to a nerve block causing a regional loss of sensation. The patient may be wide awake for the procedure, but typically is mildly sedated. 3) Monitored anesthesia care (MAC), also called local standby. This occurs when the patient is monitored as with a regional or general anesthetic, but receives only mild to moderate sedation and does not require an airway device. Sometimes the surgeon may inject a numbing agent at the surgery site to assist in pain control.

Regional anesthesia, which includes a wide variety of nerve blocks for various parts of the body, has become increasingly prevalent and popular, both as a primary anesthetic technique, and in conjunction with a general anesthetic to decrease the amount of pain experienced by the patient when he or she awakens by causing a prolonged loss of sensation in the surgical area.

Nevertheless, general anesthesia remains the most common type of anesthesia, probably because it can be adapted to almost any type of surgical case, because it is safe, and because it has an extremely low failure rate. Thus, much of residency training is directed toward mastering the technical aspects and challenges related to administering a general anesthetic. A very basic understanding of the physiology of the cardiovascular system and the respiratory system is helpful to appreciate the challenges faced by the anesthetist. The following diagram gives an overview of the two systems.

Cardiopulmonary System

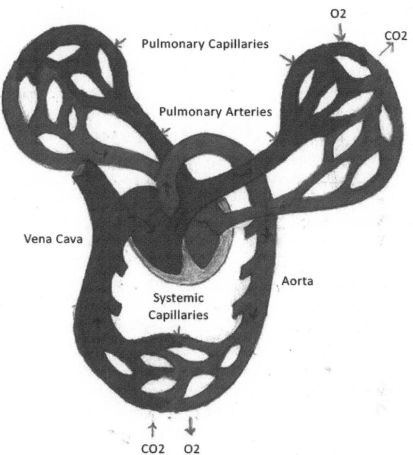

An average cardiac output is about 5 liters per minute. An average effective ventilation of the lung is about 4 liters per minute, not counting the dead space or ineffective ventilation. Note, the circulatory system actually consists of two circuits connected in series: the pulmonary and systemic circulations. A critical interaction between the cardiovascular and respiratory systems occurs in the lungs where the pulmonary blood flow interfaces in the alveolar (small lung compartments) with the ventilating "air." This is where the blood gives off excess carbon dioxide (CO_2) from the body's metabolism, and accepts oxygen (O_2) from the lungs, which in turn combines with hemoglobin in the blood. The blood will also take up other substances, such as anesthetic vapors, if they are present in the air, with O_2 used to ventilate the lungs. The O_2 and any other dissolved gases are then transported in the blood to the rest of the body, including the brain, where they produce a variety of effects. The O_2, of course, is vital to life at the cellular level as a means to release energy for life. The anesthetic gases, on the other hand, will cause the conscious brain to shut down when transported to the brain by the systemic circulation.

There are two main portals or pathways that may be used to induce a state of general anesthesia. As suggested above, the lungs may be used to introduce an anesthetic drug (anesthetic gas or vapor) that can cause a state of general anesthesia when transported by the blood to the brain. Alternatively, anesthetic drugs can be injected directly into the circulation via a peripheral vein, which causes the drug to be transported back to the heart and then to the end organs (including the brain) where it can induce a state of anesthesia. Either pathway may be used to induce anesthesia and maintain a state of general anesthesia without use of the other. With a typical anesthetic, however, the intravenous route is used to induce anesthesia because it is quicker and more pleasant; and the anesthetic gases, introduced via the lungs after anesthesia has been induced, are used for long-term maintenance of the anesthetic state. Babies and small children are an exception to this rule. Induction is usually via ventilation since IV access is more challenging in this age group, and gaseous induction is not as slow as in adults.

This brief didactic background helps elucidate the two main challenges for the anesthetist, MD, or nurse anesthetist. They are simply: 1) obtaining access to the venous circulation (usually a peripheral IV in the arm or hand), and 2) obtaining a reliable airway, usually by placing an endotracheal tube via the mouth, but sometimes with other devices. The venous access can be used not only to give anesthetic drugs, but also to replace body fluids and to replace blood loss if needed. The airway is used not only to give anesthetic gases but also additional oxygen, and to assist ventilation with positive pressure breaths. A senior resident advised me that as long as I had a good, reliable IV and a good, reliable airway, I would have no problems giving anesthetics. This is not totally true; there are rare conditions such as anaphylactic shock and malignant hyperthermia that can be life-threatening despite having good venous access and a good airway. Knowledge of the pathophysiology of these problems; i.e., what is wrong at the cellular and metabolic level, can be critical to saving the patient's life. There is much more to the specialty of anesthesia than IV access and airways. However, accomplishing these two maneuvers is critical to the safe administration of a general anesthetic, and is an appropriate focus for the beginning resident.

Starting an IV usually constitutes the first major interaction of the anesthetist with the patient on the day of surgery. If it goes well, as it usually does, this sets the stage for building confidence and good will with the patient. If one does a thousand IVs in one year, however, inevitably a few will prove difficult and require multiple attempts. This is partially because some people have very small, curvaceous, or "deep" veins; they are "hard sticks." But it is also true that occasionally a good anesthetist (MD or nurse anesthetist) will blow a good vein. It is difficult to do any simple task, like putting your socks in the laundry basket, a thousand times in a row without occasionally missing. Or, as I tell my patients, even Michael Jordan misses a layup every now and then. (Perhaps I should change that to LeBron James now.) The time, energy, and sweat every anesthetist spends over the years obtaining IV access is considerable.

The cumulative angst of obtaining IV access, however, is relatively small compared to that of obtaining a reliable airway. This is not because the majority of airways are extremely difficult to place. A well-trained and conscientious anesthetist may be able to intubate close to 99.9 percent of the general population, though not without considerable effort with many. A lesser skilled anesthetist would fare a good deal worse. The source of anxiety of intubation failure lies in the consequence of that potential failure. In some cases a breakdown in the process of intubation could mean cancellation of the surgery. In rare cases it could result in harm to the patient, e.g., if the anesthetist could not ventilate the patient by an alternate means such as mask ventilation with an oral airway or ventilation via a laryngeal mask airway (LMA device). A very rare case might need an emergency tracheotomy (a surgical incision in the anterior neck leading directly into the trachea). I have had the need for one such surgery in about thirty-eight years of private practice; the patient was a young female who had postop bleeding after surgery on the neck.

The most common form of airway desired and used for major surgery is the endotracheal tube: a long, hollow plastic tube with a 7 to 8 mm internal diameter for an adult. This is most typically placed via the oral cavity (mouth) into the glottis or opening of the trachea, after the anesthesia is induced, using a handheld laryngoscope, which when placed into the mouth enables the anesthetist to see the vocal cords and hence the opening of the trachea.

There are various sizes and shapes of blades that attach to the laryngoscope handle that adapt to various patient sizes and shapes and to individual preferences of the anesthetist. For shorter, less major cases, an oral airway—a small, curved plastic device that helps keep the tongue from obstructing the airway—may be used instead of the endotracheal tube. Today, the laryngeal mask airway (LMA), a device intermediate between an oral airway and an endotracheal tube, can provide a useful airway device for many short to intermediate surgeries. They have their own set of advantages and limitations, and have become very popular in recent years. They weren't available when I was in training. The endotracheal, however, remains the standard for major surgeries into body cavities or where positive pressure ventilation is a necessity.

So the major concern with placing the endotracheal tube is that it is extremely difficult to achieve in a very small percentage of patients. Furthermore, we can't always tell which patients will prove to be problematic with just a cursory external examination. Yes, we can make an educated guess by examining the neck and facial features, but this is not foolproof. If an extremely difficult intubation is anticipated today, a standard alternate technique is to do an awake intubation using a fiber optic intubating scope. The patient's airway is first numbed topically with lidocaine or other local anesthetic; then the slender scope is gently inserted through the mouth or nose with the patient awake and breathing spontaneously. Again, these scopes were not available to me during my residency.

It should probably go without saying that teaching good intubation skills is an important part of the anesthesia residency program. No other skill carries such weight as a hallmark of a good anesthesiologist. The anxiety of failure and egotism involved can make for much drama surrounding the intubation, especially for those in training. I once observed a senior resident supervising a less experienced resident with an anesthetic induction and intubation. When the junior resident failed to accomplish the intubation in a smooth, timely manner, the senior resident took over abruptly to complete the task. The less experienced resident, having felt sure he was on the verge of success, was angered that the procedure had been stolen from him. The senior resident, however, was convinced that he had saved the patient from near catastrophe. Lesson learned: leave your ego at the door when performing critical procedures on patients. Some doctors feel the need to parade their abilities, while others have trouble accepting help. It's always better for everyone involved to accept help graciously, needed or not, and to avoid drama or condescending behavior in the OR.

By the end of my second year of residency, I had completed several rotations in the OR at the VA Hospital and at Shands. I had also spent four or five months in the ICU. It was just beginning to sink in that in just one year my residency training would be through, and that I could hope to gain a position in private practice. Medical school and residency had taken a toll on my personal life, but I was beginning to see daylight. On slower rotations I actually had some time to do some nonmedical reading and even occasionally to play my acoustic guitar, though the calluses on my left hand's fingertips had almost disappeared.

Also in my second year of residency, I discovered I could use the university's athletic facilities, including the weight room. I could sneak in when the gym was closed. More importantly, I had dated several RNs, both from the VA and Shands, and was beginning to enjoy life a little. However, at the end of my second year, there was still uncertainty about major life issues: Whom would I marry? And where I would find a private practice position in anesthesia? Both of these questions were answered in my third year of residency.

In July 1977 I met Heidi Jensen, an OR nurse at Shands. The first memorable conversation we had concerned a canoeing date in July. Just three months later, in October, we were talking about moving in together and planning a Christmas wedding. The marriage lasted twelve years and produced three healthy children, all now in their early to mid-thirties, and all with successful careers.

Heidi and I were both somewhat athletic and felt at home with outdoor activities such as hiking, swimming, and canoeing. Both musical, we shared a love of guitar and contemporary folk and soft rock music. She was more outgoing and interactive; I was somewhat reserved and philosophical. For a time it seemed we complemented each other in a positive way. In those days my professional life and personal life seemed to be thriving in harmony.

My last year of residency contained more ICU and OR rotations, including a month of cardiac anesthesia. The cardiac surgery program at Florida had been lacking in consistent leadership, but a new cardiac surgeon from Duke, Dr. James Alexander, came in the summer of 1977 to help boost the program's reputation. Dr. Alexander's daughter, coincidentally, is a popular OB-GYN physician, working currently in Concord, North Carolina, where I live today.

Two other brief rotations were noteworthy that third year of residency. A month spent on nephrology with Dr. Robert Cade was very worthwhile. The kidneys are responsible for removing anesthetic drugs and their metabolites from the bloodstream, and excreting them into the urine for removal from the body. Therefore, knowledge of renal (kidney) function is important for predicting the duration of action of many anesthetic drugs. Dr. Cade, in addition to being a good renal doctor, was famous for being the inventor of Gatorade. He originally developed the drink for the Florida football team to help them replace vital body fluids after excessive sweating. Besides water, Gatorade also contains ample salts (NaCl and others) to help avoid a serious drop in the body's electrolytes during the rehydration process. Eventually, however, Dr. Cade realized the universal utility of Gatorade and marketed it to the general public. He became embroiled in a legal battle with the university over the right to do this, since they claimed he developed it with the university's resources. I believe he came out okay financially from that contest.

Another worthwhile rotation was a month spent in pulmonary medicine under Dr. Philip Boysen, a pulmonologist. Pulmonary (lung) function, of course, is primarily important for supplying oxygen to, and removing CO2, from venous blood. It also serves as a means to introduce anesthetic gases to the patient. A significant decrease in lung function, as occurs with severe COPD or morbid obesity, can be a critical factor determining how the patient does with major surgery, especially in the immediate postoperative period. Interestingly, Dr. Boysen, shortly thereafter, did a residency in anesthesiology, and became double board certified. He subsequently moved to Chapel Hill, North Carolina, and became chairman of the Department of Anesthesia for the University of North Carolina Medical School, a position he held for several years.

By the spring of 1978 I was married and nearing the end of my three-year training program. My confidence was high and I was looking forward to discovering what private practice was all about. I recall a case at Shands near the end of my residency that proved to be a great learning and humbling experience. Coming as it did just before entering private practice was probably fortuitous. The patient in question was a middle-aged man who was a smoker and suffered from PAD (peripheral artery disease). That is, the blood flow to his lower legs was greatly reduced due to the buildup of plaque (atherosclerosis), which caused a partial blockage. He was scheduled to undergo a femoral-popliteal bypass surgery (insertion of a graft above and below the obstruction) to improve blood flow to his lower leg muscles. He had undergone an angiogram (an X-ray with dye injected into the artery) to delineate the blockage. I had reviewed the chart and talked to the patient the evening before surgery.

On the day of surgery I put the patient to sleep in the usual manner, intubating him and placing him on a ventilator to assure he was adequately ventilated. In addition to the anesthetic gas (ethrane), I chose to give him intravenous fentanyl, a narcotic, and intravenous curare, a muscle relaxant. The patient did well in surgery. At the end of the case, I reversed the muscle relaxant with neostigmine and turned off the gas. When the patient began responding to commands and breathing on his own—without help from the ventilator—I removed the breathing tube and transported him to the recovery room.

At first everything seemed to be fine. His vital signs were normal, except he was breathing a little rapidly, a condition known as tachypnea. As he woke up more fully, however, it was clear something was not quite right. He seemed to be struggling to get his breath with rapid shallow breathing. It appeared that he was still weak from the muscle relaxant, curare. As indicated, I had given the standard reversal dose of neostigmine for curare. Under normal circumstances, the reversal drug should have been adequate to overcome the blockade caused by curare at the neuromuscular junction. What was the problem?

The attending anesthesiologist thought I needed to intubate the patient to help his breathing. I thought he would probably get by okay if we just raised the head of his bed more, to make breathing easier, and gave extra oxygen. I did reintubate the patient, however, as the attending suggested, and placed him on a ventilator. I then reviewed his chart to search for clues to explain his prolonged reaction to curare. It was then that I discovered his creatinine was 2.0 the morning of surgery, whereas it had been only 1.1 a couple days earlier. A rising creatinine strongly suggests a decrease in renal (kidney) function. Thus, the patient's ability to get rid of the curare by excreting it into the urine was greatly reduced. The "curare" effect, or relaxation of the muscles, was prolonged, and the standard reversal dose of neostigmine was inadequate to overcome the increased effect of curare. Evaluation of the degree of muscle relaxation (curarization) is greatly aided by using a twitch monitor. This device delivers a small electric current to a superficial muscle in an anesthetized patient to evaluate the strength of the contraction. It can still be difficult in some patients, however, to accurately determine the degree of relaxation.

In about one hour I reevaluated the patient for possible extuba-tion. He could now raise his head easily off the pillow, indicating good muscle strength. I extubated him again. This time he showed no evidence of weakness. His breaths were deeper and slower; he was not struggling. The rest of his recovery was uneventful.

I was embarrassed by the case, and somewhat defensive. I had conscientiously administered the anesthetic, and followed all the recommended rules and procedures, including accurate curare doses and standard reversal drugs. Yet I failed to realize the patient had a sudden decrease in renal function, probably due to the angiogram dye. But it was a good learning experience for me. Some residual weakness from muscle relaxants is not uncommon, though usually at a clinically insignificant level. I have gradually come to appreciate the benefits of such experiences. They make one wiser, more humble, and hopefully a better doctor.

The drug curare comes from chondrodendron tomentosum, a vine that grows in the Amazon River basin of South America. The name comes from the Tupi Indian words for "bird" and "to kill." Extracts from the vine have been used by the Tupi Indians, and others, on the tips of arrows or darts, to help immobilize the prey when shot. Curare was first used in surgery in 1942 by Harold Griffen, an anesthesiologist in Montreal, Canada, to supplement general anesthesia with ether.

In theory, the anesthetist can get by with a lower dose or concentration of anesthesia when used with curare, possibly making the anesthetic safer. In 1954, however, Beecher and Todd published a paper revealing a much higher incidence of respiratory problems in the recovery room during the ten or so years since the introduction of curare. Other papers disputed these findings. The use of muscle relaxants, however, helps illustrate that new innovations in medicine usually have a risk-benefit equation associated with them. An improvement in muscle relaxation in surgery and a decrease in other anesthetic drugs are associated with a need for greater vigilance and a focus on adequate reversal of muscle relaxants.

We no longer use curare in anesthesia. Newer and improved muscle relaxant drugs have a shorter half-life, and are easier to reverse than curare, So we are also somewhat more sophisticated in detecting muscle weakness. The term "curarization," however, arising from the early use of curare, is still used to denote a state of muscle relaxation or weakness, even though rocuronium or some other drug was used. Hence, the "curare effect" lives on through other drugs.

Finding a Place to Practice

—∞∞∞—

The process of choosing a place to begin private practice began in the fall of 1977. I had toyed with the idea of looking in the Oregon or Washington State area because of its natural beauty and mild climate. However, I learned that these areas were well saturated with doctors already. I then decided to focus on the state of North Carolina because of its location between my home state of Tennessee and Heidi's home state of Florida, as well as its natural beauty and moderate climate. I learned through a bulletin from the NCSA (North Carolina Society of Anesthesiologists) that there were a number of practices in the state that were looking to hire new doctors. I chose five practices from that list that seemed desirable. They were located in the following cities: Gastonia, Concord, Raleigh, Rocky Mount, and Fayetteville. I contacted each of these practices and made an appointment to visit with and be interviewed in December 1977. After forty years each interview is still a vivid memory.

My first interview was at Gaston County Hospital with Tom Wingfield. We had a nice tour of the medical facility and were taken to the country club for dinner. We were made to feel welcome in Gastonia. From there we drove to Concord and met Bill Swan, who showed us Cabarrus Memorial Hospital and the town of Concord. We liked both the town and the hospital and were treated very well. Next up was Raleigh, where we visited Memorial Hospital of Wake County. This is

the only stop at which the vibes were less than welcoming. It's probably the reason I don't remember the name of the anesthesiologist who
interviewed me. The fourth interview was in Rocky Mount at Nash
General Hospital with Dr. Vincent Andracchio. He was quite pleasant
and drove us around the area after the interview. I really liked Dr.
Andracchio and the town. The final interview was in Fayetteville at
Cape Fear Valley Hospital with Dr. David Beckham. Coincidentally,
a surgeon who trained at Florida, Dr. Russell (Rusty) Clark, a former
UNC basketball star, had recommended this practice to me. We were
treated well by Dr. Beckham and his wife.

Back in Florida we assessed our interviews. We quickly ruled out
the hospital in Raleigh because of the poor reception. Nash General
in Rocky Mount was the next to go, not because it wasn't a desirable
practice situation, but because it seemed so isolated from the rest
of the world. Cape Fear Valley Hospital in Fayetteville was a strong
contender. Its proximity to Fort Bragg, however, made it less desirable. Thus it came down to Gastonia and Concord. Dr. Wingfield had
been very encouraging during our interview. A strange coincidence,
however, attracted us to Concord. It just so happened that Dr. Bill
Swan had grown up in Concord, Tennessee, in an area now known
as Farragut (for the high school) in West Knox County. This is the
same area that I grew up in. He had attended the same high school,
eighteen years before me. It seemed to be my destiny to practice in
Concord, North Carolina. Two anesthesiologists from Concord,
Tennessee, would now be practicing in Concord, North Carolina. The
synchronicity of it all was hard to resist. Of course, the hospital had an
excellent reputation. It was a nice-size hospital (457 beds) situated in a
medium-size city. Concord had a warm, charming downtown area, as
well as a fairly new mall, and was located only twenty miles northeast
of Charlotte, North Carolina's largest city.

I finished my residency training on June 30, 1978; therefore, I had a
month off before I started my employment with Cabarrus Anesthesiologists PA. In July 1978 we spent some time visiting Heidi's cousins in

Groveland, Florida, and then with her sister, Holly, and husband, David, an engineering professor at UF; they lived right outside of Gainesville.

Sometime on or around July 15, we packed all our belongings in a small U-Haul trailer, which was attached to Heidi's 1974 Plymouth Fury, and headed for Concord. I had traded my '65 Ford for a '77 Chevy Nova, so one of us pulled the trailer in the Plymouth and the other drove the Chevy. Gabrielle, the cat, had a first-class ticket, so he could ride wherever he wanted. He seemed to prefer the floor of the Plymouth, and tended to snuggle with our feet. I kept a very detailed record of our expenses involved with transferring all our worldly goods from Florida to North Carolina. Below is an accurate reproduction of that list in detail.

1) 24 hour rental for small U-Haul trailer: $50. That's it.

Okay, I guess we did have to buy gas, and we probably also stopped at a McDonald's somewhere in South Carolina.

We got to Concord late that afternoon. I called Marilyn Carroll, the wife of Dr. Charles Carroll, a pathologist at the hospital, from a pay phone in downtown Concord. We needed keys to their rental house on Gold Hill Road. They kindly accepted $150 in cash for the rent for the last half of July; our agreed upon monthly rent was $300. The house was a rustic weekend cottage on a small lake just outside of town. It was adequately furnished with a decent kitchen. We unpacked, grabbed a bite to eat, and then fell asleep. Thus started my long adventure in Concord, North Carolina.

My contract stated that I was to begin employment with Cabarrus Anesthesiologists PA on August 1, 1978. However, Dr. Swan had a family vacation planned for the first week of August. He thought I should delay active practice until he returned. So my first actual day working in the OR was Monday, August 10. During that first week I made frequent visits to the hospital to learn the lay of the land. I met most of the nurse anesthetists, as well as the OR and recovery room nurses. I also met several of the surgeons with whom I would be working.

I quickly learned some of the hospital's history. The hospital opened for business in 1937 as a county hospital with forty-six beds and ten bassinets. But it was largely through the efforts of Charles A. Cannon of Cannon Mills and his associate, George Batte, that the hospital was created. Cannon Mills needed an adequate hospital to serve its employees, both in Concord and its sister city, Kannapolis, just to the north. Cannon Mills contributed generously to its startup and continued operation. It was rumored that a trust fund with several hundred million dollars was created with Cannon money to subsidize the hospital. Some people jokingly referred to Cabarrus Memorial Hospital as Plant No. 13. Mr. Cannon died of a massive stroke in 1971, but his ethos was very much alive when I arrived in 1978.

When I began, the hospital had 457 beds. It had 67 doctors on staff. Dr. James Keel, Dr. Doug Clark, and I were numbers 68, 69 and 70. We had a busy emergency room and a modern ICU. There were about twelve 1200 deliveries a year and 7,000 surgery cases a year counting those with local anesthesia. The OR suite had eight usable ORs. These were well-equipped with modern HP ECG monitors with pressure module for invasive blood pressure monitoring. There were modern Ohio Medical anesthesia machines in most rooms, but a few of the older little green machines (3000 series) were still around. OR number three had a window that looked out over Church Street with a good view of Shoney's, Concord's finest restaurant at the time. I remember seeing a few of the old copper kettle vaporizers, an old-timey anesthesia gas dispenser made by Forreger and developed by Lucien Morris in 1951, but these were not in use. Overall the hospital was well-equipped for its time.

Interestingly, there were two doctors out of the 70 on staff who were on the original hospital staff when the hospital opened in 1937. They were Dr. Lance Monroe, an OB-GYN physician, and Dr. Russell Floyd, a general surgeon. Occasionally I had the opportunity to hear them talk at the lunch table (yes, we got relieved by a nurse anesthetist to go to the cafeteria one floor below). When they talked about "Old

Mr. Cannon" they were referring to James W. Cannon, born 1852 and died 1921, not Charles A. Cannon, born 1892 and died 1971. Charles A. Cannon had helped make Cannon Mills and Cannon Towels a well-known brand name. James W. Cannon, his father, however, had started the first textile plant around 1888 as Cannon Manufacturing Company, in Concord.

In 1905 Cannon bought about a thousand acres of farmland seven miles to the north where he opened a much larger plant in 1908. He also built mill houses and schools and a YMCA, calling the resulting new town Kannapolis, the city of Cannon. The business flourished in the 1920s, producing over three hundred thousand towels per day. At that time it was the largest producer of textiles in the world. The towels produced by Cannon Mills were a very coarse, absorbent cloth known as cannon cloth, which made them very useful and popular.

Another reason for the success of Cannon Mills was that it integrated the whole process of making the towels, from the raw cotton to the finished product, all at one site, instead of needing to subcontract some of the steps to other sites. The Cannon YMCA was the largest in the world when it opened. When in 1921 James Cannon died of an unknown illness, his son Charles Cannon took over as head. He had already been playing a major role in running the company. The Cannons contributed generously to the community in the form of libraries, schools, and the arts. We all know what happened to the textile industry in the 1980s and 1990s as foreign competition increased. But at the time I arrived, Cannon Mills was still by far the biggest employer in the area.

Consistent with the philosophy of Charles Cannon, the hospital was known as a low cost provider. In a survey of about two hundred hospitals in North Carolina in 1980, Cabarrus Memorial Hospital was the lowest cost of all except one. Likewise, the professional fees of Cabarrus Anesthesiologists PC were well below average for the time. In 1978 the corporation billed nine dollars per relative value unit (RVU). When I joined the practice, it increased to ten dollars. As a curiosity Dr. Swan showed me a copy of a bill for anesthesia services from the 1940s. The bill was for two dollars.

In 1975 the Federal Trade Commission (FTC) sued the American Society of Anesthesiologists (ASA) for price fixing after it published its ASA RVU guidelines. These guidelines merely assigned a relative value for different anesthetics, depending on their degree of difficulty. For example, the RVU for an inguinal hernia may be four; for cholecystectomy, seven; and for a carotid endarterectomy, ten. Normally one point is also added for each fifteen minutes of anesthetic time. Therefore, the RVU charge for an inguinal hernia that lasted one hour would be eight (four plus four). The RVU charge for a cholecystectomy that lasted one hour and fifteen minutes would be twelve (seven plus five). The conversion factor is set by the provider, depending on the cost of living and other factors in his practice area. So in 1978 an inguinal hernia lasting one hour would get a charge of eighty dollars (8 times $10) for anesthesia in Concord. The RVU guideline is not price fixing; it is merely a means to standardize relative values. The FTC lost the case against the ASA. RVU guidelines are now the standard for billing in anesthesia and many other specialties.

Anesthesia was administered at Cabarrus Memorial Hospital (CMH) by CRNAs and MDs like myself, who had training in anesthesia. CRNA is an acronym for certified registered nurse anesthetist, known simply as nurse anesthetists. CRNAs are RNs who have undergone two more years of rigorous training in a certified program. In addition, they also have to do a year or two of intensive nursing, such as in the ICU, before they can be accepted by the training program. It's quite competitive. As a result almost all graduates are highly qualified. The terms are a little confusing, because the term "anesthetist" literally means one who administers anesthesia. MDs who do a residency in anesthesia are generally referred to as anesthesiologists. The term "anesthetist," however, could in theory refer to either a CRNA or an MD.

When I arrived, the normal OR schedule consisted of five ORs with elective cases, with staffing to open a sixth room, if needed, for emergencies. This increased to six elective rooms with one backup room about a year after I started. We ran one elective room on Saturdays for a half day. There were ten CRNAs employed by the hospital. The surgery load consisted of a good mix of ENT, urology, GYN, orthopedic, and general surgery. CMH was not a major trauma center, although an occasional episode of domestic violence or automobile accidents provided enough cases for us to keep our trauma skills honed. One surgeon did an occasional thoracotomy, and two other surgeons did a fair amount of vascular surgery, including AAAs (abdominal aortic aneurysms). This was enough to keep our skills in invasive monitoring from getting rusty.

Dr. Swan and I did our own cases, and CRNAs did their own cases. We did not directly supervise the CRNAs in the current standardized mode of supervision. Consequently, we did not bill for cases that were done by the CRNAs. There was, however, always at least one CRNA floater available to relieve one of us in case someone needed help with a difficult intubation, a difficult IV, or some other anesthesia-related challenge. We also met with the CRNAs in the morning to go over the daily schedule and we provided in-service education for them, usually on Wednesday afternoons. We also managed personnel issues such as hiring, firing, sick leave, and rare discipline problems in conjunction with the administration. To compensate, the hospital paid the corporation a monthly stipend.

Overall, I was happy with my choice to join Dr. Swan in practice in Concord. It was fairly busy, but without an undue amount of trauma or middle-of-the-night surgery. We alternated taking off every other Wednesday and every other Friday. Therefore, every other week I had a three-day weekend. This was a significant improvement over residency. We did not take in-house calls, as the CRNAS did, since there were only two of us. We did, however, come in to help with almost all the big cases. Dr. Swan had a rule in place when I arrived: the CRNAs could proceed with doing either an appendectomy or a Cesarean section case without calling one of us to come help. This policy would obviously be unacceptable anywhere in North Carolina today. But it seemed to work adequately at the time.

I can remember only one time in the first few years that I was called in from home to help on a case already in progress. The CRNA was unable to intubate a patient undergoing an emergency Cesarean section. She was able to ventilate the patient adequately by mask for fifteen minutes until I arrived to do the intubation. I am not aware of any major complications arising from this policy. I'm glad, though, that it's a thing of the past.

The quality of the surgeons and the medical staff at large was outstanding. Board certification was close to 90 percent, very good for the time. I found it easy to have a high level of respect for the professional skills and abilities of the staff. Many had trained at Duke, Bowman Gray (Wake Forest), or UNC (Chapel Hill). They all showed great respect for me and my professional abilities. This atmosphere of positive mutual reinforcement led to high expectations of success.

The demography of the staff was uniformly white male, with the exception of one Filipina, Elsa Yap, who was one of three pathologists. The staff tended toward conservative politics, with Senator Jesse Helms being a favorite son. The atmosphere was cordial, even genteel. It was customary for all physicians to wear a coat and tie to work. Almost every physician on staff belonged to the county medical society, which met on the first Thursday of the month, except in the summer. After "Where are you from?" and "Where did you go to medical school and do your residency?" the most common question asked a new doctor was, "What church do you plan to join?"

Alcohol was served at medical society functions, and most of us imbibed modestly. There had been some problem drinkers in the past years, but there didn't seem to be any when I arrived. Cabarrus County was dry and would remain so for another fifteen or more years, so the medical society meetings served as the social focus for the medical community. These were pleasant occasions to share a glass of cabernet with one's colleagues.

Despite the cordial welcome by all, I couldn't help but feel a little bit like an outsider to the medical community. At twenty-nine years old, I was the youngest doctor on staff. Furthermore, Heidi was only twenty-three years old, by far the youngest spouse. Neither of us was especially politically active. But we did look at world issues such as Vietnam, Watergate, and racial problems from a different viewpoint than most of the older doctors. We were more inclined to put less emphasis on style and tradition, and tended to look at issues from a global perspective.

To my knowledge, I was the first doctor to come to work routinely without a coat and tie. It seemed pointless, since I would only change into surgery scrubs almost immediately after entering the hospital. At that time of day (about 6 a.m. in those days), I would be seen by few people. No one said a word to me about this matter, but I suspect it wasn't unnoticed. I did not dress in blue jeans, T-shirts, or other overtly unprofessional outfits, merely what would be described as office casual. Today it's common to see some physicians come to the dressing room in blue jeans and T-shirts or in jogging clothes. These physicians are highly respected and professional in all other respects. Clearly, there has been a huge shift in dress over the last thirty-eight years.

One other feature of Cabarrus Memorial Hospital that I failed to mention earlier was its close relationship with Duke Medical School. In 1973 Tom Long, a GI Fellow at Duke, along with Galen Wagner, also at Duke, helped initiate a continuing education program at CMH. In this program, Duke physicians provided medical consults and continuing education on a regular basis. Each department at Cabarrus interacted with its counterpart at Duke. In the case of the surgery department, (anesthesia was included in the surgery department in those days), we had monthly conferences with a Duke surgeon usually involving a review of interesting cases. Surgery residents from Duke also did brief rotations at Cabarrus, working alongside the private practice surgeon. I was told that Dr. William DeVries, famous later for the first artificial heart implant (the so-called Jarvik 7) in 1982 in the patient Barney Clark, was one such resident. About once a year for several years the chief of surgery at Duke, Dr. David Sabiston, would visit and give a brief talk.

The Duke conferences were genuinely interesting and helpful at times. They certainly added a veneer of sophistication and academia to the medical staff. Dr. Swan and I attended many of the surgery conferences. It was, admittedly, also a big ego trip to have world famous physicians come visit us.

Early on I recognized that I had found a unique and desirable practice setting in a nice mid-sized town. And Heidi was pregnant. It did not take long, therefore, to get the itch to own our own home. In October 1978 we decided to find a medium-sized home in the country. We had visions of a country homestead with children, a garden, and maybe horses. We found a sixteen-hundred-square-foot modern house with thirty acres on Sapp Road, about eight miles from the hospital. We made an offer of $72,000 contingent on a six-month rental period with a rent of $500 per month. The offer was accepted. We needed the six-month period to save for a down payment that we later extended three more months.

On November 1, 1978, we packed all our belongings again and moved to Sapp Road. We had some new furniture delivered to the house. I recall we had acquired a washer and dryer, which were a little problematic to move by ourselves. It was all very exciting, but moving again so soon was exhausting. We collapsed in our new home that evening.

In the wee hours of Monday morning, November 2, Heidi began cramping. We went to the emergency room about 5 a.m. She had a miscarriage requiring a surgical evacuation with anesthesia. We were physically and emotionally drained. It was a real low point. After a few days' rest, Heidi returned to Florida to her parents' house to recuperate emotionally and physically.

The Early Years of Practice

— ∞∞∞ —

The early years of practice were exciting and hopeful years, especially after Heidi returned from Florida and we got settled in our new home on Sapp Road. We embraced our new community and became active in Central United Methodist Church, where we both joined the choir and later became counselors for the youth group (MYF). Though I still felt a little like an outsider in the medical community, this feeling was gradually diminishing in intensity.

In those early years, several people extended a hearty welcome by inviting us, and other newcomers, to their house for dinner: Bill and Ann Cannon, Dr. David and Betty Sue Lockhart, Dr. Vince and Laurabell Arey and Dr. Marvin and Maryann Rozear all stand out. My partner Bill Swan and his wife Lillian also had us over a number of times. This was an old school tradition in the medical society which seems to have all but died out today. Too bad. I think it was one of the bright spots of yesteryear. I guess I feel a little guilty for not doing my part to continue the tradition.

The practice with Dr. Swan was challenging, but not overwhelming. Most cases were bread and butter surgeries; i.e., tonsillectomies, cholecystectomies, hysterectomies, prostatectomies, etc. Except for Cesarean sections, we didn't cover OB. Labor epidurals would come much later. As with any busy practice, we had our share of difficult airways, problematic venous access, and occasional unexpected hemorrhage with hypotension (drop in blood pressure) that kept things exciting. Some say that anesthesia is 99 percent boredom and one percent panic. Although I can't speak to the boredom, I can certainly attest to the panic.

There were two types of cases that could cause an adrenalin rush and demand an all out effort on the part of the anesthetist (MD or CRNA). The first was an emergency Cesarean section for fetal distress. It was believed that the well-being of the baby depended on how quickly the obstetrician could remove the fetus from the uterus when its heart rate had dropped. The fear was that the umbilical cord was not delivering sufficient blood, and hence oxygen, to the fetus, possibly due to it being wrapped around the neck: or there was some other mechanical problem. When we were paged for this type of case, everyone from anesthesia who was not tied up, would drop what they were doing and rush to OB to put the mother asleep so the operation could begin ASAP. I am sure at times we overreacted, but it wasn't our job to question the call. No one wanted to be blamed for a bad outcome.

The second maximum effort scenario was a ruptured abdominal aortic aneurysm, also called an AAA. When a patient's main artery leading from the heart to the lower body (abdomen, pelvis and legs) gets diseased, it tends to dilate and form an aneurysm. The aneurysm eventually can rupture rapidly, causing sudden death, or do so more slowly allowing time to be repaired, but only with quick skillful intervention. Whenever we got a call alert of a ruptured aneurysm, usually from the emergency room, we would furiously rush to get an OR ready with multiple IV solutions and invasive monitoring sets (arterial line and central venous catheters) and assure an ample stock of emergency drugs (sodium bicarbonate, epinephrine, lidocaine etc.) were immediately available. Typically, there would be an anesthesiologist (Dr. Swan or myself) and one or more CRNAs helping. These cases were labor intensive. In addition to rapidly starting multiple IVs and invasive monitoring, multiple hands were needed for transfusing blood, giving drugs, managing the anesthetic, and last but not least, keeping an accurate record of the proceedings.

We had two excellent surgeons who knew how to rapidly repair a leaking or ruptured aneurysm with a prosthetic graft. Because of this, and the rapid response of the anesthesia team, we never in those days had a ruptured aneurysm patient die on the table in the OR. This was quite a feat considering their prevalence. I do recall we had one death, but that was many years later with a new anesthesiologist and different surgeons.

There were other cases that were very demanding of course. Difficult airways and unexpected hemorrhage always called up our fullest effort. Trauma cases, though not common, could be among the most challenging.

One case in the early '80s stands out as one of my most remarkable in a career of almost forty years. One summer evening, the police discovered a young man lying dead on the side of the road outside Concord. He had multiple serious wounds, the apparent victim of a brutal altercation. On closer inspection, however, they noticed he took a breath. Someone thought they felt a pulse, but weren't sure. Apparently, he was only mostly dead. They brought him to the emergency room where the ER doctors detected a pulse and were able to start an IV. They were also able to obtain a sample of arterial blood, probably from the femoral artery, to send to the lab for analysis of PH, PO2 and CO2 (also called blood gas analysis). They called the general surgeon on call and also the OR to prepare for the emergency surgery. The OR called me to come immediately.

I met the patient as he was wheeled into the operating room. He was breathing, but unresponsive. His blood pressure was difficult to measure, but seemed to be in the 50s systolic. He was in profound hemorrhagic shock. It was urgent that he receive blood and fluid replacement ASAP. It was the surgeon's task to prevent any further bleeding by surgically exploring the abdomen to control the source. Meanwhile, the blood gas report came back showing a severe acidosis. The PH was 6.9. He could not live long in that state.

The case presented a dilemma for me. I needed to give him an anesthetic, so I could intubate him and also so he would hold still for the surgery. However it was probable that the usual anesthetic drugs; i.e., sodium pentothal in those days, would cause a further drop in blood pressure and certain death. Using ketamine might decrease, but not totally eliminate this risk. Years before this, during a summer rotation at Walter Reed, someone told me that after the Pearl Harbor attack on December of '41, several trauma victims lost their lives due to the induction of anesthesia in a state of hemorrhagic shock. I realize this is hearsay, but it is very plausible, and came from a credible source. So, before I induced the anesthetic, I gave him four ampules of sodium bicarbonate to treat his acidosis. I also opened up the IV to allow a rapid infusion of ringers lactate. This caused his blood pressure to increase into the 80s. Only then did I put the patient to sleep and intubate him. At this point I gave him two more ampules of sodium bicarbonate and started an arterial line in his right radial artery where I could feel a weak pulse. It was now time to send another sample of arterial blood to the lab for a repeat blood gas analysis.

While I was waiting for the blood gas results I prepped his neck with betadine and then inserted an 18 gauge needle into his right internal jugular vein. After inserting the guide wire through the needle and using a dilator to open up the hole, I inserted a large bore catheter over the guide wire into the internal jugular vein, which fed it into the superior vena cava. The PH came back 7.1; still very acidic, but improving. Over the next several hours I administered multiple units of packed red cells, fresh frozen plasma, platelets as well as ringers lactate solution. I rechecked the PH and gave sodium bicarbonate as indicated. At the end of the case, he was much more stable. The surgeon was able to surgically control the bleeding. He required a total of twenty ampules of sodium bicarbonate to treat his acidosis. He was taken to the ICU and left on the ventilator overnight. The next morning, he was extubated. Miraculously, he made a full recovery.

Later in my career, I had another patient with a PH of 6.9 due to hemorrhagic shock who also survived; but, in my estimation, this case remains the most dramatic save of a patient in severe shock. Had the patient been much older, or had significant co-existing heart or lung disease, it's likely he would not have survived.

Overall, I felt the department was well-run. People showed up on time and worked in harmony to get the job done. One surgeon was predictably ten minutes late for his 7:30 am case. Everyone seemed to accept this without much kick-back.

Dr. Swan was technically adept and set high standards in that department. I felt compelled to meet his standards. I don't recall that either of us ever canceled a case due to inability to intubate in the eleven years that we worked together. There were several cases of minor dental damage, however. And an occasional fat lip.

In 1979, Dr. Swan suggested it would be helpful if I would serve, as he did, as a medical examiner for Cabarrus County. Medical examiners in North Carolina are physicians who investigate deaths of people who die unattended (without a primary physician), or due to foul play, trauma, or other unusual causes such as drug overdose. In other words they serve the same function as a coroner does in other states. The medical examiner system gives the state the advantage of a death investigation by an MD. A coroner on the other hand, is an elected official who may or may not be a physician. The downside of the medical examiner system is that all physicians who serve as medical examiners do so as an extracurricular activity. It is not part of their practice. They may, therefore, have little experience in forensic medicine.

I served as a medical examiner (ME) from 1979 until 1997. I estimate that I investigated approximately a hundred deaths. Most of these cases were merely elderly patients without a regular doctor to sign the death certificate. For the most part I didn't mind serving as a ME seeing it as a form of community service. We got paid only $25 per case. In a year or two that would increase to $50. The ME job had no direst relevance to my job as an anesthesiologist, except that it would occasionally interfere. This was especially true one evening in the early 80s when I had to investigate a crime scene in the county. A murder victim had been buried in a shallow grave for some time. My job was to help the police recover the body intact. It wasn't enough that the task was as noisome and foul as one could imagine, but as the police were giving me a ride back to the hospital around midnight, I received a stat page to come to the OR. It seems a young man was shot in the chest and was crashing. We were unable to save him despite our best efforts. Fortunately, in most cases the body was brought to the morgue in the hospital where I could examine it and draw blood samples for alcohol or toxicology studies, without being far from the operating room.

In the late '70s and early '80s there began a major shift from using reusable to disposable supplies and equipment in the OR. A prime example of this was the anesthesia breathing circuit that delivers gas flow from the anesthesia machine to the patient, and then returns the exhaled gas from the patient through a CO_2 absorber, and finally back to the anesthesia machine. During my residency in Florida, and during my first year or two in private practice, these tubes were made of black rubber which could be cleaned and reused multiple times. There were several disadvantages of this system. The first was the risk, however remote, of transferring bacteria or viruses from one patient to the next. Secondly, the hose, when in normal use, absorbed anesthetic gas. This resulted in both a slightly slower delivery of gas on induction, and a similar slowing in gas clearance from the patient on emergence. But the critical factor, as usual, was money: the rising labor cost for the cleaning and recycling process, and decreasing cost of mass producing plastic hoses. The economics favored disposables.

The pressure transducer was also on the disposability chopping block. This simple device translates the pressure of a liquid on a flat surface, into a proportionate electrical signal that can be projected on a screen. In the '60s and '70s, these devices were washed, sterilized and reused. By the 1980s they were disposable and could be made in great numbers very cheaply. The same thing was happening to gowns and drapes. The looming AIDS epidemic in the '80s added fuel to the fire that was raging against reusable supplies. Again, however, the economics of cheap mass production of disposables was a key factor.

One of the latest items to become disposable are laryngoscope blades. These are the lighted probes, attached to a handle, that are inserted into the patient's mouth to help visualize the vocal cords in the intubation process. I am not totally sure they will completely replace the old reusable metal blades, but they are off to a running start.

Other changes involved the anesthesia machines themselves. Somewhere in America In the late '70s an anesthesiologist entered an OR and put the patient to sleep in the usual manner, and then turned on the vaporizer to deliver a standard flow of anesthetic gas to the patient. After several minutes he noted the patient's blood pressure and heart rate dropped much more than expected. He decreased the percent of gas below customary level, but the blood pressure remained critically low. The patient's condition deteriorated; she did not do well. After the case, it was noted that the patient was actually receiving two different anesthetic gases from two different vaporizers. Apparently, a vaporizer had been left on from the evening before. The anesthesiologist had turned on the other vaporizer, unaware that the first was still on. Thus the hapless patient received a double dose of anesthetic. Fortunately we have resolved this situation.

By 1980, most anesthesia machines, (Ohmeda and Dragger) were equipped with a locking system, that mechanically prevented, anyone from turning on a vaporizer if a first were already turned on. About this time, most all machines became equipped with a fail-safe system that prevented anyone from turning on nitrous oxide if the oxygen was not already flowing. These safety features are taken for granted today and they make mechanical errors in gas delivery extremely unlikely.

In the early years, we made friends with many of the new doctors and their wives. The following, with their date of arrival in Concord in parenthesis, were among the first; Dr. Jim and Rosemary Loftus (1979), Dr. Peter and Nancy Chikes (1979), Dr. Frank and Marilyn Pancotto (1981) and Dr. Vincent and Eileen Keipper (1977). All these people remain good friends after over thirty-five years. The town of Concord, despite the lack of gourmet restaurants, was charming, and had some beautiful historic homes on North and South Union Streets. The old historic courthouse (1876-1976) was no longer used by the county, but was used by a newly formed theatrics club to stage amateur productions for the community. It was called "The Old Courthouse Theatre". What they lacked in originality, they made up for in enthusiasm.

Cabarrus County was settled in the 1750s by German immigrants in the eastern part of the county, and by Scotch-Irish immigrants in the west. The new county needed a seat, so the two factions settled on a site between the two in harmony or concordance, hence, the name Concord. The town was formed in 1796 and incorporated in 1806. The Concord area was primarily a farming community until textiles became big in the late 1800s. We felt that we were part of the Concord community, even though we lived a few miles outside town, because of our membership at Central United Methodist Church, one of the pivotal Concord institutions, and because of my work at the hospital.

Besides three big churches, downtown Concord also had three banks, the Hotel Concord, a court house, a police station, a number of shops and was home to the Concord Telephone Company (CTC). CTC was founded in 1894 by Daniel Coltrane, a Civil War veteran, and his son, Lester D Coltrane. One of Daniel Coltrane's grandsons, Lester D Coltrane II, had a beautiful home with a garden and park facilities about ten miles south of town called Rosecrest. He allowed the hospital and other organizations to use the facility for picnics and special occasions. I attended several outings there as an associate department head with the hospital, and also for special functions of the church. Another grandson of Daniel Coltrane, Frank Dusch, just recently died in the summer or 2015. He was ninety years old.

We were amused to discover that Cabarrus County had been the site of the first major gold discovery in this country. In 1799, Conrad Reed, son of a deserted Hessian mercenary soldier, found an unusual 17 pound. rock in Little Meadow Creek one morning. His father, John Reed, used it for a doorstop for three years until he sold it to a jeweler in Fayetteville for $3.50. The jeweler in turn sold it for $3,600 when it was correctly identified as gold. John Reed was able to get a $1000 finder's fee after his error was discovered. Subsequently many people came to Mecklenburg and Cabarrus counties to seek their fortune. In 1832 there were fifty gold mines in the area. The Charlotte Mint, a branch of the United States Mint specializing in gold coinage, came into existence on March 3, 1835. Up until 1848, when gold was found in California, North Carolina was the leading gold producer in the country. Reed Gold Mine remains as a tourist attraction where tourists can still pan for gold for a small fee.

The most important events for me personally in my early career years were the births of my three children. They were William Jensen (Billy) 6/20/1980, Dustin Louis, 9/10/1981 and Corey Ann, 7/19/1983. They all weighed between 8 lbs 10.5 ozs and 8 lbs 12 ozs; all full term and healthy at birth. After the miscarriage in November 1978, we wondered for a while what the future would hold. But October 1979 laid our concerns aside when we discovered Heidi was pregnant.

Since I was an MD, Heidi an RN, her father a family MD and her mother a CRNA, we didn't feel we needed any special classes in childbirth or Lamaze classes for pain control. In retrospect, this may have been a little arrogant on our part, but I doubt it would have made a major difference. The actual labor and delivery process was more of an ordeal than we anticipated, and the details of how it progressed, was a reflection on us and the state of medicine in Cabarrus County in 1980.

Heidi was admitted to CMH around 9 p.m. on June 19, 1980 in early labor. I remained with her through the night as labor progressed slowly. The obstetrician was Dr. Clayton Jones, whose son, Dr. Michael Jones, is a popular obstetrician today. Dr. Jones was very attentive and was concerned about the slow progress of labor. Around 4 a.m., he told us that if progress did not pick up in the next few hours, a Cesarean section might be indicated. He also thought that an epidural for her increasing labor pains might be helpful. He asked me if I would be willing to do the honors.

The situation was something of a dilemma for me. For starters we didn't routinely provide epidurals for labor patients at that time, so the OB nurses were not accustomed to managing them. I thought I also remembered a rule somewhere that prohibited doctors from performing procedures on their own family members, although I knew of one orthopedic surgeon who performed a minor elective procedure on his wife.

On the other hand, the obstetrician was probably more objective than I was. Labor pain can be very severe, and the placement of a labor epidural is medically and legally considered an emergency procedure. I considered myself "pretty good" at placing epidurals, and my wife was physically fit, which made an epidural placement less perilous.

I watched as she moaned with each contraction. I held her hand intermittently. At about 5 a.m. we decided to go ahead with the epidural. We turned her on her left side. I prepped her back three times with betadine. I gave one cc of lidocaine over the L34 interspace (lower back). Then I inserted the epidural needle with the loss of resistance technique, followed by the epidural catheter inserted through the needle. I slowly gave her 10 mls of 0.25 percent bupivicaine. The procedure went well. In fifteen minutes she was feeling much better. The rest of her labor was much more pleasant. We had no infusion pumps at that time to infuse the maintenance medicine, so I had to give a bolus injection with a syringe every one to two hours. Placing the epidural seemed like the right thing to do.

Around 6:30 a.m. Dr. John Ashe came on to replace Dr. Jones on OB. Heidi was doing somewhat better by this time, but still was progressing slowly. Dr. Ashe seemed to think she could deliver vaginally, so a Cesarean section would not be necessary.

It was now Friday morning and we normally had only one anesthesiologist on Fridays. I had to run the OR for anesthesia by myself. Dr. Swan was off and had a trip planned for the weekend, so I was it. Around 7 a.m. I walked down one flight of stairs to the ORs right below the OB suite, feeling unsure about how I was going to handle the situation. But, I was in luck. There was an extra CRNA available that morning, so the CRNAs could run all the rooms and still have someone available for breaks. I would be available to help if they had a serious problem, such as a stubborn intubation. When I returned to OB, Heidi seemed more optimistic since the epidural had been placed. Pain relief can do wonders for your attitude.

Still progress was slow, but steady. I spent most of the day in OB, but about every two hours, I drifted into the OR to see if there were any pending problems or crisis. Fortunately there were none. I do remember at one point inserting an arterial line for a carotid endarterectomy for a CRNA case. Aside from that I periodically bolused the epidural as needed. The epidural worked well, but each bolus would work for only about ninety minutes.

By late afternoon Heidi's contractions were increasing, so we felt delivery was imminent. The OR schedule was mostly completed, so I could focus totally on my wife and baby. Finally, a delivery around 9 p.m., after a grueling 24-hour labor. Our baby suffered a moderate degree of shoulder dystocia due to a somewhat difficult delivery; but overall it went fine. People came from out of nowhere to congratulate us. News travels fast in the medical community. Around 9:45 p.m., Dr. Swan and his wife came by to congratulate us, even though they were in the process of leaving town for a short trip.

Thus began my weekend call. I believe it was fairly slow and uneventful. I can't remember doing much in the OR. We brought baby Billy home on Sunday. What a special time.

Did I do the right thing by placing my wife's epidural? What should I have done differently? I was playing three roles on June 20; husband and primary support for my wife during labor and delivery, consultant to the operating room, and anesthesiologist for my wife. How could I be a top notch husband when I was multitasking? On the other hand, how would her labor have gone without the epidural? These questions persisted in my mind.

Our second child, Dustin Louis, was born about fifteen months later. This time we broke down and attended a Lamaze class, trying to act like normal average expectant parents. It seemed to pay off, or maybe it was just luck. Heidi was admitted to OB in the morning of Thursday September 10, 1981. She delivered in the early afternoon, with Dr. Vince Arey as her obstetrician. He gave Heidi a caudal block to help with the delivery. It was gratifying to experience a birth with less of the anxiety and stress of the first.

Coincidentally, B.J. Keel, wife of Dr. James Keel, delivered a baby boy within a few minutes of Heidi's delivery in the delivery room directly across from ours. Dr. Arey attended both deliveries. Dustin was full term and healthy. He weighed about 8 lbs 12 ozs.

About two weeks after coming home from the hospital, Dustin began having an unusual amount of diarrhea. This went on for several weeks without a specific diagnosis. In mid October, the diarrhea abated and he was well enough to travel with Heidi to Florida to visit with her parents while I attended an ASA meeting in New Orleans. Unfortunately, Dustin relapsed, and was admitted emergently to Wuestoff Hospital, in Rockledge, Florida. I flew to Florida from New Orleans and rushed directly to the hospital to check on his status. His pediatrician put him in the ICU and had a central line placed. For a day or so we contemplated the worst. But then he started improving for no apparent reason.

Back in North Carolina, Dr. Doug Clark, our regular pediatrician, re-cultured the stool and finally discovered the culprit: salmonella. Where had he gotten it? From the hospital? At home? No source was ever identified. By Christmas, he had fully recovered. That was enough excitement for a while.

Corey was born July 19, 1983, in the afternoon. Dr. Frank Long, the obstetrician, a good friend and also a good acoustic guitar player, delivered her. By now we had our system down pat. There were no problems with the delivery, nor health issues with baby Corey. Maybe that's why she turned out to be so healthy.

Since neither set of grandparents lived nearby, we needed help with childcare in 1983, having three children under four years old. Our savior was an African-American lady who lived on Spring Street in Concord named Idella. She was in her late 50s and already had a reputation for being very good with kids. She was gentle and kind, but she would not put up with any flak from the kids. She was a life saver.

The early '80s were a time for having babies and raising them in our little house on Sapp road. We had enclosed a covered porch to increase the square footage from sixteen hundred to two thousand square feet. I also had purchased an Allis Chalmers tractor with a bush hog from Troxler Equipment Company to help with the yard work. Life rotated around our kids, my job as an anesthesiologist, and activities at Central United Methodist Church where we sang in the choir and eventually became MYF counselors.

My practice with Dr. Swan continued pretty much unchanged. We continued to do our own cases, as opposed to medically or supervising the CRNAs. We raised our RVU to keep up with inflation, but remained a low cost provider. Occasionally I would go into the hospital in the middle of the night for an emergency, and still have to work the next day. But, the three day weekend every other week, and the alternate Wednesday off had become fully institutionalized. Overall, not too hectic.

Every summer we managed a trip to Gatlinburg in the Pittman Center area in Tennessee to join my parents and two brothers, Scott and Steve, and two sisters, Karen and Susie, and their families. This is where my family had vacationed since I was five years old. We also would go to Rockledge, Florida, at least once a year to visit Heidi's parents Lou and Joy. Lou was a popular family practice physician in the Rockledge-Cocoa area. His brother Adrian was a general surgeon who practiced at Wuestoff Hospital in Rockledge.

In 1982 an athletic club called "the Sportscenter" opened up on Country Club Drive, about one half mile from the hospital. This was a joint venture between Dr. Frank Sellers, Dr. William Burchfield, and Sammy Johnson, a recently "retired" NFL running back from High Point, North Carolina. It was ahead of its time, and nicely done with tennis courts, racket ball courts, indoor track, two swimming pools and of course a weight room with both free weights and a wide assortment of Nautilus machines and treadmills and other aerobic equipment. It was said to be a million dollar facility (in 1982 dollars).

Around the same time Heidi was teaching aerobic exercise classes for postpartum women at Central United Methodist Church. She was soon asked to lead classes at the Sportscenter, and promptly became a regular instructor. My initial reaction to the Sportscenter was to ignore it. Hard to believe since I had been a hard core exerciser most of my life. But my house on Sapp Road was equipped with a small set of weights, a place to do pull-ups, and of course plenty of open roads for jogging. My tractor and yard work also provided a regular workout. We had thirty acres; three of them lawn. My philosophy was that fitness was very important, but was dependent mostly on dedication and commitment to a routine of exercise, rather than a bunch of equipment. You can't buy fitness.

Sometime in early 1983, I visited the Sportscenter. Impressed with the equipment and the opportunities for exercise, I began to appreciate the advantages of selective motion exercise. If one has an injured shoulder, back or other body part, there were machines available that enabled a good workout, without aggravating the injury. The pool was an additional venue for stretching and aerobic workouts. Cross training was a very important concept. I joined in 1983 and have been a member ever since. In addition to getting a good workout, I frequently see people in the community that I would otherwise not encounter. These are brief, but important social interactions.

Through the Sportscenter, we became friends of Sammy and Linda

Johnson. Linda was a native of Concord. Her father, Hank Utley, played baseball at NC State and then in a semi-pro league. He co authored two books about baseball in North Carolina and was also instrumental in expanding Concord's early Boys Club. Sammy, I believe was the driving force behind the creation of the Sportscenter. He had been a star running back for the University of North Carolina in the early '70s. and then had a six year career as a running back with the San Francisco 49ers and the Minnesota Vikings. He had nine career touchdowns and gained 830 yards in 206 carries.

By 1984, even with the excellent help of Idella, we were beginning to feel a little cramped and stressed in our small house outside of town. The seemingly simple task of getting all three kids dressed and in the car to go to church, or wherever, was problematic. Some days I would help a good bit with child care, but other times not so much, due to my work schedule.

Heidi thought the size of our house was a major cause of our problems. —She began to push for buying something bigger—and soon. I wasn't so sure that the house was the primary problem. I preferred to hold off a couple years, and plan our move carefully. I was afraid that if we made a rush decision, we might wind up regretting our decision, and possibly wind up paying more than market value.

We saw a marriage counselor to help manage our differences. Dr. Zerof was helpful in resolving our conflict. I caved a little. We began searching the Concord real estate market in June 1984 for a larger house in town. We made a low ball offer for a house on Northgate that was turned down. The house was sold to another physician who had begun practice shortly after me. This did not go over well.

Then we learned from Sammy and Linda Johnson that the house they were renting on Williamsburg Drive was available at a bargain price. The house was a six thousand square foot Georgian style on three levels with six bedrooms. It had gone on the market in 1981 with an asking price of $265,000. The owner, Jim Huntley and wife, were getting frustrated. He had sold his Seiko watch dealership and moved to Florida, allegedly to avoid paying state income tax (Florida has none).

In July 1984, Sammy learned from Mr. Huntley that his bottom line was $175,000. Sammy relayed this information to us, as he knew we were looking for a larger house. We jumped on it. Sammy and Linda were good friends, our kids often played together, so we were already familiar with the house. It was certainly more house than we needed; but it was a great location, slightly over a mile from the hospital and about two miles from the Sportscenter. We had managed to save $75,000 for a new house and by selling a lot we owned on Blenheim for $35,000, we were able to put down $110,000. This left $65,000 which Jim Huntley was willing to owner finance. All things considered, we thought we had gotten off pretty lucky. By the way, did I mention the house was right next door to Dr. Swan, my partner?

The house was in decent shape overall, but needed some updating with carpets, curtains and other fixtures. We began the long process of settling in. In September my parents came to see the house and stay with our kids while we took a much needed vacation. It seemed like things were going in the right direction.

One other noteworthy event of the early '80s occurred in 1982. A billionaire from California, David Murdock, CEO of Dole Foods, (not to be confused with billionaire Rupert Murdock of Australia) purchased Cannon Mills. As a bonus he promised to vitalize downtown Kannapolis with a new shopping area and to build a new YMCA. These promises were fulfilled in 1984 and 1987. That year also saw the town of Kannapolis incorporate to become the City of Kannapolis. It appeared new life had come to the mill town. In retrospect, it was really the beginning of the end for Cannon Mills. At the time no one could conceive what lay ahead in the next twenty years for the mill town, and its chief industry.

The Mid-Eighties

—∞∞∞—

Viewed in retrospect, the decade of the '80s was a very important and critical time at many levels for worldwide politics, locally for Cabarrus County and professionally for the practice of medicine. At the same time, it has been much misunderstood and even underappreciated by some. Artistically, it is sometimes considered a bland era. Consider, for example, the top two songs of the year 1986: number one was "That's What Friends Are For," a pleasant but wearisome ballad by Dionne and Friends. Number two was "Say You, Say Me," by Lionel Richie, a drab forgettable hit. (Sorry, you can do better, Lionel). Reviewing the box office hits is a little more encouraging. The top three grossing movies were; 1) *Top Gun* (Tom Cruise), 2) *Crocodile Dundee* (Paul Hogan) and 3) *Platoon* (Charlie Sheen). So maybe the '80s did have something going on after all.

Globally, the '80s are noteworthy for the politically dominating news stories at the beginning and at the end of the decade. We saw the end of the Iran Hostage Crisis in January 1981, with the release of the hostages, and the fall of the Berlin Wall, beginning in November 1989. But the decade was also shaped by such noteworthy events as the Chernobyl Nuclear disaster in 1986, the Challenger disaster in 1986 and the Bhopal chemical spill in India in December 1984. (The Bhopal disaster is known even today as the worst industrial accident of all time with over 10,0000 killed and many more injured).

But major events alone don't define an era. Perhaps more important in the 1980s were the discussions held between President Reagan
and newly elected Soviet president, Mikhail Gorbachev, which led to
improved U.S.-Soviet relations. The era was also partially defined by
the looming AIDS epidemic, both in this country and worldwide, and
by the struggle against apartheid in South Africa. Perhaps even more
subtle was the appearance of the earliest cell phones, and the rise of
the personal computer. These changes helped make us who we are
today.

The practice of medicine wasn't isolated from worldwide events.
From the AIDS epidemic, we developed the concept of "Universal
Precautions." During the early stages of that epidemic, stringent rules
for hand washing, using gowns and gloves and using extreme caution
were adopted to deal specifically with patients thought to carry the
AIDS virus. After a few years, we decided to apply a uniform standard of caution to all patients receiving medical treatment. That was
because some patients may be undiagnosed carriers of the AIDS virus,
but also because the risk of exposure to patients with the hep B or hep
C virus, or some other unknown infectious disease, was probably an
equal or greater risk to the average care giver. Therefore it was best to
use a high standard of care or "universal precautions" when dealing
with all patients, to avoid the spread of infectious agents.

In 1985, the cost of medicine had exceeded the dreaded 10 percent
of GDP (gross domestic product) benchmark, and was still increasing.
The total expenditure on medical care, expressed as a percent of GDP
was 6 percent in 1965, 13 percent in 1993 and 18 percent in 2012. Use
of more sophisticated technology, such as lasers and video equipment
in the OR and use of more expensive imaging techniques, as CT scans
and MRIs, were certainly major contributors to the rise. Increasing
drug and basic equipment was another factor. In 1978, when I first
came in practice, we used Sears tool carts in each operating room
to store our routine anesthesia supplies and drugs. By 1985, we had
carts specially made for medical use by anesthesia. I am sure they cost

a good deal more. I really couldn't see any significant improvement over the Sears carts. Rules, regulations, standards of care, quality assurance and excellence in health care, were all by words or phrases, rooted in good intentions, and validated by somebody's myopic study, to advocate the use of a certain protocol, procedure or equipment for the improvement of healthcare. Thus the practice of medicine, in the mid '80s, grew increasingly sophisticated, specialized, protocol driven and costly. The trend continues even today.

By 1985, Medicare and Medicaid had been in existence for twenty years. The reimbursement through these programs had always lagged somewhat behind private insurance companies. By 1985, the discrepancy between private insurers and government programs was becoming deeper and deeper. Depending on individual fee profiles, Medicare was paying about 35 to 40 percent compared to private insurance. The RVU of Cabarrus Anesthesiologist PC had increased to 20 by the mid '80s. This was somewhat below average so the discrepancy was a little less in our practice.

So there was increasing resentment and criticism from some physicians for the reimbursement from Medicare and Medicaid. Others felt the low payments were better than the alternative (no payment). Was the glass half full or half empty? Using the diagnosis as a guide to reimbursement by Medicare, (DRG) was a new concept initiated by the government, but not fully understood by many. The success of the HMO concept by Kaiser Permanente in California demonstrated that fee-for-service medicine was not the only valid or successful model for practicing medicine. Therefore there was a good deal of confusion, frustration and paranoia in the air over the rising cost of medicine, and the lower reimbursement from the government relative to private insurance. Everyone had their own theory about what the underlying problem was and how to fix it.

In 1986, the administration of CMH, contracted with a health management corporation out of Boston to help establish a new system of health care reimbursement in Cabarrus County. They proposed the creation of an HMO company for Cabarrus County that would be a joint venture between the hospital and the medical staff. The new entity, named CAREolina Health Plan, would function in concept as an HMO, somewhat like Kaiser Permanente. That is, patients would pay a set annual or monthly fee to the HMO in return for complete health care coverage by physician members of the HMO. The big difference was in how physicians would be reimbursed. They would not be paid directly for services rendered. Rather, they would receive a monthly payment from the HMO, directly proportional in amount to the number of people (potential patients), who joined the HMO. That is, they were "capitated" (paid per head). Whether a physician did a lot of procedures or tests on an HMO patients, or none at all, had no effect on what his reimbursement would be. This was a novel concept to Cabarrus County, but had been proven successful in California with Kaiser Permanente.

The challenges of such a system are obvious to anyone who gives it serious thought. How does one go about calculating what these capitation payments should be to each physician specialist, and how do you determine the annual fee or premium to be paid by each client (potential patient) who joins the HMO? Obviously, these calculations had to be based on some statistical norms derived from usage patterns, disease prevalence and standards of practice in other parts of the country. The Boston company was happy to provide these statistics.

The other challenge was how to deal with medical problems not covered by physicians on the medical staff at CMH. These problems were known as outliers. For example, CMH did not at that time have an open heart surgery program. Nor did they have a neonatal ICU, or a pediatric ICU, or a pediatric surgeon. Therefore, a newborn baby requiring emergency surgery for a gastroschisis (a defect in the abdominal wall allowing the intestines to extrude from the body), or a middle-aged man who needed a coronary bypass procedure (CABG) due to a blockage in one or more of his coronary arteries would have to be transferred to another hospital, not affiliated with CMH, to access the needed medical treatment. These outlier costs would have to be therefore paid to these hospitals and their physicians on a traditional fee for service basis, since they were outside the HMO. This would seem to throw a monkey wrench into the seemingly smooth capitation reimbursement system.

But not to worry. The Boston consultants had a statistical blueprint from their data banks to deal with this dilemma by calculating the incidence, and the cost of the predicted outlier medical problems the premium patients paid and the capitation fees paid to physicians. Then they could be adjusted appropriately to allow for the contingent outliers. The consultants had an answer, and a statistic, to cover most every situation. They were the gurus; we were the pupils.

So presentations were given to the medical staff. Committees were formed, and many meetings were held between physicians, administrators and the Boston consultants. Ultimately it was decided to proceed with the proposed HMO. All parties were enthusiastic and supportive of the project, but also a little leery and skeptical at the same time. The CMH medical staff was a somewhat traditional and conservative group of physicians. The proposal was an aggressive, avant-garde concept for the medical community. But who wanted to fight the inevitable evolution of medical practice in the county? Who wanted to be labeled as too narrow-minded and too myopic to grasp the changes that were about to encompass us all? Lastly, who wanted to miss out on the capitation payments, if that's the way things were headed? Better get on board, or someone else may get your seat.

Dr. Swan and I met with the Boston consultants. Conceivably, we might have opted out of the capitation system, and accepted a fee-for-service contract with the HMO, since we were a small physician group that provided a consulting service (anesthesia). They insisted we accept capitation payments. We went with the flow.

So the HMO was formed. Patients joined, usually through their employers. Services were rendered. Capitation payments were made. Outlier payments were made. Outlier medical services were subcontracted to major medical centers; i.e., Charlotte, Duke, Chapel Hill, etc. The outlier medical services were reimbursed on a fee-for-service basis as per design. We estimated our capitation payments for anesthesia services more than covered what we would have collected. We were happy and most physicians seemed pleased.

The HMO lasted about one year. Near the end of the year, we began to hear rumors that things weren't going well. Payments to physicians and for outlier services exceeded income generated by premiums. The big problem seemed to be the cost of the outlier services. The consultant's statistic's predicting the cost of the outlier medical services greatly underestimated those actual expenses. The cost of care for a few premature neonates at other hospitals and the number of patients referred for open heart surgery, greatly exceeded predicted norms.

Had the consultants used the wrong template? Did they know what they were doing? Did we know what we were doing? The HMO went broke and dissolved. The experiment failed. Back to business as usual. Understandably, the failed HMO left many physicians cynical about alternative methods of health care delivery and reimbursement. Although at the same time, many were not overjoyed with the nuances of the old system.

What did we learn from our failed experiment? Apparently not a whole lot. Incredulously, about seven years later, the medical staff attempted to form another HMO. This was primarily due to the prodding of the new CEO of CMH, Tom Revels who arrived in June 1994. In his inaugural address to the medical staff in July, he promised we would have a new system of reimbursement in place within two years. He could talk the talk. This time, however, the HMO never got off the ground. Mr. Revels left to accept another job in early 1997.

There were many good changes that occurred in the practice of anesthesia, both nationwide and at CMH in the 1980s, that we now take for granted. Everyone would agree that the risk of death due to general anesthesia was very low in 1980. Some estimates were around one anesthetic death for every 10,000 anesthetics. But everyone would also agree that it was considerably less in 1990, by a factor of ten to twenty. That means the risk of death form anesthesia in the 1990s might be in the one in 200,000 range. What was the cause of this dramatic improvement?

Before I discuss this, I think it is important to explain the calculation of the risk of anesthesia deaths. I have seen many statistics for risk of death from anesthesia from one in 500 to one in 1,000,000. Most recent statistics are trending toward the latter. However in the very aged or very sick patient the risk of death within twenty-four hours of surgery is considerably greater than the risk of anesthetic death. If someone with terminal cancer or very serious heart disease dies shortly after surgery, primarily due to his or her underlying medical condition, it is not considered an anesthetic death. Anesthetic deaths are potentially preventable deaths, directly related to the administration of anesthesia. They should be, and are, extremely rare. As a former medical examiner, I am aware that many deaths are due to multiple factors, but usually it is easy to cite the primary cause.

The first known general anesthetic was administered by Dr. Crawford Long, a surgeon, on March 30, 1842, in Jefferson, Georgia. He used the vapors of sulfuric ether to induce a state of general anesthesia in James Venable, to remove a tumor from his neck. There is a small museum in Jefferson, about 30 miles northeast of Atlanta dedicated to this event. I have passed the sign on I-85 many times, but am always in too much of a hurry to stop. It's on my bucket list.

Unfortunately, Dr. Long did not publish the account of this first anesthetic. Therefore, it was not widely acknowledged. The first public demonstration of general anesthesia occurred on October 16, 1846, in Massachusetts General Hospital in Boston. William Morton, a dentist, administered ether, via a recently constructed vaporizer, to induce a state of anesthesia in Edward Abbott allowing Dr. John Collins to perform surgery. The news of this event spread rapidly and widely in this country, and also in Europe.

Dr. John Snow, in London, was quick to adopt and study the use of ether, and later chloroform, to induce a state of anesthesia for many patients in the London area. In 1847 he wrote a textbook on the use of ether earning the distinction of being the first full-time anesthesiologist. In 1853 he administered chloroform to Queen Victoria for the birth of Prince Leopold. This did much to increase the acceptance and popularity of general anesthesia.

There were no monitors in those days to evaluate the patient status under anesthesia. The anesthetist was dependent on his observations of respirations and palpation of the pulse, usually at the wrist. Most patients did well, but occasionally someone would not survive. On January 28, 1848, Dr. James Meggison administered chloroform to fifteen-year-old Hannah Greener in Winlaton, England, for the removal of an infected toenail. Shortly after the administration of the chloroform, her pulse weakened, and she began jerking. He tried to revive her with brandy, and then by bleeding her. It didn't work. Did she die of an overdose, or did she die from aspirating brandy? We don't really know.

The incidence of death from anesthesia in those days is unknown. Very likely it was in the one percent range. General anesthesia became more common in the late 1800s and the early 1900s. Presumably, it became safer in the early 1900s due to accumulated experience and improved techniques. Still mortality statistics are difficult to find for this era. Furthermore, it is difficult to find evidence of routine monitoring before World War II, other than observation, palpation of pulse and sometimes manual blood pressure measurement.

After World War II, use of the ECG monitor for the anesthetized patient became increasingly common. The ECG monitor senses the very small electrical signal created by myocardial cells with each contraction, and transmits the signal to a screen. It is therefore helpful to follow the patient's heart rate. Sudden changes in the patient's heart rate suggest important changes in the patient's status. The shape of the electrical signal can also give clues about ischemia, or strain on the heart muscle. Very irregular rhythms can signify pending problems, so the ECG monitor is very useful to help monitor the patient's well-being under general anesthesia.

When I entered private practice in 1978 the use of ECG monitors, and the manual blood pressure cuff were a standard of care for every patient under general anesthesia. Though both excellent monitors, neither one was especially good at detecting the most feared and dangerous complication of general anesthesia: that is the failure to adequately ventilate a patient, due to a failed intubation, and/or the inability to ventilate the patient by some other means. In such a situation, the ECG and blood pressure may change very little in the first minute. What was needed was a reliable monitor to give an early warning of inadequate ventilation so appropriate steps could be taken to correct the problem. Without ventilation, brain damage will occur in four to six minutes.

Ironically, but quite fortuitously, two new monitors became available about the same time in 1985 to address this problem. The first was called a capnograph, a device to detect the presence of CO_2, in the expired breath. The second was the oximeter, a device to give an almost immediate reading of the degree (percent) of saturation of the patient's hemoglobin with oxygen. Dr. Swan and I were in total agreement with the need to incorporate both these monitors into our practice ASAP. Although neither of us had experienced a death due to a failed intubation or ventilation, we had both witnessed and experienced difficult airway problems that caused significant concern. By 1986, we had both capnographs and oximeters, in all the operating rooms.

The capnograph works on the principle of infrared spectroscopy. CO_2 will absorb infrared light so its presence in a gas mixture can be detected by passing a beam of infrared light through the gas mixture, and measuring the intensity of the beam. If no CO_2 is present, the infrared beam will not be affected. Presence of CO_2 causes a decrease in infrared beam intensity.

When an anesthetist places an endotracheal tube correctly, CO_2

from the patient's lung will be present in the tube during exhalation. If the capnograph fails to detect the presence of CO2 that usually means that it was placed incorrectly in the esophagus. The capnograph is easy to use. The device must be turned for a minute or so to warm up, and the sampling tube must be correctly connected to the expiratory side of the anesthesia circuit. Occasionally moisture can block the airflow, but it's reasonably foolproof otherwise.

The first device to measure CO2 by infrared light was made in 1943 by Karl Friedrich Luft. In 1978 the devices were first used in Holland; they first became available in this country in 1983. However, they were not widely used until 1985. In 1986, the capnograph was officially made a standard of care by new ASA guidelines for general anesthesia.

In recent years, the use of capnography has expanded from general anesthesia to other cases involving heavy sedation and regional anesthesia. Although the endotracheal tube is not used on these cases, the possibility of hypoventilation, shallow or infrequent breaths, still exists. The capnograph can be helpful to detect problems with these cases as well.

The oximeter also uses the physics of infrared light absorption, but in a much different manner than the capnograph. The oximeter measures the absorption of both red and infrared light through tissue that is being perfused by blood. Hemoglobin in the red blood cells will absorb red light and infrared light in different proportions, depending on how much oxygen is combined to the hemoglobin molecule. By analyzing the absorption pattern of two different wave lengths (red and infrared) the oximeter can fairly accurately, in most cases, calculate what percentage of hemoglobin is combined with oxygen. This is called the percent saturation, or simply the O2 sat. In other words, the oximeter is pretty good at showing how effective the patient's ventilation has been to actually provide oxygenated blood to the tissues. This requires both good pulmonary (lung) function and a reasonable cardiac function to pump the blood.

The oximeter will detect a decrease in O2 sat if an endotracheal tube is incorrectly placed, for example in the esophagus. However, this decrease in O2 sat, might not occur until thirty seconds or more after the incorrect placement of the endotracheal tube. This is because pre-existing O2 stores in the lung will continue to combine with hemoglobin to keep the O2 sats up for a while, even if ventilation stops. When the stores of O2 are depleted, the O2 sat will drop. In other words, the capnograph will detect a failed intubation more quickly than the oximeter because of this time lag.

The oximeter, however, is better than the capnograph at detecting many other problems. Anything that interferes with gas exchange in the lung itself, such as pneumonia, lung collapse or bronchospasm, will usually be detected better with an oximeter than with the capnograph. Together, the capnograph and the oximeter provide much more information about the patient's welfare, than was available before their use in the OR. Based on national statistics, mortality decreased 93 percent in the 1980s due to these two monitors. The risk of death from anesthesia is sufficiently low that it takes a very large number (millions) of anesthetics to obtain meaningful data.

One interesting revelation from the routine use of oximeters was the wide variation of baseline O2 sats among a variety of patients. Normal healthy patients generally have O2 sats in the upper 90s, even on room air. A patient with moderate COPD may have sats on the lower 90s, or even the 80s. In rare cases of COPD, patients may have sats below 80. We are concerned in general about patients with O2 sats below 90, especially in the recovery room (PACU). However in some patients it is to be expected. Their body tissues have adapted to these low O2 levels, and do just fine there. In the early days of oximeters, we sometimes made a great effort, usually in vain, to increase their sats to those of an entirely healthy patient. We had difficulty accepting that in some patients the baseline O2 sat is a good bit less than others. Occasionally, people were kept in the hospital longer than needed because of this. However, of course, it is always better to err on the side of caution when dealing with this situation.

In many cases the trend is more important than the absolute O2 sat number. A healthy patient who has a drop in O2 sats from 99 percent to 90 percent, suggest a pending problem. A COPD patient with a steady O2 sat of 89 percent is probably fine. The cause for the drop in sats in the healthy patient needs to be evaluated and corrected, lest the trend continue and a serious problem develops. It could be due to a pneumothorax (a pocket of air around the lung), pulmonary edema (fluid in the lung) or something simple like a leak in the anesthesia breathing circuit, causing only a partial breath to be delivered to the lungs. In any case, a failure to correct the problem could be serious.

It did not take us long at CMH to become very fond of the new monitors. Within a year or two we began to wonder how we ever functioned without them. I would certainly not want to try today. But having practiced a number of years without them gives me a deeper appreciation of their worth.

Other than the addition of the capnograph and the oximeter, our practice in the mid-'80s was pretty much unchanged from 1978, when I first entered private practice, on a day-to-day basis. Several new drugs were introduced that had some advantages over existing drugs. Propofol, introduced in 1986 by Astra Zeneca, eventually replaced sodium pentothal as an induction agent because of its quicker onset and clearance. Midazolam (versed), replaced Valium because it was water soluble and had fewer side effects. Several new muscle relaxants helped make the achievement of muscle relaxation, and reversal at the end of the case, a little more efficient. But overall, our practice in 1986 was fairly similar to that of 1978.

Several issues brewing in the background by 1986 were to have very significant long-term effects on how anesthesia was practiced at CMH. The first was a steady and increasing plea, especially from the OB-GYN physicians, to provide a labor epidural service to assist laboring patients with pain control. Labor epidurals were increasingly popular and prevalent in major medical centers, but were not uniformly available in smaller hospitals in 1986. It was hard to argue that they were a medical necessity for routine labor, but given the choice, many women would prefer to at least have the option of receiving an epidural. Conceivably, CMH could lose patients to Charlotte because of their ability to provide epidurals.

By the mid-'80s, a few of the OB doctors began performing their own epidurals for laboring patients. This included Dr. Frank Long, Dr. James Moon and several family practitioners who covered OB. Also in 1986, a new hospital, University Hospital, opened up to serve the growing population around UNCC and Harrisburg, situated between Concord and downtown Charlotte. The pressure to compete was increasing. The number of deliveries at CMH remained fairly constant in the mid-'80s. However, in retrospect, we lost the opportunity to experience a major growth spurt by failing to capture the market, which could have been a source of growth for pediatrics and other specialties.

To provide labor epidurals we believed we would need at least one more anesthesiologist, possibly two. Women in labor might request an epidural anytime, 24/7. Inevitably, this would cause our workload in the evening, and the middle of the night, to increase. We would definitely be spending more time in-house. Consequently we began attempts to recruit another physician in 1984. Over the next several years we interviewed a good number of physicians and most were near the end of their residency training. I believe many were reluctant to join a practice in which they would be on call every third night even though Dr. Swan and I were doing fine splitting the call between the two of us. Several seemed very interested, but negotiations fell through at the last minute. We did temporarily stop our recruitment efforts during the year of the failed HMO, due to the uncertainty of its financial impact on our corporation. But then we resumed our efforts when it went under. As the '80s progressed, our failure to recruit became a bigger issue.

Another change that seemed to have its roots in the mid-'80s, was the increased concern and interest in decreasing post-operative pain, both in the PACU, and for the first several days after surgery. As the risk of major serious anesthetic mishaps became smaller (after the capnograph and oximeter became a standard of care) attention turned, naturally, toward making the surgery and anesthesia experience more pleasant; or perhaps we should say less unpleasant. This process took off in the mid-'80s and continues today.

In October 1984, I attended the ASA annual meeting in San Francisco. The ASA meeting is a huge convention, held over several days, and attended by anesthesiologists from all over the country. The purpose of the meeting is to provide inservice education opportunities for physicians seeking CME credit, to learn what new trends are developing in our specialty, to see displays from pharmaceutical and medical supply companies and occasionally to connect with old friends and colleagues. They are generally held in a major city to add entertainment and sightseeing options to the agenda.

I remember this meeting from over thirty years ago very well. Several incidents stand out in my mind. One evening we went to Fisherman's Wharf and dined at Scomas, an Italian seafood restaurant. The scallops were great, the service was good and it had a nice atmosphere. Another day I boarded a public bus and handed the driver my ticket. He refused to take it. Why? He had noticed that I had held it briefly in my mouth while I searched for change in my pockets with my hands. The AIDS epidemic was a big deal in San Francisco in 1984. Obviously the epidemiology was not widely understood. Lastly, I remember browsing the exhibit hall where companies display their latest and greatest products.

A display by Abbott Laboratories caught my attention. It was called a PCA pump. I had read about it recently in one of our medical journals, and was intrigued. It was basically a programmable infusion pump that connected to a patient's intravenous fluids allowing the patient to self-administer a small amount of narcotic at a predetermined dose and time interval. The type of narcotic, the dose, the time interval between allowed doses and usually a maximum total allowed over four hours is ordered by the physician and programmed into the pump. Except for the initial setup and instructions by the RN, this system freed up the RN from needing to bother with routine pain medicine administration, normally a labor intensive activity.

At this time, 1984, the most common route of narcotic administration for post-op pain was an intramuscular shot (IM), usually in the thigh or buttocks. This worked fairly well, but had several disadvantages. It required a nurse to obtain the controlled substance from a locked cabinet of some sort, confirm the existing hand written order, administer the shot and then follow up for repeated shots. The onset of pain relief usually required at least ten to fifteen minutes. The shot itself was moderately painful. Lastly, when multiple shots were given every three or four hours, there was a possibility of over sedation, due to the accumulative effect of multiple doses. Total clearance of a drug given IM is much slower and variable than when given in the vein.

Using frequent small IV doses of narcotic was one alternative to IM shots. This overcame some of the disadvantages of the IM shots, but it was very demanding of the RN. This technique was used frequently in the PACU, and occasionally the ICU. It was less commonly used on post-surgical floors.

It therefore seemed that the PCA pump could solve the logistical problem of getting frequent small IV boluses of pain medicine. The machine could do it. While this is taken for granted now at the time it was a novel concept.

When I returned home from the ASA meeting in San Francisco, I met with the chief of staff, Dr. Clayton Jones, sometime in late October of 1984. I gave him some brochures from Abbott Laboratories, and told him I thought the hospital should purchase several pumps to use for post op pain control. He said he would present my idea to the executive committee at the next meeting.

I had no financial motive or political agenda in promoting the PCA pump for post-op pain control. I merely thought it might help alleviate some of the logistical challenges in delivering post-op narcotics. There were legitimate questions raised concerning the PCA pump. How reliable was the pump? What if it malfunctioned? How safe is it to give IV narcotics routinely on the floor (as opposed to the PACU or ICU)? The proposal to buy and use the PCA pumps was bounced from committee to committee. The questions and debates continued for some time. Finally, in early 1986, the first PCA pumps arrived. The first surgeon to order the PCA pump for a patient was Dr. Robert Beaver, a good friend, who used it on an eighty-five-year-old female after surgery for a broken hip. It was a success. The use of the PCA caught on quickly; by 1987 it was in wide use at CMH. It turns out the risk of machine error is less than that of an RN following a doctor's written orders. The risk of over dosage is minimal, due to the rapid clearance of IV drugs, the need for the patient to be coherent enough to push the PCA button, and the four-hour maximum dose which puts a ceiling limit for the total dose in that time. The only problem I have seen has been from misguided family members who push the button for their loved one, when he (she) is too sleepy to self-administer. That action negates the safety feature of the PCA; if the patient is too sleepy to push the PCA button, he should not receive more narcotic. Family members should be advised against helping their loved one.

The PCA pump is not the best solution for post-op pain control for every surgery. However, it is the most widely used technique, and is the gold standard by which many other modes are measured. The primary niche for use of the PCA is on the post-op surgical floor, not so much in the immediate post-op period; i.e., the PACU.

Perhaps the most dramatic improvement in post-op pain in the '80s occurred in the PACU. If one could compare a sound track of a typical PACU in 1975 to one in 1995, there would on most days be significantly less moaning and groaning in the latter. This would be due to a major change in anesthetic technique that gained momentum in the 1980s. By combining a regional anesthetic, such as an epidural, with a general anesthetic one could combine the benefits of a general anesthetic (loss of awareness and control of the airway) with that of a regional anesthetic to give numbness and absence of pain. Typically a patient would emerge from anesthesia in the PACU with minimal pain with this technique. It was a big help with big upper abdominal cases, such as abdominal aortic aneurysms and thoracotomies for lung masses. In such cases, the presence of severe surgical pain makes it unlikely or difficult for the patient to take deep breaths or cough effectively. Therefore, the patient is prone to accumulate secretions and develop atelectasis or lack of full lung expansion with a resulting drop in O2 sats and occasionally pneumonia. A properly placed epidural can produce just enough numbness in the right area to greatly reduce pain and allow better breathing and coughing to take place. Not only is the recovery more pleasant, but the risk of developing respiratory complications is less.

In addition to decreasing pain immediately post-op, epidurals could be used for prolonged pain relief, up to six days or so, after surgery. The epidural catheter can be left in the back during that time, and an infusion of local anesthetic such as 0.1 percent bupivicaine, can be given continuously. A typical rate may be 10 cc per hour. This was usually sufficient to alleviate the worst surgical pains. Many larger anesthetic teams in bigger hospitals began using epidurals for post-op pain routinely in the mid to late 1980s. At CMH I used epidurals for post-op pain a few times during this era with some success. A full team of anesthesiologists to assist with epidural placement and follow-up daily pain rounds is helpful to fully implement this post-op pain service. At CMH, we began to fully implement this program in the early 1990s when we had more anesthesiologists; but the trend truly began in the mid-1980s.

Coincidentally, a new discovery made in 1979 complemented this surge in epidurals for post-op pain. Tony L. Yaksh et. al., showed that morphine, when injected in the spinal sac, served to greatly reduce the rats response to pain. Again in '79 Joanne Wang et. al. showed that morphine, placed in the spinal sac, was effective in alleviating pain in cancer patients. This discovery clashed with traditional thinking. Everyone knew that narcotics worked in the brain by centrally reducing the pain response. When evidence was discovered that narcotics worked by affecting receptors in the spinal cord as well we knew we might have a new tool. In the next several years, research reinforced this finding, implying that narcotics could be instrumental in a two-pronged attack on pain. They could also be combined with a local anesthetic as bupivacaine to be given as a mixture in the epidural space for post-op pain relief. Thus the mid '80s saw the introduction of morphine, and later other narcotics, as a medicine to be used in the epidural space along with the local anesthetic for post-op pain relief. It became our standard practice at CMH, and in most places, to use a combination of local anesthetic and narcotic together, when using an epidural for post-op pain relief, and also for the pain of labor and delivery.

By the 1990s, the epidural became the most popular, and probably the most important, tool for decreasing pain in a number of major surgeries. It was not a panacea, however. For one thing, in the late 1980s and early 1990s, more anticoagulants, such as Coumadin, or IV Heparin were employed in an attempt to prevent blood clots in veins, and possible emboli (clots migrating to the lung). This may have been due to an increase in the number of very sick patients having surgery who were at greater risk of forming clots, and to a more aggressive attempt to prevent the clots' emergence. The problem was that epidurals were contraindicated in the presence of these drugs, due to the resulting risk of bleeding around the spine.

The use of nerve blocks, such as the brachial plexus (for the arm and shoulder), and the femoral, sciatic and saphenous nerves for knee and foot surgery, became more popular in the 1990s, but began gaining interest in the 1980s.

CMH had no pain clinic per se in the 1980s. As one of two anesthesiologists, I would get occasional consultations for pain problems, about one per month. Some were post-op patients, but many were just unfortunate people with chronic or acute pain from an injury of some type. The most common procedure I did was an epidural steroid injection. The second most common procedure was the stellate ganglion block to treat chronic pain of the hand.

The treatment of pain, both acute and chronic, was beginning to gain a foothold as a major focus of medicine, especially for anesthesiologists. Pain clinics were formed in many larger practices. The 1990s and 2000s saw a continued growth of treatment options, including new drugs, therapy and invasive procedures. I was less affected at CMH by this trend than I would have been in many larger practices. But in retrospect, I can see how the concerns for better pain management was starting to drive the marketplace.

Lest one think my practice was entirely conventional and straight forward in the 1980s, I must relate the tale of one of my most interesting and beloved patients, Mrs. Faye Hockenberry. She was arguably the most interesting and challenging patient from the medical and physiological point of view. The management of her problems encouraged me to think outside the box, and use a novel approach. As a human being, I came to view her as a shining example of how the human spirit can rise over physical handicaps, she was easily the favorite patient of my career. I eventually began to view her as a gift.

Like many gifts, Mrs. Hockenberry came disguised as a problem. Sometime around 1985 the general surgeon told me that he had a patient in her mid fifties coming to have her gallbladder removed. She might present some challenges from an anesthesia point of view due to her long standing disability from polio. Phone calls were made and a meeting scheduled with Mrs. Hockenberry about a week prior to her scheduled surgery. At first glance, I could indeed tell that Mrs. Hockenberry would be a challenge. Wheelchair bound, and accompanied by her faithful husband, Forest Hockenberry, she was anything but a normal healthy patient. In a lengthy three-way discussion, I learned she had been stricken by polio in 1945 at age thirteen. Like many polio patients, she lost her ability to walk and breathe normally. Initially she required ventilator assistance with the tank ventilator, or iron lung, but eventually learned how to do glossopharyngeal breathing, also called frog breathing. Since her diaphragm function was wiped out by the polio, she could no longer inhale air by expanding her lungs to create a negative pressure to entrain air.

To survive, she had learned how to use her cheeks, tongue and pharyngeal muscles to gulp air, and then force it into her lungs. This resembles the mechanics used by amphibians to breathe and is hence referred to as frog breathing. I had heard of the term, but I was still a little skeptical. Then I noticed how Mrs. Hockenberry seemed to be swallowing or gulping air in between words. Forest handed me an envelope containing several medical articles explaining frog breathing. I was impressed. To survive this long, primarily by frog breathing, must require a phenomenal will to survive, or phenomenal supportive care, or, as I suspected, some of both. Could she possibly have a little diaphragmatic function (normal breathing) to supplement her frog breathing? I couldn't tell. Either way I had to give her the benefit of the doubt. She had her act together, and presented her case clearly and calmly, exhibiting a tenacity that reflected great inner strength. I had to admire that.

It seemed their primary worry was that she might need prolonged mechanical ventilation after surgery, and possibly wind up with a tracheostomy, a surgical hole in the neck. If that happened, whatever quality of life she had now would greatly diminish. A tracheostomy would eliminate her ability to frog breathe. She would be completely dependent on a ventilator for the rest of her life. Considering her age and frailty, it would be difficult, if not impossible, to relearn how to frog breathe after a tracheostomy. Becoming ventilator-dependent was her greatest fear. I suspect she had seen this happen to other polio victims and I couldn't blame her for her that fear. It did present quite a problem for me, however.

At that time, a week before surgery, I had time to sit back and quietly consider my options for dealing with Mrs. Hockenberry's approaching surgery and anesthesia. Here is what I came up with.

My first thought was to recommend that we send her to Duke, the world famous medical center, with whom CMH had a pre-existing relationship. The case was out of our comfort zone; we had no experience with this specific problem. But, there was little karma in outsourcing; the patient preferred to have the surgery at CMH, and the surgeon, of course, wished to do the case here. Furthermore, I was chairman of the Respiratory Therapy Committee, and had trained at a facility (University of Florida) that was among the most innovative in dealing with respiratory problems. That pretty much put the spotlight on me. As a resident, the joke was, "Don't worry if they don't have a ventilator available for your patient, they can make a new one in the basement in a few minutes." Besides, what could Duke do that we couldn't? So I put the Duke option in my back pocket.

Another alternative would be to attempt to do the surgery without a general anesthetic, and therefore without intubation and ventilation control. It is possible that the surgeon could infiltrate the skin with lidocaine in the right upper quadrant of the abdomen, and then make a surgical incision there to remove the gallbladder. We could sedate her slightly to tolerate the procedure. Or, we could administer a regional anesthetic, such as an epidural or spinal block, in an attempt to anesthetize the upper abdomen selectively, proceeding with mild sedation. Either way, there would be a great risk that it would be unpleasant for the patient and require heavier sedation. Given her slim reserves in pulmonary function, it was likely she would need some type of ventilatory assistance. And it's worth noting the additional stress for the surgeon and the anesthesiologist. These are all factors that affect outcome. I felt, if we tried this route, we would have at least a 50 percent chance of needing to abort the plan and intubate her anyway. I wasn't enthusiastic about this plan.

My third option would be to proceed with a general anesthetic with intubation as usual, but use extreme caution in titrating the anesthetic drugs to avoid prolonged effects, and extreme vigilance when attempting to wean her from mechanical ventilation in the immediate post-op period. Perhaps with enhanced diligence in care, we might have a better than 50 percent chance of weaning her successfully from the ventilator within twenty-four hours of surgery. If for any reason we were unable to wean her, and she became ventilator-dependent, it would be tragic for her, but nobody could blame us too much. We would say we did our best with the standard available resources and her physiological reserves were inadequate to the challenge. What more could we have done? This option was very tempting. But then I remembered that her fear of becoming ventilator dependent was the very reason she met with us in the first place. Were there any other ways to approach this challenging situation?

This dilemma on how to deal with Mrs. Hockenberry's pending surgery encouraged me to review the literature on ventilation and polio patients. The first modern ventilator to gain wide use was developed by Phillip Drinker and Louis Shaw, professors at Harvard. It was essentially a large airtight metal box (iron lung) with an electric motor to create a negative pressure while the patient was inside the box. The negative pressure would cause room air to be entrained into the patient's lungs. The first patient to be placed in the "Drinker" was an eight-year-old girl with polio, who was near death due to respiratory failure. When placed in the Drinker ventilator, on October 12, 1928, she was immediately resuscitated. The dramatic success of this first case did much to popularize the use of the iron lung.

In 1931, John Emerson produced an iron lung based on the same ideas of the Drinker, but with much improved efficiency, and at a somewhat lower cost. The patient could be rolled in and out of the tank on a sliding bed. Despite the fact that Dr. Drinker sued Emerson for patent violation, the Emerson became the workhorse ventilator for polio patients in the 1940s and 1950s. It was just a better machine. Drinker lost the suit because Emerson argued that his product was too valuable for saving lives to be legally restrained in use. He also claimed that the components of the Drinker iron lung were all simple products already well-established in the market.

The advantage of the iron lung was that the negative pressure ventilation which it produced was physiologic in nature; that is, it mimicked natural breathing. It didn't cause an increase in airway pressure, which can cause a risk of impeding venous blood flow in some cases, or occasionally minor trauma to lung structures, as may happen with positive pressure ventilation. It did not require intubation or tracheostomy, but could take place without any man-made airway device. The disadvantage of the iron lung was that it was large and cumbersome, limiting mobility. It also had less efficacy on patients with very stiff or non-compliant lungs.

In Europe the polio epidemic of the 1950s saw a new technique introduced. In 1952 at Blegdam Hospital in Copenhagen, Denmark, doctors began intubating polio patients, and placing them on positive pressure ventilators. Positive pressure ventilators quickly replaced the more awkward iron lungs. The new ventilators were smaller and easier to move about. They also worked better with patients who had very stiff lungs. By 1959 there were only twelve hundred estimated iron lungs in use in this country. By 2004 this was down to thirty-nine. During my residency and private practice, I had used only positive pressure ventilators. The iron lung was considered a dinosaur. Nevertheless, they were more physiologic than the positive pressure ventilators. What's more, they did not require intubation!

I reconsidered my options for Mrs. Hockenberry. In theory it would be nice if we could use an iron lung for her in the operating room, but that was impossible. The iron lung was too big and cumbersome to fit in the OR. However, provided we could actually find such a ventilator in working condition, it was possible we could use it in the ICU to assist weaning from positive pressure ventilation used in the OR. Conceivably, she could be placed in the iron lung right after surgery and extubated. The negative pressure ventilator could then take over until she was strong enough to begin frog breathing again.

We were in luck. The Hockenberrys had an acquaintance with

polio in Mount Pleasant, a nearby town, who owned an iron lung. He was not using it currently and might be willing to loan it to us.

I do not recall what strings we had to pull, or what bureaucratic hurdles we had to jump, but the day before Mrs. Hockenberry's surgery, we had the bright yellow Emerson tank ventilator, the iron lung, set up in the ICU. It was a curiosity. Several people came by to gawk. The surgical procedure (cholecystectomy) and anesthetic proceeded without incident the next day. Immediately after surgery we brought her intubated to the ICU. Shortly after placing her in the tank ventilator, we removed the endotracheal tube. Except for being a little claustrophobic, she did well. She only needed the assistance of the iron lung ventilator about twenty-four hours, until she was able to resume her normal breathing unassisted. She did as well as could be expected.

In the next fifteen years or so, I saw Mrs. Hockenberry several times when she came back for minor procedures not requiring intubation. She always displayed an inner peace and confidence of her future, despite her handicap. Many people with lesser handicaps become bitter. Some try to the soak the system for all they can get. I can't blame them too much. If I suddenly became severely handicapped, I am not at all sure how I would handle it. It was refreshing to see someone handle their situation with grace and dignity. Why can't we all behave like Mrs. Hockenberry?

I found out some time later that she was a devoted member of Calvary Baptist Church in Kannapolis. In my presence, she never flaunted her religion or attempted to moralize or preach. She merely taught by example. That was her gift.

One day in late August 2009, I returned home from a brief trip. A voice mail from Forest informed me that his wife had died August 24, 2009. She was 77 years old. Unfortunately, I had missed her funeral. I recently phoned Forest to get his permission to discuss her medical management, and to verify my recollections. He stated that she finally did become ventilator-dependent and eventually required a tracheostomy, many years after our initial meeting. To survive to age seventy-seven with her disability was remarkable.

I have never seen or heard of any of my colleagues use an iron lung for post-op ventilation. It is not considered a tool of modern medicine. It does, however, have some unique advantages over positive pressure ventilation and perhaps deserves consideration for unique situations. Its niche, however, would be extremely small.

* * *

In the mid-'80s my personal life seemed to be going well. We lived about a mile from Beverly Hills Elementary School where all three kids began kindergarten around age five (Billy 1985, Dustin 1986 and Corey 1988). The principal, Scott Padgett, ran a good school. He later was elected mayor of Concord in 2001 and he is still mayor as of this writing. All three kids seemed to like school. Several good friends, Jim and Jean Scarbrough, Sammy and Linda Johnson and Frank and Marilyn Pancotto had children about the same age at Beverly Hills. This was convenient for us parents. We continued to use Idella, at least one day a week to help with housework and child care. She was almost like a member of the family.

I became a regular at the Sportscenter, going at least three times a week. I found it most convenient to go straight from work to work-out and then home. I developed the habit of doing a good run on the weekend (usually Sunday morning) and a shorter one during the week. Weekends, when I wasn't working, centered around the kids and family activities. Some of the weekend activities included trips to Discovery Place, the children's science museum in Charlotte, Carowinds and the train museum in Salisbury. Longer trips to Knoxville, Tennessee or to Rockledge, Florida to visit grandparents continued on at least an annual basis. The kids were lucky to have two full sets of devoted, loving grandparents.

In 1985 Heidi gave me a new acoustic Alvarez guitar for my

birthday. It is a very playable acoustic guitar with a sweet mellow tone. I still own it and play it occasionally. This rekindled my interest in soft rock and folk music. On several occasions we had parties at our house centered around playing music with a number of friends.

Around this time, Heidi and I were asked to perform at the wedding of one of her childhood friends from Florida. It took place in Seven Lakes, North Carolina, a small community just west of Pinehurst. Later we played for two other wedding parties: one a nurse from the OR and the other the son of our billing clerk. I recall playing "Evergreen" by Streisand and The Lord's Prayer among others.

At least two other people inspired and influenced our musical endeavors. The first was Char Solomon who lived in downtown Concord on Academy Street with her husband Tom Oakley and two children Sean and Katie.

All three of our children studied piano and or guitar with Char. Consequently they all grew up with a deep respect for music of all kinds, and a general appreciation of the arts. I can distinctly recall that Dustin, at age six (1987), declared that music would be his life's profession and love. He is now living in Marietta, Georgia, with his wife Adrienne and son Jude. He is, in fact, a full time professional musician, equally outstanding on the keyboard and the guitar. He is well-respected on the Atlanta scene where he is a regular with Schooner, an '80s niche band. He also plays in bars and coffee shops with Adrienne, for weddings, a traveling Gershwin show and many other venues. He has made several CDs with his wife. His reputation in the Atlanta area is strong and steadily growing. I couldn't be prouder. He is doing exactly what he dreamed of as a child, and making a decent living. How many people can say that? I give major credit to Char for her positive early influence.

In addition to teaching music, Char is a freelance writer and speaker. She has appeared in documentaries and given presentations at museums, libraries, universities and book clubs concerning her biography of Tatiana Proskouriakoff, a pioneer in the field of Mayan archeology with whom she worked as a volunteer assistant in 1972-73 at Harvard's Peabody Museum. Char obtained access to her personal diaries and became inspired to begin research on her in 1996. That biography was completed in 2002.

I had the privilege of taking acoustic guitar lessons from Char for about six months in 1987. I was somewhat obsessed with samba guitar music by Antonio Carlos Jobim. She helped me work out a playable version of "The Wave," "The Girl from Ipanema" and several others. Thanks Char.

The second person to influence me artistically was Gerry Dionne. Gerry is originally from New Hampshire, but has been in the Charlotte area since the mid 1960s. He dropped out of college in the late '60s to be a full-time musician for several years. He toured the southeastern United States with a band called the Sandalwood Candle. Later he became a regular with the Arthur Smith Show, syndicated from Charlotte. He once played with Hank Williams Jr., Kitty Wells and a young Crystal Gayle. Eventually Gerry finished college and married a local girl, Quin Troxler, in the early '80s.

Quin and Gerry settled in Concord and joined Central United Methodist Church, where Quin's family attended. We had met Quin briefly when we first moved to Concord while she was still in high school. I got to know Gerry when he joined the church choir. One Wednesday at choir practice I discovered he had a love of acoustic guitar music as I did. We invited Gerry and Quin to our house for a causal visit. He seemed savvy about music in general, but I had no idea of his extensive background or talent. After Heidi and I played a couple songs we had rehearsed, we watched as he removed his blond acoustic Guild from its case and proceeded to play "What a Fool Believes" by Michael McDonald and Kenny Loggins. I was blown away. His wrist glided up and down the neck and his fingers smoothly morphed from one jazz chord to another without a glitch. Meanwhile his sonorous baritone voice blended the lyrics with the musical tones as if they were all coming from the same source. How does he do that? Over the next few years I watched him play and garnered some tips on improving my style. Not all professional musicians are willing to take the time to help a less skilled amateur; most important and lasting music learning is usually done on one's own. An occasional inspiring performer, however, can make a major difference.

Gerry and Quin still live in Concord on Eastcliff Drive. I don't think he performs a lot these days except occasionally in church. For a couple of years he has been writing editorials for the Concord Tribune Sunday edition. He has a broad repertoire of experiences to draw from and possesses an offbeat sense of humor.

Social life in Concord remained somewhat mundane. This was fine for a family with small kids. Unless you belonged to the Cabarrus Country Club (we didn't) you needed to go to Charlotte for a cocktail and a gourmet meal. I can remember a few visits to Slug's Ribs and Dickadee's Front Porch, but these were only a few times a year. Occasionally a new restaurant would open in Concord for a year or two, and then disappear. Shoney's, K&W Cafeteria,Villa Maria, the Red Pig and Troutman's barbecue were the most reliable and successful restaurants.

The small Carolina Mall, adjacent to the hospital and the active business area of downtown Concord, made the trip to Charlotte rarely necessary. Concord's S&D Coffee Company, started in 1927 by Roy Davis Sr., was beginning to supply major restaurants, and gain recognition on the national scene under the leadership of Roy Davis Jr. It remains a major player in the coffee world: a true success story for a Concord-based business.

In Kannapolis, events seemed to accelerate in the 1980s. After purchasing Cannon Mills in 1982, David Murdock kept his promise to revitalize downtown Kannapolis in 1984, and to build new YMCA which was completed in 1987. Under his influence, Kannapolis voted to incorporate on December 11, 1984. Rents soared from $40 per month to $320 per month. Kannapolis would never be the same.

An ongoing struggle to unionize Cannon Mills by ACTWU met

with defeat in October 1985 by a vote of 3,530 to 5,982. Thus unlike the vote in favor of the union in 1974 at J.P. Stevens in Roanoke Rapids, North Carolina (portrayed in the movie *Norma Rae* starring Sally Fields), Cannon Mills was able to avoid the unions once again.

The really big news was the sale of Cannon Mills by Murdock in December 1985 to Fieldcrest Mills in Eden, North Carolina. The new entity was called Fieldcrest Cannon. The sale price was around 250 million dollars, with Murdock keeping most of the surrounding real estate, including downtown Kannapolis. Before the sale, Mr. Murdock received federal approval to terminate Cannon's pension plan with assets of about 103 million dollars. He replaced the pension with an annuity contract purchased from Executive Life Insurance Company for 67 million dollars. Apparently he kept the "excess" cash of about 30 million for himself. These proceedings were all above board and compliant with federal pension laws.

Unfortunately, Executive Life had invested heavily in junk bonds advocated by Michael Milken of Drexel fame. Both Executive Life and Michael Milken were convicted of securities fraud. The net result was a major reduction in payment to pension holders. Understandably, this created ill feelings in Kannapolis that lasted for some time.

* * *

The summer of 1988 marked the ten-year anniversary of my private practice in anesthesia. This fact gave me cause to reflect on, and evaluate my career so far. On the one hand, there had been major advances in intraoperative monitoring as discussed earlier and improvements in drugs of all kinds and in the anesthetic machine itself. These enhancements made administering anesthesia a little more pleasant, and increased the safety margins. On the other hand, our practice model had ossified. Dr. Swan and I did our main cases, alongside the CRNAs, assisting them on an as-needed basis. The volume and types of cases did not change much. The laparoscope was just beginning to be used for gallbladder surgery; a trend that would grow and spread to other types of surgery such as hysterectomies and eventually nephrectomies.

In an average year I was on call about 52 percent of the time, and did at least 52 percent of the cases for the corporation, Dr. Swan doing the rest. Dr. Swan remained the president and sole shareholder of the corporation. We had ongoing discussions about how I might become a shareholder, and how we would incorporate a third anesthesiologist, if we were ever successful in recruitment. The corporation's daily operations were conducted fairly and competently, but the shareholder issue grew in importance in my mind.

We had an excellent anesthesia practice. Nevertheless, there were several areas in which I believed some changes were desirable. The foremost was in the policy of providing labor epidurals. Some of the obstetricians were doing epidurals for their patients. This was a little embarrassing to me. I continued to do an occasional request case. At first, we didn't have the fancy infusion pumps especially made for epidurals. At one point I used an oxytocin syringe pump to infuse sensorcaine into the epidural catheter. This seemed to work okay, but the pumps made by Baxter were more flexible in their infusion rates and very welcomed when they showed up in OB. The pressure to provide labor epidurals added impetus to recruit more anesthesiologists.

Providing better post-op pain relief with epidural infusions on selected cases, was also an area of concern. I had used an epidural for thoracotomies a few times with some success. Another time I used an epidural for a large abdominal surgery. The surgeon didn't like it and ordered it to be removed in the PACU. This was unfortunate. I put this concern on hold until we had more support, but it was always on my agenda.

Another area where I felt change would be appropriate was in our use of blood and blood products. This was certainly a sensitive issue, since sudden unexpected blood loss could be a nightmare for both the surgeon and the anesthesiologist during an operation. Some surgeons still advocated proactive aggressive blood replacement on cases in which significant blood loss was likely. Many people, however, were advocating a more conservative blood replacement practice by the mid '80s, for several reasons. The risk of transferring the AIDS virus, or other infection through transfusion, though very small, was not negligible. Furthermore, some studies suggested that patient outcomes might be negatively impacted with multiple transfusions. Lastly, there existed blood substitutes that could achieve the same goal as that of transfusing blood, but at a significantly lower cost. There are valid counter arguments to be made for all of these points. An effective screening test for the AIDS virus was eventually developed which removed that risk. Our blood supply is extremely safe, though short of perfection. Certainly special situations exist where aggressive blood replacement is appropriate and desirable. However, transfusion practices became considerably more conservative in the 1990s than it had been in the 1970s nationwide. Perhaps some practices went too far in decreasing transfusions. Nevertheless, I advocated for re-evaluating our transfusion practices.

I believe all these issues were pivotal for our practice at CMH in the late 1980s. However, my advocacy was not appreciated by all. Indeed, changing one element of a complex treatment procedure, or protocol, may not always work well unless other adaptations are concurrent. This helps explain some resistance to change. Nevertheless, I felt I was pushing in the right direction.

So as I "celebrated" my ten-year anniversary of private practice, there were significant issues brewing in the background. Our day to day practice continued pretty much as usual; on the surface things appeared calm. These issues were important to me, but I was patient. I expected things to evolve slowly. Little did I know, that in the next twelve months, I would experience a total overhaul of my professional career, and a dramatic change in my personal life. That is a story in itself.

Of course, business as usual could still include very stressful cases.

As I mentioned earlier, a difficult intubation can frequently be the most demanding aspect of an anesthesiologist's practice. Certain cases stand out in one's memory; the specific circumstances and details of the intubation tend to be etched in your memory, and filed under "situations to avoid if possible."

In our practice at CMH during the late 1980s, there were several types of surgery that could potentially cause a problem with intubation and airway management in general. These included thyroid surgery, anterior cervical disc fusion (ACDF), carotid endarterectomy and others. We were fortunate to have very skilled surgeons and correspondingly excellent outcomes for all these surgeries compared to national norms. I would have gladly undergone any of these surgeries at CMH, if I had a need for the procedure. However, even in the best of hands, some patients experience bleeding at the surgical site in the first few hours after surgery. Occasionally, this requires that the patient return to the operating room and be re-anesthetized, so the surgeon can drain the hematoma, and stop the bleeding. With the surgeries mentioned, the main difficulty was presented by the proximity of the surgery site to the airway (trachea). In some cases, the hematoma could compress the trachea and cause an obstruction to air flow resulting in respiratory distress. This made a return to the operating room even more urgent.

A senior CRNA had such a case one morning during this time frame. I was not directly involved, initially, since I was doing my own cases, but I was aware of the surgery. The patient was an elderly male who underwent surgery in the late morning. The induction, the intubation and the anesthetic proceeded without great difficulty or problems of any sort.

In the late afternoon, however, the surgeon needed to re-explore the site of surgery due to a moderate degree of bleeding and swelling. The CRNA who did the case and myself were on call that afternoon. I decided to allow the CRNA to do the bring-back case, since she had worked with the patient earlier in the day; and I made a point to be present in the OR to assist, if needed.

In the operating room we connected the patient to the ECG monitor, the oximeter probe and the automatic blood pressure cuff, and then administered 100 percent oxygen to him via the anesthesia breathing circuit. The right side of his neck was somewhat swollen due to the hematoma. It did not appear that the trachea was greatly displaced as can occur sometimes; there was only a mild degree of respiratory distress. Of course, the concern was that tracheal compression and distress could develop rapidly at any moment.

We induced the patient rapidly with propofol and anectine while he was breathing 100 percent oxygen. We hoped to place the endotracheal tube in the trachea ASAP to minimize the risk of regurgitation and aspiration, since he had recently eaten. (He had obviously not expected to have more surgery that day.) I stood nearby as the CRNA opened the mouth to skillfully place the MAC 3 laryngoscope blade in the mouth. I held gentle pressure on the cricoid cartilage, to help prevent any stomach contents that might appear from entering the trachea. As the CRNA adjusted the laryngoscope in the mouth in an attempt to visualize the glottis, she suddenly frowned. After attempting to visualize the tracheal opening for about thirty seconds, she turned to me anxiously and said, "Dr. Cottrell, I can't see a thing." That meant it was my turn.

I grabbed my Miller 3 blade and slowly inserted it down the right side of the pharynx, looking for normal anatomical landmarks that would guide me to the tracheal opening. I saw none. The mucosal tissue was red and much more edematous (swollen) than one would have guessed by the external swelling. I estimated that I had about sixty seconds to place the endotracheal tube and begin ventilation before a major decrease in the O2 sats raised the intensity level another notch. If I was unable to place the endotracheal tube correctly by that time, I would need to ventilate the patient by some other means. Normally this would be with an oral airway and an anesthesia mask, but the neck swelling and the presence of food in his stomach would make this not only difficult, but risky for possible aspiration of stomach contents into the lungs. An emergency tracheostomy might be necessary if I was unable to ventilate by the usual methods.

I adjusted the angle and depth of the Miller 3 blade for about thirty seconds. All I saw was red swollen mucosa. Then I saw a faint horizontal indentation midline in the mucosa. Could that be the epiglottis? If so, I might get lucky, and slide a small endotracheal tube under it, hoping it entered the trachea. If I was wrong, however, not only would I fail to achieve desperately needed ventilation, but I might damage the mucosal tissue, and further distort the anatomy. Then I saw a bubble appear from under the indentation, confirming that it was the epiglottis, covering the opening of the trachea. I grabbed a 6.0 mm endotracheal tube with my right hand, and carefully slid it under the ridge where the bubble appeared. It looked hopeful. When I connected the anesthesia circuit to the endotracheal tube, and manually squeezed the anesthesia bag, the capnograph indicated that the tube was properly placed--that is CO_2 was detected in the exhaled gas. The hematoma in the neck was quickly evacuated and the bleeding was controlled. The patient did well. He was watched closely after surgery for any signs of further bleeding or respiratory distress. There were none.

Today we readily have available both a fiber-optic bronchoscope and a video laryngoscope in the anesthesia work room, either of which could have made the intubation less daunting, though not necessarily easy. We had neither in the anesthesia department in 1988. The CRNA who attempted the intubation was very adept, having practiced anesthesia longer than either Dr. Swan or myself. She had intubated the patient without difficulty earlier in the day. The quandary is that even a modest swelling externally on the neck can translate to a major swelling and distortion of anatomy internally, making intubation very problematic. Dealing with this type of abnormal situation is my job and responsibility. I readily accept the challenge. At the same time, I am always searching for ways to help decrease the occurrence and minimize the risk involved with a difficult intubation. Many people, including the majority of physicians, are not especially focused on, or aware of the dilemma and hazards associated with a difficult intubation. That's understandable. The problem is the anesthesiologist's to handle without special fanfare or acknowledgement. Most busy anesthesiologists face a number of such predicaments in their careers. Nevertheless, I was a little dismayed by a physician's summary of that day's events when he stated the next morning, "The patient did well overall with his surgery; his only problem has been a sore throat caused by the anesthesiologist."

The Crisis Years 1989-1990

—◦◦◦—

The years 1989 and 1990 were pivotal times for me both on a professional and a personal level. In retrospect it was almost like I began
Act Two of a play with a new script and a new cast. How much of the
play was due to my own decisions and actions (wise or foolish as they
may be) and how much was the inevitable unfolding of events due to
the political climate, changes in the medical community, and individual personalities, I cannot say, even with the advantage of hindsight
and years of reflection. All I can do is relate the events from my own
viewpoint.

As I mentioned earlier, I had concerns about some issues in the
late '80s, but I felt that overall we had a good practice situation. The
safety and welfare of our patients was always our top priority. We ran
a conservative, efficient and low cost anesthesia service.

The practice of anesthesia had become significantly safer by the late
'80s, as was mentioned earlier, due not only to the recently introduced
monitors, but also from the efforts of many to make patient safety a
specific focus. As a reaction to safety concerns, the ASA created the
Anesthesia Patient Safety Foundation (APSF) in October 1985. Thus
the specialty of anesthesia became recognized as a leader in patient
safety. The APSF became the model and inspiration for the larger
National Patient Safety Foundation (NPSF) initiated by the AMA
eleven years later in 1996. Due to the efforts of APSF and others, a

"culture of safety" became strongly ingrained in the practice of anesthesia both nationwide and at CMH. This "culture" included not only improved safety features on anesthesia equipment, but also better alarm systems for low pressure in the breathing circuit, better labeling of drug vials and syringes, plus routine safety checks on anesthesia machines. Safety and anesthesia became almost synonymous terms.

As a result of this increased safety awareness, experts created aviation analogies. Incidents with safety concerns were referred to as near misses. The theory was that multiple small problems have the potential to snowball into a full blown mishap. For example: a fatigued caregiver, a poorly labeled syringe and a breathing circuit with a leak, all increase the possibility of an "accident." The more small problems that can be prevented; i.e., by better syringe labeling or low pressure alarms, the less likely any type of major mishap will occur. These principles were well established by the late 1980s. Therefore, much time and energy was directed toward multiple small changes and improvements to decrease the risk to the patient.

The last half of 1988 was filled with a number of personal and professional challenges and burdens that collectively weighed me down, although I didn't acknowledge them at the time. I can see in retrospect how they took their toll. Could it be that the safety issues in anesthesia have counterparts on a personal level? It seems plausible that a number of ongoing burdens and events were working synergistically to destabilize my life as I knew it. It's helpful to review what those burdens were in order to weigh their significance in my mind. I will start with the least important and work up to the bigger issues.

Since 1979 I had continually served as a Medical Examiner for Cabarrus County. The majority of ME cases were elderly people who died of an apparent natural cause, but without the attendance of a primary physician. These became ME cases by default. Our role was merely to sign the death certificate and state the most likely cause of death such as a heart attack or a stroke. Most unnatural deaths were sent to Chapel Hill for an autopsy by a pathologist for medical-legal reasons. The ME would then sign the death certificate based on his own knowledge of the case and the findings of the autopsy. Vehicular accidents and burn victims were among the more common unaturals. Homicides were less common although I had several. One poor soul fell in a sewer processing pool and drowned. Another man was electrocuted while pressure washing a building near high voltage power lines. Serving as ME for Cabarrus County gave me a somewhat moribund outlook on life, but also made me more safety conscious and provided a service to the medical community. Only once was I requested to testify in court. This was concerning a death involving a motor vehicle and cyclist. I don't believe my testimony was critical to the outcome.

Serving as a Medical Examiner was voluntary and I saw it as a form of community service. When I started serving in '79 we had ten to twelve physicians doing a similar service. In 1990 the number had dwindled to six. Ideally we took ME calls when we were also on call for our specialty practice. But with fewer physicians participating, that ideal became problematic. In the mid eighties it became my turn to make out the ME call schedule. This made me the defacto coordinator for the ME system in Cabarrus County. I was unable to pass this job to another physician until around 1992; there just weren't enough physicians serving as ME. The Medical Examiner system in North Carolina was ailing, and was finally revamped in the mid '90s, I was one of the last few physicians who served in those ailing years.

In 1987 I was nominated to be an officer in the Cabarrus County Medical Society. By tradition this meant I would serve as treasurer for two years, then as vice-president or program chairman for a year, and finally as president of the society the fourth year. This was not a heavy duty job. The County Medical Society served as the social club for the medical community. As the treasurer (1987-88) my job was to balance the bank account and purchase the wine and booze for the monthly meetings held at the Cabarrus Country Club. The job of program chairman was a little more demanding. This involved finding speakers or entertainment for the monthly meetings. Finally, as president in 1990 I had to preside at the monthly meeting and deal with an occasional complaint directed toward a doctor in the community. I was happy I had the opportunity to serve in this capacity. But it came at a time when my career underwent some major transformations and therefore added somewhat to my work load.

I continued to be quite active at Central United Methodist Church. No longer a youth counselor, I continued to sing in the choir and serve on various committees. In 1988 the minister, Donald Beatty, asked me to spearhead a committee to raise $80,000 to have an elevator installed in the church to assist elderly and handicapped church members gain access to the second floor. I accepted the challenge and gave a brief pep talk on Sunday morning to the congregation. After successfully completing this mission by getting the commitment for the 80,000, I felt a sense of accomplishment and received praise form the church staff. I felt I had done my civic duty for a while.

It was not to be. Shortly after the successful elevator campaign, Reverend Beatty asked me to be chairman of the finance committee for the church. This was a little out of protocol. I had not even as yet served as a regular member of the finance committee, and lacked familiarity with the budget and the budget-making process. What was I getting into? Church committees can be hornets' nests. It seemed there was an ongoing internal conflict within the congregation. Many, including the church staff, felt that the salaries and benefits of the minister and other church employees had fallen behind those of comparable churches in the area and needed to be bolstered. Another faction of well-respected and loyal parishioners felt the church's income had not grown adequately to justify such an increase; it would be financially irresponsible to do so. The minister correctly guessed that I would sympathize and side with those in favor of the increase.

I agreed to accept the job as the chairman of the finance committee for Central United Methodist Church starting in 1989. By all accounts I had plenty on my plate between the medical society, duties of the

Medical Examiner and church choir. And did I mention that I had a busy anesthesia practice plus a wife and three kids? There is no impelling argument why I should have felt obligated to take the job of finance chairman. Certainly, if I had known of the events about to transpire in 1989, I would have declined. I confess, I had a problem saying no. I suppose this may have been due to a personal flaw, or just faulty wiring in the part of my brain that was supposed to make my mouth say no. I was vigorous, not yet forty, but had a problem seeing my own limitations.

The conflict in the church came to a climax at an official board meeting in late 1989. A number of board members vocalized strong opinions for and against the proposed budget increase. I spoke in favor of the increase. My argument was that the welfare and enthusiasm of the church staff was a key element in attracting more members and encouraging growth. The proposed budget increase passed by a small margin. After this critical meeting, my duties as chairman of the finance committee consisted of more mundane chores related to the routine financial operation of the church.

In addition to these extracurricular activities, there were two major events adding to my stress level in late 1988. Both were mostly beyond my control, but demanded a good deal of emotional energy.

The first was a malpractice suit filed in 1987 against me. The summary judge dismissed the case in late 1988. This meant I got no "black mark" or any negative points against me in the National Data bank for doctors. The case disappeared. The amount of time I had to spend with lawyers and the malpractice insurance company and the financial outlay were minimal. But I'm sure it sapped a good deal of emotional energy. The best way to describe the experience was that I felt I had a dark cloud over my head. It did not seem to affect my ability to function on a day to day basis or to interact with others, but it did cast a shadow on my outlook in general. When the case disappeared the cloud went away and I could see the light again.

The greatest personal burden I had in late 1988, however, was dealing with my father's terminal illness due to a misdiagnosed cancer. He had undergone a partial colectomy in 1965 for colon cancer, but was generally in good health. In May 1987 he had the onset of abdominal cramps and other GI symptoms resembling those of 1965 when he was diagnosed with cancer. His primary doctor sent him for an upper and lower GI study with barium in Knoxville. Nothing remarkable was noted on the X-rays. No further tests were done despite continued symptoms. In February 1988 he underwent an emergency operation for severe pain due to a perforation in his colon. The surgeon found evidence of recurrent colon cancer which had spread throughout his abdomen. There was little he could do but repair the perforation. We all knew what this meant. We were shocked; he was not yet sixty-four at the time.

He recovered enough to travel to England with my mother in the spring. He had an unpleasant summer, but appeared to be holding his own while taking chemotherapy. When I last saw him in early October at his home in Tennessee, however, he was very weak and frail. I knew he couldn't last very long.

On October 9, I was back in North Carolina administering anesthesia at CMH when he passed. Someone called the main anesthesia office to notify me and the word quickly spread through the ORs that my father had died. In a few minutes a CRNA entered the OR where I was working to relieve me. I knew the minute she came through the door what had happened. She didn't have to say anything. This was the first death or tragedy of any kind to occur in my immediate family; it was a heavy blow. But I had prepared myself emotionally for the shock since I knew from my last visit that death was imminent. I did not want to project any image of weakness or vulnerability, so I thanked her for her offer to relieve me and reassured her that I did not need to be relieved at that moment. I expected the case to be over soon.

I was not a stranger to death. As a physician with ten years of experience, I had witnessed it several times in the ICU and emergency room. As a medical examiner I was even more acquainted with death than the average physician. I knew how the body's functions shut down one by one until the last glimmer of life lingers a few precious moments and then fades into eternal oblivion. I knew the various ways that people cope with tragedy and about the four stages of grief. It came with the territory.

Furthermore, as an anesthesiologist, I had trained myself to suppress my personal feelings in order to perform the task at hand with unfailing professionalism. If I had been up working the night before, and so tired I could barely function, I had the uncanny ability to focus all my energy on those critical procedures like placing an endotracheal tube or obtaining venous access when necessary. What about the time I became suddenly ill at work? Well, I vomited in a trash can and two minutes later administered an anesthetic. There was no one to relieve me at that time; it had to be done. So, in a sense, dealing with my father's death was not unlike any of the other challenges I had to face. The key was to be able to focus on the case at hand. I appreciated the CRNA's offer to relieve me and made a mental note to thank her later. I had the situation in control. It was just a death in the family.

The CRNA left and I continued my case. It was not an especially difficult one. Everything was going fine. I rechecked the breathing circuit, the anesthesia gauges and the vital signs. No problems. I would call my mother and siblings as soon as the case finished.

But then I noticed some changes in the Dinamap blood pressure monitor. The numerals, once sharp and distinct, were now blurry and ran together. Other objects in the room displayed a similar phenomenon. It seemed as if I was experiencing some type of visual disturbance. What could it be? Something was interfering with the usual ability of my lens to refract the light and form a sharp image on my retina. It appeared a thin layer of fluid had formed over my cornea. Some had even overflowed and run down my face. This would never do. I used a towel to remove the evidence. I felt fine, but the visual disturbance was a problem and a source of embarrassment. Part of my lower brain had initiated a lacrimation process, I had not authorized it. I asked the OR circulator nurse to ask the CRNA to return to relieve me so I could deal with this problem. When she returned I quickly turned the case over to her and left the room.

My goal was to return to my office as discreetly as possible to deal with my situation. From Room Three in the OR, I went through the anesthesia work room and then through the old call room into the main hallway, thus avoiding the break room and the main entrance to the OR where I might be seen. In the hallway it was a direct shot into my office area where I would be out of sight. I entered the office and went right to my desk. Our secretary came to my aid immediately with a box of Kleenex. Despite having no background in medicine, she had made the correct diagnosis and quickly provided the remedy. The only problem was she didn't bring enough.

My father, William Barber Cottrell, was born April 17, 1924, in Brooklyn Hospital in New York City. His father, Royal Lee Cottrell, was a teacher and principal in the New York school system, which is where he met and married Helen Barber, my dad's future mother. He grew up in a four-story row house at 209 Greene Avenue in Brooklyn, and attended New York City public schools. His summers were spent at Cobossee Colony, a rustic summer hotel his father owned and operated on Lake Cobosecontee near Monmouth, Maine. All family members including his mother, brother and half-brother participated in the operations. His younger brother, Henry, was born in cabin ten on July 17, 1925. The hotel consisted of a main lodge, a boat house, fifteen to twenty cabins and a primitive golf course. There were plenty of chores to go around. Golf caddying earned seventy cents per eighteen holes, with a good tip it was possible to make a whole dollar. Wood patrol, fishing guide and restaurant errands filled the day. They loved it.

They were back in Brooklyn every year to begin the new school year after Labor Day. In addition to school his family was active in the local Seventh Day Baptist church. His grandfather, Ira Lee

Cottrell, was an ordained minister in the church. For a while they rented the top floor of their row house to a German immigrant, Bruno Timmermann, in exchange for violin lessons for my dad and his brother. Allegedly Bruno had fled Germany before WW I to escape manslaughter charges. He initially found work playing in the "pit" for vaudeville shows. The Depression, however, was hard on musicians. In 1936 (age twelve) my father entered the Brooklyn Technical Institute, a high school within walking distance to his home, and arguably the best public school in New York City at the time. He graduated in 1940, at age sixteen, 17th out of 550 students. He had been able to skip a total of two grades earlier in his schooling. I am sure his father's influence as a teacher helped facilitate his rapid advancement. Also noteworthy was an IQ score of 153 as a senior in high school, and a score of 161 on the army entrance exam.

He entered Alfred University in September 1940, and graduated in December 1943 with a major in math and physics. Alfred was a small university in western New York founded by the Seventh Day Baptist in 1836. It was near Richburg, New York, home of numerous Cottrell ancestors, and where his half-brother, father and grandfather had attended. In January 1944, shortly after graduation, he married my mother, Jeannette Milnes, a classmate from Buffalo. Shortly after getting married in New York, he accepted the job offer from Tennessee Eastman Corporation, a subsidiary of Eastman Kodak. The job offer was dated October 2, 1943. Starting salary was to be $49.50 per week. This included some allowance for expected overtime. I have a copy of the letter. The closing sentence of the letter was; "For a young man with your training, we know of no position in which you could better serve your country, and on this project you need not feel at all apologetic about serving the industrial rather than the military army." Although he was eventually drafted and underwent basic training in June 1945, he was released in February 1946, along with a number of other scientists, so they could continue their research or teaching careers.

So in January he traveled with his new bride to Knoxville, Tennessee, for job processing and soon began work in a research area about 20 miles to the west. His earliest assignment was with the research group XAX in Building 9735 known as an experimental alpha calutron unit. These were the early days of the town later known as Oak Ridge. The research was part of a large effort known as the Manhattan Project which was carried out at Oak Ridge, Hanford, Washington and Los Alamos, New Mexico. The idea was to separate the isotopes of uranium (235 and 238) to acquire enough uranium 235 to sustain a rapid nuclear chain reaction with the release of tremendous energy. That is, make a functional atomic bomb. We know from Hiroshima, August 6, 1945, and Nagasaki, August 9, 1945, that the Manhattan Project accomplished its goal. Fortunately, or unfortunately, depending on your point of view, the world was changed forever.

In 1959, Dr. Alvin Weinberg, director of the Oak Ridge National Laboratory (ORNL) asked my father to edit and supervise a technical journal, *Nuclear Safety*. Originally a quarterly publication, it became the primary focus of his career for the next twenty-five years. Having such responsibility in the physics world without an advanced degree in physics was somewhat unusual.

In the early 1970s, the nuclear industry was under attack by Ralph Nader and others for safety concerns. My father had to testify on behalf of the industry in hearings in Washington, D.C. In December, 1971, he authored a letter to the regulatory branch of the AEC concerning some design flaws or safety issues with proposed new reactors, specifically for the cooling systems. For this he incurred criticism from the AEC heads for being a stumbling block to progress. The AEC claimed the letter was unauthorized, an apparent reference to his lack of PhD credentials, and returned it. The letter was officially snubbed. Dr. Weinberg defended him despite pressure to fire him from the AEC. Weinberg refused to be blackmailed, but was himself eventually pressured to resign. My father kept his position as editor of *Nuclear Safety*, but lost some other responsibilities. He was eventually vindicated by the ECCS (Emergency Core Cooling Systems) Hearing Panel in December 1972. The results were published in *Nuclear Safety* Vol. 15 (1) January-February 1974 and reprinted in the "Atomic Energy Law Journal" 16 (4), Winter 1975. In a strange coincidence, Milton Shaw of the AEC, after pressuring Weinberg to resign, was soon pressured to resign himself by the new AEC chairman.

In 1984 he was offered the possibility of being director of the Atomic Energy Museum in Oak Ridge. He wisely opted for full retirement. Probably a good move, he would only live four more years.

In 1953 I accompanied my dad to an auction in the Farragut community, 25 minutes from Oak Ridge, for a thirteen acre tract of land and a 3,500 square foot house. His bid of $25,000 was the last one. Hence in 1953 our family moved from Oak Ridge to the Concord-Farragut area in the western part of Knox County. Both he and my mother became active in the Concord United Methodist Church. In addition to serving as finance chairman and chairman of the official board, he authored a book in 1985; *Concord United Methodist Church. The History of a Church and Its Environment.* He also served as a commissioner of the first utility district of Knox County from 1956 to 1978, and as its president the last sixteen years. Under his leadership the local water supply was eventually fluoridated in the 1970s. He received no pay for these services.

My father was generally an upbeat and cheerful person, an eternal optimist my mother would say. One of his endearing characteristics was to frequently whistle when working around the house. From rooms away we would hear "Serenade in Blue" a big band song written by Harry Warren and popularized by the Glen Miller Orchestra in 1942. My dad's memory and that song are inseparable and irreplaceable.

I used to view my dad as being a little eccentric. He was different from most Southern dads. Was he a little out of synch with fashions, or was he just a little ahead of the times? He liked paisley ties and colored socks. But those fashions come and go. In the long run I came to see him as much more traditional in his later years. He was widely respected in the church and community. As a physicist he received a decent salary, but considerable less than even a beginning physician. I never heard him complain or express anger over the failure to diagnose his cancer in a timely way. Conceivably it may have been curable in May 1987, if properly diagnosed.

My dad and I shared a high mutual respect and never underwent any major estrangement like many baby boomer children I know. I had a high respect for physicists and he for physicians. However, because of our busy schedules, mostly mine in the last ten years, we rarely had much bonding time in our adult lives. I would like to have had the opportunity to play a few rounds of golf with him, other than the obligatory family golf outing each summer in Gatlinburg. I had little attraction for the game as a child and in medical training, so I did not relate to his enjoyment of it. That's certainly changed.

I never really thought about it much until reviewing his autobiography, but our jobs really had a lot in common. As a safety engineer, he had to analyze nuclear reactors and defend against any weakness in the system that would allow a possible accident. It was all about safety. As an anesthesiologist my job was to defend and protect the patient from possible harm during surgery. I was concerned not only with individual cases and procedures, but also using systems and protocol that minimized risk. I was a safety engineer for the surgical patient. He was a safety engineer for nuclear reactors. Out of necessity, our mindsets were much the same.

The funeral service was at Concord United Methodist Church on October 12, 1988. The burial was at Pleasant Forest Cemetery in Concord, about two miles from our home on Admiral Drive immediately after. My last visit to the Cemetery was August 4, 2006, when my mother was interred. I am overdue a visit.

December 1988 brought the end of a somber year and January 1989 rolled around with little fanfare. Anesthesia services continued as usual. Our failure to recruit another anesthesiologist was becoming more and more a concern of the administration. I heard rumors that a hospital board meeting was to be held in late January to discuss the future of the Department of Anesthesia. I was not invited, so I don't know who said or did what; all I can do is relate the events from my vivid but biased memory.

On Saturday morning following the meeting, Dr. Swan was on call at the hospital and I was at home with Heidi and the kids. It was around nine o'clock when he called the house and asked me to come in to discuss some business issues. This was most unusual; something must be up, but I had no idea what.

I went directly to the hospital and met Dr. Swan in his office. He said he was stepping down as chairman of the department and that furthermore he was totally quitting the practice of medicine. As a consequence he was giving me a sixty-day notice of termination of employment with his corporation, Cabarrus Anesthesiologists PA. Since he had a ninety-day term for cancellation of contract with the hospital, he would continue to practice until May 1. My term would be up on April 1. He gave me the impression that he had been asked to resign. Other people told me they thought he had offered to resign. It didn't matter. He was quitting. I was stunned. I didn't see it coming. Not this. He was only fifty-seven years old.

We continued our practice as it had been before the meeting for two months. I began talks with the administration about building a new group to provide anesthesia services for the hospital. They seemed interested in working out a deal. They gave me a letter of intent to develop a contractual relationship, but refused to enter into an agreement while Dr. Swan was still around.

Dr. Swan began practice at CMH in 1960 after finishing his residency at the Ohio State Medical University College of Medicine in Columbus, Ohio. Two other anesthesiologists practiced briefly in the 60s or late 50s, but he was the first one to bring stability and longevity serving as Director of Anesthesia for twenty-nine years. Under his leadership the department was run efficiently and economically. The core business was general anesthesia and some regional anesthesia for bread and butter cases in the main OR and occasionally for Cesarean sections in OB. No bells, no whistles. There were very few services rendered outside of the main OR or OB. The RVU charge in 1989 was 23, to my knowledge one of the lowest in the state of North Carolina. What's more, there was only one charge per case; either for the MD or the CRNA who were employed by the hospital. Mishaps were rare. The patients received good service for their money. The main weakness was a perception that the department was a bottleneck to growth. A failure to provide labor epidurals and 100 percent MD coverage at night were concerns. Nevertheless, the experience of doing my own cases, and assisting the CRNAs as needed under that system, provided a strong core of experience. It honed my clinical skills and also helped shape my outlook on the practice of medicine.

Since I was not a shareholder in Cabarrus Anesthesiologists PA, my last payment from my old employee would be in early April, paying me for my work in March. I would receive no further accounts receivable or other assets. The hospital wanted to work out an agreement with me, but would not sign until the end of April. Although I always thought an agreement was probable, all this left me dangling.

In March '89 I learned a few of the elements in the hospital's tentative agreement through discussions with Bob Conroy, the COO of CMH. A key provision of the contract would be a requirement to recruit at least three more anesthesiologists within twenty months of the initiation of the agreement, which turned out to be midnight April 30, 1989. Furthermore, each of these recruits would be required to obtain their board certification within four years of the completion of their residency. I vehemently argued for an increase to six years. I was not opposed to the requirement of boards; board certification is a good thing. But if certification were to become an ultimate criterion for the practice of medicine in at CMH, I argued it should be a generous term. The hospital acquiesced.

Dr. Swan might continue to practice if he so chose, either as an independent practitioner, or as an employee of the new corporation.

Either way he would count as one of the required three physicians that I had twenty months to find. I thought that was an appropriate appeasement for him, but he declined the opportunity to practice by either regime.

The contract contained the usual legal jargon about providing appropriate and quality medical services and treating all patients equally. In addition, the "on call" anesthesiologist should be available after 4 p.m. within at least thirty minutes for emergency cases. Looking back this was a fairly lax standard, but seemed about right at the time.

The contract was to be exclusive; that is if I agreed to the terms, no one else would be allowed to practice anesthesia at CMH unless they worked for my group (with the possible exception of Dr. Swan). Exclusive contracts were the trend for hospital-based practices. The advantages for the hospital administration was that they could hold one entity responsible for quality, adequate coverage and personnel issues. In theory it made services more efficient and economical. I realized that the exclusivity concept was at least a little controversial and resented by some practitioners. When I expressed some reluctance to include the clause, I was informed that if I did not accept the term of exclusivity, CMH would find another physician who would. If that happened I could be conceivably excluded myself from practicing medicine at CMH, despite the fact that I was then vice president of the Cabarrus County Medical Society, and had almost eleven years of service at CMH under my belt. Welcome to Medical Politics 101. Nothing devious; it was simply obvious who held the cards. The hospital owned the physical plant and equipment and employed the CRNAs, the RNs and other employees that I required to practice my medical arts in the manner to which I was accustomed. They had deep pockets. Mine were shallow. I decided to agree to the exclusivity clause.

In addition to the foregoing considerations in the contract proposal, the administration recommended to me that we initiate an entirely different arrangement for providing anesthesia services. Instead of administering anesthesia services directly ourselves, alongside CRNAs who were doing the same, they advocated a system whereby all, or nearly all anesthetics would be directly administered by the CRNAs, but also with an attendant MD (anesthesiologist) to supervise. Regional anesthetics would be administered by the MD, but with a CRNA also involved to help sedate and monitor the patient. This meant that the MD would do an adequate preoperative evaluation of the patient, be present and assist with the induction of anesthesia, be present at frequent intervals in the operating room, assist with problems or difficult aspects of the case, and assure good care of the patient in the immediate post-operative period in the OR and in the PACU. The advantage of this system is that every patient would have an MD involved, either as the primary anesthetist, or as a medical supervisor of a CRNA. Either way, an MD's name was on the anesthetic record. Not so under the old system. Even though we responded well to the needs of the CRNAs, we had not been meeting the definition of "medical supervision" by the new standards.

The political, logistical, financial and practical consequences of the proposed new system for administering anesthesia were considerable. One could write a lengthy thesis on the resulting changes. For starters, each case would require not one, but two anesthesia caregivers to be present in the OR before a case could start. If one caregiver was briefly tied up in the PACU, or needed to run to the restroom, it would cause a slight delay in the induction of the anesthetic. Everyone, especially surgeons, hates delays in the induction of anesthesia. Also, each patient would now receive two bills for anesthesia, one for the hospital-employed CRNA, and one for the anesthesiologist.

The advantages, however, were indisputable. Each case would now have a pilot and a copilot. The safety net was strengthened. Their collective knowledge, skills and observations would work synergistically to help assure a good outcome. I'll say it again, it's all about safety. This system was already established in nearby Mecklenburg County

(Charlotte). It rapidly became the standard system in North Carolina and most of the eastern and central parts of this country. It was not my duty to challenge the macro political trends in my specialty. Was the new system of supervision superior, safer or more cost effective than MD only, or even CRNA only anesthesia? It is virtually impossible to get well-controlled data on outcome to answer this question objectively. I can only say it was the path most anesthesiologists were taking and it was the path we took. I warmed to it.

As April approached, it seemed probable that I would reach an agreement with the hospital, even though they chose not to sign it yet. It was necessary, therefore, to do the ground work to form a medical corporation and to set up a billing and accounting system. This was done with the help of Robinson, Bradshaw & Hinson, a large law firm in Charlotte; Medical Finance Company, an anesthesia billing company started by Scott Spellman in Charlotte; and Sue Rinehart CPA, a local accountant. Thus in April my new corporation, Concord-Kannapolis Anesthesiologists PC, was launched. I began providing services through my corporation in April before I went solo in May. I signed the contract in late April, and on May 1 I entered a new phase of my medical practice when Dr. Swan retired.

I stopped to assess my situation. I was the only full-time anesthesiologist in a 457 bed hospital that did 7,000 surgical cases and 1200 deliveries a year. To provide needed anesthesia we needed at least four full-time anesthesiologists to compete with comparable sized hospitals. I was contractually committed to adding at least three more in twenty months. On the plus side I had eleven years of clinical experience, I was in good health and I had a positive outlook on the situation. But, I was politically naïve and had mediocre business skills. Looking back, I can see I was a little too trusting in human nature. I thought grit and sweat could conquer just about anything.

To help me get started, CMH agreed to pay me a small stipend for three months, then I was on my own. They had paid Cabarrus Anesthesiologists PA a significantly larger stipend for years and years to manage the department, but that was under the old system. To assist me in recruiting new MDs, CMH arranged a meeting for me with a headhunter service with which they were working. After the failure to recruit a new doctor in five years, CMH didn't trust me to recruit without help. I preferred to take someone directly out of training to help build a new department. By May, however, most residents graduating in July had already found jobs. Good new doctors were scarce. Given the urgency of the situation and my political inexperience, I felt it wise to use the headhunters with whom CMH had a pre-existing relationship. They ultimately discovered three of the first four doctors I hired.

Meanwhile, I had to practice medicine. It would likely take at least several months until a new full-time MD could start and I needed to cover six surgical rooms a day plus night call and weekends. To help with the coverage I contacted Kron Medical Corporation, a locum tenens company founded by Alan Kronhaus in 1980 in Chapel Hill, North Carolina. Kron Medical was able to consistently provide a qualified anesthesiologist from May 1 until August when Dr. Beach, my first full-time recruit arrived. I recall there were only two days in that stretch without a locum doctor. I was very busy on those days.

During those early days, the locum doctor and I would each cover three rooms. Given the inexperience of the locums and the novelty of the new system (supervision versus MD anesthesia) I think things went fairly smoothly. Occasionally a room might need to wait a minute or two for the anesthesiologist who may be tied up elsewhere, but it didn't seem to be a huge problem. I split call with the locum tenens doctors, but I could no longer take every other Wednesday or Friday off. As a matter of fact I worked every other weekend, Saturday and Sunday. On my "off" weekend I worked Sundays to give the locum doctor a day off and to decrease expenses. Hence in a typical fourteen day cycle, I was only totally off on one day (every other Saturday). Sundays were usually not very busy. So I used them to catch up on accounting and other office work.

There was very little cash flow (income) in the first two or three months for my new corporation. This was due to the glacial pace of processing insurance claims. To remedy this I had opened up a line of credit with Wachovia, signed by Robert Brannan III and myself on April 5, 1989. I was approved for up to $100,000. By September the cash flow had picked up significantly.

As the summer progressed, along with my lawyers, I made decisions about the terms of employment to be offered a new recruit and how the business would be run. Since not being a shareholding partner had been an issue for me, I was willing to make partnership easy to obtain by loyal and capable new employees. Initially I decided to require only one year to partnership. Eventually I increased this to three years. I didn't make board certification a prerequisite for partnership. Although failure to pass oral boards on the first attempt was not unusual, statistically most graduates of qualified residency programs in the U.S. were successful within six years.

As the president of the new corporation and as the new department chairman, I did not give myself special perks. I had no paid days off, no extra salary or other considerations. I based my income on productivity as I did for the new recruits. The extra five or ten or more hours a week I spent on administrative, accounting and legal business for the department and corporation were not reimbursed per se. As the initial shareholder, I did eventually make a significant profit on the locum tenens productivity, but this was a one-time occurrence. My income under the old system with Dr. Swan was a good 25 percent or so less than a comparable MD in Charlotte. I learned this through my new billing manager, Scott Spellman of Medical Finance Corporation. It appeared under the new corporation and system of supervision that our incomes would be on par with those in Charlotte. Therefore, after the first few months, I was not especially concerned about my income or the extra workload that I incurred. I expected that my considerable office duties would level out and eventually lessen. They never did.

Some of these early decisions about how the corporation would work internally were not in my best interest in the long run, but I made them in good faith for the growth of the department and the medical community. One other issue was that the hospital agreement was a little ambivalent and problematic. Under the old system with Dr. Swan, we had worked closely with the CRNAs, not as medical supervisors per se as with the new system, but almost like employers. Dr. Swan did employment interviews, annual reviews, dealt with sick leave, vacation and other personnel issues. We provided an excellent in-service education program and met with them daily. For these services Dr. Swan's corporation was paid a generous monthly stipend. As I became involved in these activities, I also profited from this income. But under the new system there were no such monthly payments from the hospital. Who would handle these issues now? As the department grew who would recruit and interview the much needed new CRNAs? Who would smooth over inter-personal problems and help defend them in confrontations or differences with MDs, either surgeons or anesthesiologists? The hospital agreement seemed a little vague on the details.

In 1989 I assumed those duties for the hospital along with my other corporate, department and medical responsibilities. I continued to provide these HR services free of charge for the hospital for several reasons. First of all I was accustomed to assisting with these tasks under the old system with Dr. Swan. It "felt" appropriate to do so. Secondly, maintaining an adequate quantity and quality of CRNAs was essential to our style of practice now more than ever. A major loss of CRNAs would be a nightmare for our practice. Ultimately, I was able to recruit a retired colonel, Clem Markarian, to serve as a "super" chief CRNA and assume most of these managerial duties. I negotiated an increased salary on his behalf with the administration and assisted in finding temporary housing for him. I was highly motivated to relieve myself of those extra duties. However that didn't happen until 1993.

As my corporation's contractual and financial agreement were being ironed out, our medical practice was beginning to expand rapidly. We were not yet covering labor epidurals routinely, but the main OR was as busy as ever. Although patient outcomes were uniformly good, one case in those early days was noteworthy for the political controversy surrounding it. I will relate from memory the essential points of the case minus names and some details.

One weekday afternoon around 2 p.m. an elderly diabetic male experienced some dizziness and weakness on his left side for two or three minutes while working at home. His symptoms resolved quickly, but his wife brought him to the ER promptly. He was admitted by a primary MD that afternoon and scheduled for an arteriogram around 10 a.m. the next morning. The concern was that a major stroke could occur due to emboli or other causes. He was taken to radiology around 9:30 a.m. The angiogram showed a high grade blockage on the right carotid artery that was likely the source of an embolus the day before. The main concern now was avoiding the possible occurrence of a major stroke. At some point the surgeon was notified of the results. Around 1:30 p.m. the surgeon called the OR to post the case. He would leave his office early, around 3:30 p.m. hoping he could start the case by 4 p.m. at the latest.

Shortly after the case was posted, I left the OR briefly to interview the patient and discuss the anesthetic. Entering his room at approximately 1:45 p.m., I saw he was sitting up in bed calmly talking with family members. Immediately in front of him was a lunch tray of mostly empty containers. He had just finished eating. Who ordered this lunch? He was scheduled to have an urgent surgery in about two hours to fix a carotid blockage. I was appalled. I asked him who told him he could have lunch. He answered, "the surgeon." Later he changed his answer and said it was the radiologist. Well, it had to be the radiologist; it would have been unthinkable for the surgeon to order food shortly before a needed operation. Nevertheless, this left us with two options, neither of which was totally satisfactory.

The first option was to proceed with the surgery at 3:30 or 4:00 p.m.

despite the inappropriate lunch, some of which was sure to remain in his stomach when it came time to induce anesthesia. A rapid sequence induction of anesthesia with cricoid pressure would minimize, though not totally eliminate the risk of aspiration. Bleeding around the trachea post operatively could certainly further add to this risk, but that was fairly unlikely. The other choice would be to delay the case until 9 or 10 p.m. so we would be more comfortable that his stomach would be empty. The risk here is that he might have a massive stroke while waiting the extra few hours for surgery. I thought this risk was quite small though not negligible. It was dilemma.

Which course of action was best for the patient? The patient would probably do okay either way. Option one put a little more stress on the anesthesiologist to protect the airway from aspiration. Compared to someone who was not fed "by accident," there was some increased risk for the patient. Option two made the case very inconvenient and carried a very slight risk of stroke while waiting. I weighed the options in my mind.

The risk of death due to aspiration of stomach contents into the lungs was first described by Curtis Mendelson, an obstetrician performing emergency Cesarean sections back in 1946. With the increasing number of Cesarean sections occurring in the 1930s and the 1940s, a number of patients were noted to aspirate food matter into their trachea and lungs during the induction of general anesthesia. Death might occur acutely due to food particles obstructing airflow in the trachea. Or the stomach contents might cause a chemical burn in the lungs causing a life threatening pneumonia. This syndrome is known as aspiration pneumonia or as "Mendelson's Syndrome" after Dr. Mendelson. Although pregnant women may be at somewhat increased risk, this same syndrome can potentially occur in any patient given a general anesthetic who has significant liquid or solid matter in his stomach.

According to *Principles of Anesthesia* by Vincent J Collins, "For each patient whose heart has stopped during anesthesia because of drug effects, the hearts of dozens of patients have stopped because the larynx was flooded with vomitus. There have been more anesthetic deaths from aspiration of vomitus than from any other cause." To say an anesthesiologist is concerned about the airway and possible aspiration pneumonia, would be like saying a sky diver is concerned about his parachute, or a SCUBA diver is concerned about his breathing apparatus. It is the heart of the matter, and comes with the territory.

For normal elective surgery the ASA guidelines require eight hours of fasting or NPO (nothing by mouth) for a large meal, but only two hours NPO for clear liquids (clear liquids empty much faster from the stomach than solids). To make things a little more complicated, we now require only six hours NPO for a light meal. If this is a little confusing, don't feel bad, I still struggle with it after forty years. What about a thirty-year-old man who has been NPO of everything for fourteen hours, except that he forgot and ate two blackberries from a bush in his yard five hours before a planned inguinal hernia? This is an actual case I had recently. I elected to proceed. The surgery was not around the neck and he had a class one (easy) airway. He was in technical violation of the guideline. Black coffee is considered a clear liquid and hence requires only a two-hour wait. However, if you add a little cream to the coffee, this technically now requires a six-hour wait. Now I have seen studies that show little difference in emptying time for coffee with or without cream. I am therefore somewhat lenient with these types of issues, especially if I am confident of my ability to intubate the patient. One has to look at the overall picture.

However, if a surgical case is considered an emergency, all these guidelines take a back seat to the urgency of the case. Let's say Mr. Smith is a diabetic with an infected foot who expects to need a below the knee amputation, but is receiving IV antibiotics in an attempt to delay the inevitable. He eats breakfast at 8 a.m. At 10 a.m. Dr. Goodknife makes rounds and thinks the leg looks worse and post Mr. Smith for a BKA (below the knee amputation). At 10:30 a.m. the anesthesiologist interviews the patient and discovers he ate at 8 a.m. He therefore recommends the case be done not before 2 p.m., a six-hour postponement to minimize the risk of aspiration. At noon, however, Dr. Goodknife has finished rounds and becomes concerned about the delay. He declares the case an emergency. This declaration renders the NPO guidelines irrelevant. The anesthesiologist has little alternative but to proceed with the case. Good technique and diligence can minimize the risk of aspiration. This is how the system normally works. The urgency of the surgery generally outweighs the risk of anesthesia and aspiration in most cases.

The weakness of this system is that not all emergencies are equal. Not all patients are at equal risk for aspiration, and not all airways are of equal difficulty to manage. Occasionally the anesthesiologist may attempt to "negotiate" a more desirable time with the surgeon to minimize his concerns of aspiration. He does so at his own peril and often winds up giving in to the surgeon if he is adamant about the need to proceed. If that happens, the anesthesiologist might not only be held accountable for a possible aspiration pneumonia, but may also be labeled recalcitrant. What is needed is an objective way to evaluate all the risk factors of each option, and choose the option that is best for the patient. Would that it were that easy.

That afternoon the surgeon wanted to proceed with the surgery, despite the fact that he had recently eaten. I preferred to delay it several hours. Feeding the patient at 1:45 p.m. was a distinct error; not necessarily the surgeon's fault. Nevertheless, it put the patient at some increased risk; and the onus was on me. I didn't back down. The surgeon was unhappy. Rather than do the case late at night, however, we both agreed to come in the following morning and do the case when we were both fresh. It was to be my day off, but I readily agreed to this option. The patient did well. I thought the case was well-handled.

After this noteworthy case, surgery continued as usual and many doctors congratulated me for taking a controversial stand for the benefit of the patient... in my dreams! In the real world word spread through the surgery section that I had defied a senior surgeon and was a problem. No less than three clout-heavy physicians (two surgeons and one family practice doctor) strolled by my office during the next week or two to give me a warning. They all said the same thing: "I was a nice guy, not a bad doctor, but I had better watch my step or my days may be numbered." Not those exact words, but essentially that message. At the next surgery meeting in July, I took a whippin'. I would show you the scars, but the lashes were verbal. One surgeon proposed that the surgery section pass a rule that an anesthesiologist could never cancel a case unless the surgeon agreed to it. This proposal failed to pass. Now, keep in mind that, at age forty, I had eleven years of experience and was the most senior anesthesiologist in a 457 bed hospital. Also keep in mind that at age forty I was the youngest anesthesiologist in a 457 bed hospital. Come to think of it, I was the only anesthesiologist at the hospital, other than the locum tenens MD. I realized that a polit- ical victory here was an unrealistic goal. I opted for survival instead. Trying to lecture a body of thirty-five surgeons on the dangers of aspi- ration pneumonia, and the virtues of an adequate NPO status, would be like a teetotaler lecturing on the dangers of alcohol to a convention of wine connoisseurs. You may make some valid points, but they are more focused on other issues. I may exaggerate a little. Several physi- cians did sympathize with me. But you get the idea.

The furor over this case eventually died down. There was a lot work to do. I felt that most surgeons "forgave" me for my transgres- sion. I was putting in seventy -hour work weeks, but a lot of it was behind-the-scenes administrative activity. Most people were unaware of these duties. I can sort of understand what happened. I challenged a senior physician's decision. The system defends seniority over junior troublemakers. Fair enough. I get it. I took my punishment. What concerns me is that the system never addressed the underlying problem. The physician who ordered the meal inappropriately for the patient got off scot-free. The issue of miscommunication about the need to be NPO for surgery was never addressed. Was it a nursing error, a missed phone call, a dietary department miscue, or a false assumption by the radiologist? Rather than placing blame, would it not have been more productive to analyze the system of communication that led to the error and then take steps to make a system change or improvement to minimize the risk that it ever happen again. To my knowledge, nothing like this ever happened.

I struggled to find some guiding principles in the literature or text books to support or condemn my decisions concerning this case. The best I could do was consult the definitive textbook on the subject, *Anesthesia and Neurosurgery* by Cottrell and Turndorf, 2nd edition 1986. A word of caution about supporting one's position by quoting textbooks or relevant articles. Unless the issue is cut and dried (most aren't) it is not too difficult for any physician to cherry pick opinions and place one's own spin on the evidence to support almost any position he desires. This caveat, of course, applies to myself as well as those I may disagree with.

Dr. James E Cottrell (no immediate relation to myself), the primary author, is recent past Chairman and distinguished professor of the Department of Anesthesia at SUNY Downstate in Brooklyn, New York. He was also the regional Chairman of Anesthesiology at Long Island College Hospital, Lutheran Medical Center, Downstate at Bay Ridge and past chair at Kings County Hospital Center. He has served on the New York State Education Board of Regents, served as past president of the ASA, President of the Society of Academic Anesthesiology Chairs, President of the Society of Neurosurgical Anesthesia and Critical Care (SNACC), Board Examiner for the ABA, Editor in Chief of the Journal of Neurosurgical Anesthesiology, Rovenstine Lecturer, founding member of the AIDS Action Foundation, honorary member of foreign medical societies, co-authored three major text books, authored 140 publications and delivered over 250 presentations. I could go on with many more distinctions and honors of Dr. Cottrell, but I think you see the point. He has gone as high in the field of anesthesia as anyone I have known of, and then some. His specialty is anesthesia for neurosurgery cases, which includes carotid endarterectomies.

In chapter 19, entitled "Anesthesia for Carotid Endarterectomy", there is a discussion about the indications for carotid endarterectomy. On page 445, one may read: "TIA's lasting longer than an hour and associated with angiographic evidence of severe stenosis can also be considered an indication for urgent operation." So the question is, what about a patient with a TIA that lasts only two or three minutes early one afternoon? Should it be done the following afternoon two hours after a full meal? We have guidelines and principles, but nobody can teach us how to think.

In retrospect I can say the following about my actions. I thought at the time that the decision I made was in the best interest of the patient. I can't prove that, of course, but going with the flow and doing what is best are not necessarily the same thing. The choice I made was not the easy way out. It would have been much easier to do the case on a full stomach and hope for the best.

The system of supervising CRNAs and using a locum tenens from Kron Medical Corp seemed to work well in the summer of '89. Despite their inexperience they all adapted well to the situation. Most surgeons were reasonably pleased. The headhunters had found a resident at Vanderbilt, Dr. Laurie Beach, who would finish on July 1. She seemed interested in starting her practice with me in August. I also got a call out of the blue from a Dr. Bruce Hines. He was finishing up his residency at Charity Hospital and wanted to move to this area and so I invited him to stop by. By September the cash flow had picked up and I expected to pay off my Wachovia loan soon. Despite the earlier controversial case, my new practice was starting to fire on all cylinders. I had very little time off, but I was expecting things to get better. My goal was to help create a desirable practice situation for new doctors, and also take on some new endeavors such as labor epidurals and to use more regional techniques (mostly epidurals) for post-op pain control. This would take a little time. I was overworked but I was hopeful.

* * *

Apparently, Heidi was not hopeful. I don't remember the date, but on the last Saturday in June, she packed the Jeep with my three children and their belongings and drove to Gainesville, Florida. Initially she moved in with her parents. It was about 10:30 a.m. when she rolled down the driveway. The image of my three kids, aged nine, seven and five in the back seat will stay with me forever. My faults as a husband and father were acts of omission rather than acts of commission. If I seem blasé about this event, that's a major misinterpretation. It is just that I could not do anything about it at the time. I was so busy with my work that I couldn't afford the luxury of self-pity. Besides, I really thought they would all return in a few weeks or at least a few months. That turned out to be wishful thinking.

In a nine-month period I had experienced three major life changing events: in October '88, I had experienced the premature and tragic death of my father at age sixty-four. In late January '89 I received a notice of termination of employment with Cabarrus Anesthesiologists PA. And in June '89, my wife and children departed for greener pastures. Each blow was severe, not to be trivialized. Nevertheless I was down, but not out. What sustained me was a belief that I had a purpose and an important role to play. I clung to that thread.

I tried to keep my problems in perspective. It would seem that I now had all of the key ingredients of a hit country song. I just needed to think of a few words that rhymed with nuclear physicist, anesthesiologist and flower child and the song would practically write itself.

As mentioned above, my first full-time physician recruit was Dr. Laurie Beach who began employment August 1, 1989. She had just completed her third year of residency at Vanderbilt. Before that she had completed a residency in internal medicine in Boston. She was originally from Cookeville, Tennessee. Since she was discovered; i.e., recruited by headhunters, I was obligated to pay a $17,000 placement fee. No worries, I had a line of credit up to $100,000 and was expecting my cash flow to pick up soon. Actually, I was happy to pay it. I offered her a reasonable starting salary with a generous bonus after the first year if things worked out; my plan was to make her a shareholder after one year. I helped her find temporary lodging. It happened to be an apartment in an old Victorian house on South Union Street near downtown Concord that had served as Dr. Niblock's office for his pediatric practice. I think she liked it.

At that time the surgery section enjoyed an image of excellent standards, skillful surgeons and great erudition. There were close connections with medical icons at Duke (Dr. David Sabiston) and other institutions. As a whole it was highly respected. But it might also be characterized as a little stodgy. The surgeons and anesthesiologists were all white males, mostly middle-aged. Their views on medical, social and political issues were respectable and predictable. Nothing wrong with that per se. It just seemed overly homogeneous.

Laurie helped change that image. Whereas other physicians discussed issues in *Time* magazine, *The Wall Street Journal* or the upcoming game between Duke and the Tar Heels, Laurie read *Rolling Stone* magazine and talked about concerts she was hoping to see. Some of the older surgeons teased her some about this. She seemed to hold her own fairly well. A hard worker, I was glad to have her on board, despite the culture clash.

Around this time Dr. Bruce Hines came by for a visit. He was from New Orleans and had just completed his residency at Charity Hospital. We had a nice chat. He seemed well-grounded and had a pleasant demeanor. I had not noticed from my earlier phone conversation that he was African American. There were currently no full-time African American physicians on the medical staff at CMH. Why not? His credentials looked good. He graduated from Xavier in 1981 with a BS in Chemistry. He had done a summer session at Harvard in 1979. He graduated from Tulane University of Medicine in 1985. I thought he had strong possibilities. The ultimate question was would he be an asset to the functioning of my new corporation, Concord-Kannapolis Anesthesiologists PC?

I decided to offer Bruce a trial employment for four months, September through December. If things went well I would offer him a full-time contract starting in January 1990, similar to that of Dr. Beach. It seemed wise to stagger new employees because it gave me time to evaluate how the new players would work together. I thought a culture change would be a good thing for the surgery department, but too much change too fast might be disruptive.

In my estimation, Cabarrus County was pretty average or middle of the road when it came to issues like integration and racial equality. It was not on the forefront of progressive causes, but neither was it a hot bed of Klan activity or regressive thinking. Cannon Mills (by then Fieldcrest Cannon) slowly became more integrated. A suit filed by the Nixon administration in 1969 against Cannon Mills for violation of the 1968 Fair Housing Act, Title Vll of the 1964 Civil Rights Act and Title Vlll of the 1968 Civil Rights Act was finally settled in 1982. Cannon Mills denied any wrongdoing. In 1979 a "Death to the Klan" rally, staged by "communists" in nearby Greensboro, resulted in five marchers being shot dead by Klansmen and neo-Nazis. The Klansmen and Nazis were acquitted by an all-white jury. However in 1985, law enforcement officials were found guilty of collusion with the Klan. This bizarre incident was worrisome, but seemed far removed from mainstream politics. At any rate, neither of these aberrations seemed sufficiently relevant to discourage me from offering an aspiring young doctor from New Orleans a chance to begin his career at CMH.

So in September 1989, Laurie was in her second month of employment and Bruce had just started his trial employment. One day that month offers some insight into my mindset. I was still living (by myself) in the large house on Williamsburg Drive, about a mile from the hospital. Around 5 a.m., Friday morning September 22, I received a phone call from a CRNA informing me that she could not make it into work because a tree felled by strong winds was blocking her driveway. Then several more calls. By 5:30 a.m. four CRNAs had notified me that they would not be able to make it into the hospital that morning because of the storm.

We were not a huge department. We could survive a no show of one CRNA. If two were out we might squeak by, but only by a hair and with no lunch breaks or other luxuries. With four CRNAs out, there was no way we could cover the schedule. It was a manager's nightmare. What would the administration and surgeons do when I failed to provide the services I had guaranteed to provide by contract.?

Around 5:50 a.m. I started my car down the driveway. Luckily I had no big trees blocking my progress. But the neighborhood was a disaster area. I had heard the high winds last night, but had no idea it had been this bad. Branches, trash and other debris were strewn everywhere. I slowly crept up Burrage Road going about seven or eight mph looking for trees or other debris that might be hazardous. Then I heard a "creak" and saw a large black cable diagonally in front of the windshield. I felt the car jerk to a stop all at once. I saw no sparks. I put the car in reverse and slowly backed up. Fortunately the line was not hot. I drove to the hospital via the Branchview and Lake Concord Road route. When I reached the OR I found that virtually no one was present. Then I met Dr. Hector Henry in the hallway outside the ORs. Hector was a Vietnam veteran, a reservist, a former college football player, and a leader in the surgery section. If any surgeon would make it to work, it would be Hector. Together we discussed the situation. The storm had been devastating. The danger of getting doctors and patients to the hospital out-weighed any benefits of elective surgery, so we cancelled those appointments. Aside from the major holidays, it's the only time in almost forty years that I have witnessed the ORs being closed on a weekday. I think we did one emergency case later in the evening.

Hurricane Hugo hit the South Carolina Coast around 12:30 a.m. that morning just north of Charleston with 140 mph winds. It was the strongest hurricane in twenty years to hit the U.S. coast and was the costliest to date (seven billion dollars damage in U.S. and Mexico). Usually such storms slow when they encounter land. But Hugo defied all forecasting and made a bee line for the Charlotte area. When it reached Charlotte, around 6 a.m, it was down to a Category one, but still had winds up to a 100 mph. There were twenty-seven deaths reported in South Carolina. One child died in nearby Union County when a tree fell on the house. No deaths were reported in Cabarrus or Mecklenburg County. However, about a week or so later, my seventy-five-year-old neighbor, three houses away, was using a chain saw on a tree felled by the storm in his yard. The section he was cutting dislodged and crushed his chest. After a valiant struggle he eventually succumbed about a month later in the ICU.

I finally took a week off in November. I used this time to revise the policy and procedure manual for the Department of Anesthesia. Since we had adopted a whole new style of practice, this took some doing. After a few days, however, I still had time left to drive to Gainesville to visit my three children. I was relieved to find they had all adjusted to the new school with no major attitude or behavior problem. What more could I ask for? This discovery helped me convince myself that all my efforts were not in vain. It made the eight-hour drive back to Concord more pleasant.

By January 1990 both Dr. Beach and Dr. Hines were working under similar full-time contracts. In addition, a husband and wife team, Dr. Chekan and Dr. Caruso, found by the same headhunters who recruited Dr. Beach, seemed interested in seeking employment with my corporation sometime later in the year. Act Two of my professional career was in full swing with new actors entering the stage right. In 1993 we would recruit Dr. Mark Ellis, 1994 Dr. Vernon Merchant, and in 1995, Dr. Frank Schwalbe.

By early 1990 I felt comfortable taking on some new challenges. With three full-time anesthesiologists, and two more starting in June, I thought it was time to begin a commitment to providing labor epidurals on a full-time basis. With twelve hundred deliveries a year, we might expect to do about eight hundred labor epidurals per year. The remaining deliveries would be elective Cesarean sections or natural childbirth. This would mean an average of two or three labor epidurals a day. The emphasis here is "on average." Some days may have none, other days may have request for five or more. They may also come at the most inconvenient time: at 6 a.m. when trying to start a busy surgery schedule in the main operating room, or at 3 a.m. after just lying down after a marathon day in the main surgery suite. However, that's what we signed up for. Babies don't consult the anesthesiologist about when to arrive. The epidural service grew slowly but steadily. In two or three years we saw the first real growth in the number of deliveries at CMH in decades. This was soon followed by the first real growth in surgery cases in decades. This growth was certainly due to many factors, including the increasing number and sophistication of patients. I like to think that I played a small but significant role in this growth.

By May I was getting used to living alone and realized the possibility of reuniting with my wife was remote, and getting remoter. However, I really was not prepared for the ominous looking pack of legal papers I got from the lawyers in Gainesville, Florida. What the heck! It looked like the bad news I got a few years ago when I was sued. I nervously pulled the papers out of the big envelope. I felt a little nauseated. Then I saw my wife's name and the word divorce. So that's how you do it. You sue for divorce. It seemed so draconian. This not what I had wanted, but under the circumstances, maybe I should just go acquiesce.

We worked out a financial settlement. This included a property and asset split, alimony and child support. The child custody issue was not too difficult to deal with. We would have joint custody with their primary residence being with Heidi. I would get them for eight to ten weeks in the summer, plus during the Christmas season. That was the game plan we used for eight or nine years.

The theory was that in Gainesville, Heidi would have not only her parents, who were both in good health, but also her sister and brother-in-law (Holly and David Bloomquist) to help out. With Heidi working full-time, and or going back to school full-time (she eventually got a degree in architecture at University of Florida), she would need plenty of help. The theory of multiple relatives helping to raise children had some merit. The weakness was in the execution of the theory. Predictably there were many gaps in the child care coverage after school and early evenings. I am surprised everyone did as well as they did in those days.

With my marriage drawing to an end, I had to re-evaluate my domestic situation. Being the sole occupant of a six thousand square foot house only served to exacerbate the feeling of loneliness. It had been almost a year since Heidi left, so time for a change. In May, I opted to buy a thirteen hundred square foot condominium on Lake Concord Road, directly across from the hospital. The price was right, $84,000, and the advantages were significant. The condo was quiet and energy-efficient. It was small, but still big enough for all three children during the summer and holidays. Best of all it was across the street from the hospital. I could walk to work. I was now closer to the OR suite, whether on call or not, than any other member of the surgery department. It would be my home for three years, 1990-1993. I slept better there than I had for quite some time. Meanwhile I was able to rent my large house to my new employee, Dr. George Chekan, and his family. Some things seemed to be working out.

The last noteworthy event I recall in 1990 was several months later, I drove to downtown Charlotte to Reliable Music Store on Stonewall Street. The store has since gone out of business. There I purchased a new guitar that I had my eye on, a jumbo Taylor acoustic model number 815CE. It had a "cutaway" on the body to facilitate playing on the higher frets and a built in acoustic pickup to connect directly to an electric amp. I was happy with my purchase. On my way home, however, the heavy traffic caused some delay. Motionless in the fast lane I experienced another problem. For the second time since October

1988, I experienced a visual disturbance associated with excess ocular fluid. I was glad nobody could see me. I could think of no logical reason why it should occur at that time. By the time I eventually got back to my condo, the disturbance had dissipated, and all evidence of its existence had vanished. I was glad to get that over with. I parked my car and brought my new purchase into the condo. I unpacked the guitar and played a few simple chord progressions. It had very mellow base tones for a Taylor which tend to be brassy, the finger action was a little stiffer than I would have liked, however.

So the years 1989 and 1990 were the two years of greatest change for me both personally and professionally. Many more dramatic events were in store that rivaled these in importance, but nothing surpassed them in intensity. My responsibilities as chairman for the finance committee for Central United Methodist Church and as President of the Cabarrus County Medical Society periodically demanded my attention, but these were minor compared to the demands of my job. Fortunately I was still able to find time to jog and workout at the Sportscenter several times a week. This helped me keep my sanity. Playing my new Taylor in my condo was also a good stress reliever. I had survived the chaos in good spirits and good health except for a few psychological bruises that seemed to be dissipating. What more could I ask for? The changes were unexpected, but things happen for a reason. Some may have handled them better, but I thought my prospects were good. Eventually I began dating, later in 1990 as time allowed. Perhaps there was life after divorce after all.

The Nineties

—◦◦◦◦—

The '80s might be viewed as a sleeper decade, an era that appeared tranquil on some levels but had a lot going on inside. This proved to be true in world politics and also locally. It was certainly true personally as evidenced by the major changes I experienced in '89 and '90. Likewise the '90s would be no slouch when it came to newsworthy events both worldwide and locally. Many of the big stories of the '90s can be viewed as extensions of those of the '80s. For example, the collapse of the Berlin Wall in 1989 is closely linked to the reunification of Germany in 1990 and the collapse of the Soviet Union in 1991. The ongoing fight against apartheid in South Africa and an increased recognition of human rights globally in the '80s directly contributed to the release of Nelson Mandela in 1990 and his election to the office of president in 1994.

In addition to the global awareness of human rights, the '90s is also known for the explosion of technology related to data storage, processing and communication. This explosion seemed to have its roots in the mid '80s with the introduction of the personal computer and early cell phones. Moore's law, which predicted the doubling of processing power of computers at least every two years was proving to be true again and again. But who could have foreseen the growth of the worldwide Web starting in 1993 with companies such as Amazon, founded in 1994 by Jeff Bezos and Ebay founded by Pierre Omidyar and Jeff Skoll in 1995? Meg Whitman would come later. These businesses and many others (often not as successful) helped create what became known in retrospect as the tech bubble. Many technological innovators, investors, speculators, professionals and everyday people knew we were onto something new and valuable, but they were not very accurate at estimating the value of individual companies, and figuring which companies would fail and how our everyday life would be affected. I distinctly recall TV ads with a young techie man dressed in blue jeans and T-shirt viciously lambasting a traditional Wall Street broker dressed in suit and tie holding a briefcase in one hand and a *Wall Street Journal* in the other. These ads curiously disappeared around the year 2000.

What did the tech explosion and the resulting financial bubble have to do with the practice of medicine, particularly my practice of anesthesia in Cabarrus County? One direct result was the increased use of technology in our day to day practice. Medical records began the long process of becoming computer based: the physical chart would grow smaller. Communication between doctors and RNs was enhanced by in-house Cisco cell phones. But doctors were not immune, collectively or individually, to the unbridled enthusiasm for the new technology and possible increased rewards that might be associated with it. The "smartest guys in the room" at Enron seemed to prove you could make a lot of money even if your business was doing poorly. There was some kind of high tech accounting method, too difficult for the average person to understand. We were all sucked in a little and some were more gullible than others.

A little worrisome in the '90s was an apparent trend toward increased episodes of violence in this country. In 1992 there were riots in LA following the Rodney King verdict. Fifty-three people were killed and 11 billion dollars of property damage resulted. On April 19, 1993, a raid by the FBI on an offbeat religious sect, Branch Davidians, in Waco, Texas, resulted in 75 deaths including twelve children under five. The details and justification of this confrontation are still being debated. Exactly two years later Timothy McVeigh detonated five thousands pounds of explosives at the Alfred P. Murrah Federal Building in Oklahoma Building in Oklahoma City killing 168 people. This was allegedly in retaliation for the raid at Waco two years earlier. Then there was that incident on February 26, 1993 where two Middle Eastern men detonated a bomb in a yellow Ryder truck in the parking garage of the North Tower of the World Trade Center in New York City. Their plan was to topple the North Tower, causing it to crash into the South Tower. This episode was worrisome, but seemed too remote and audacious to be a major concern. What could a handful of terrorists in New York City do to harm this country and upset my sense of peace and tranquility? What did they want anyway?

Some people remember the 90s for the iconic events, good or tragic, that made the headlines. In 1997 Tiger Woods won at the Masters and Princess Diana died in a car crash in France. 1998 brought the movie *Titanic* and the Clinton impeachment. Others found significance in the final publication of "Calvin and Hobbs" and Gary Larsen's "Farside," both in 1995. I recall the '90s as an era of great change both personally and professionally as I remarried in 1993 and saw a total overhaul of the anesthesia department in 1997, both ultimately for the good.

The '90s was the decade that the baby boomer generation rose to their level of greatest importance both politically and in the business world. A scary thought! We accepted our successes and failures in stride as had all previous generations. On the one hand we knew we weren't the "greatest"; that title was rightfully secured by our parent's generation. On the other hand we were eager to prove that we weren't a generation lost in space as Don McClean suggested in his epic hit "American Pie."

Fieldcrest Cannon continued to have problems both with profitability and challenges from the labor union (ACTWU) to unionize. The attempts to unionize were barely defeated in 1991 and again in 1997. Both times the results were very close but favored Fieldcrest Cannon.

Both time, however, the National Labor Relations Board (NLRB) took the company to court for election violations or for intimidating workers who sympathized with the union. A third election was set for June 1999. The union (now UNITE) won by 2,270 to 2,102. The company, Pillowtex, which had purchased Fieldcrest Cannon in late 1997, conceded and recognized the union as the bargaining agent for its workers. Unfortunately the company was in a downward spiral.

Most doctors were aware that the textile mills in Kannapolis were undergoing difficult times. The working force, already streamlined by Murdock, was about 7,500 in 1991 and down to around 4,000 in the year 2000. Some years, however, saw good profits; i.e.. $30 million in 1994 and $43 million in 1998. It would therefore be inaccurate to say that the industry was in an obvious straight line decay in the '90s. By the year 2000, however, its prospects looked bleak.

Ironically, CEO Hanson blamed the financial problems on new high tech equipment that slowed production due to required training. Furthermore, he claimed that the new computer system caused problems by failing to ship orders on time, thus hurting business. Whether this was the true reality or just contrived excuses is difficult to say. Nevertheless, by 2000, many wondered what effect would the total demise of the area's leading industry have on the survival and well-being of its population? What industry would replace it? How would these events affect our practice of medicine? Though not as disastrous as some may have feared, the answers to these questions are still being answered today.

Although the nineties were not great years for the textile industry in Rowan and Cabarrus County, they did not seem to be too bad for the practice of anesthesia. I have already mentioned how we began to provide an epidural service for laboring women in 1990. Shortly thereafter, in 1991 and 1992, we began providing epidurals for controlling post-op pain for certain operations performed in the main OR. I had actually done a few epidurals for post-op pain management in the mid to late '80s, but full implementation of this practice required a team of anesthesiologists for preoperative placement, intra-op management and post-op rounding. By 1991 we were adequately staffed. The technique of using epidurals for post-op pain management was very similar to that of using epidurals for labor and delivery in obstetrics. The big difference was that labor epidurals are typically used for six to twelve hours, whereas post-op epidurals are used for three or four days. They proved most useful in big cases such as thoracotomies or abdominal aortic aneurysms though any case with a large abdominal or thoracic (chest) incision would benefit. As with any new technique, it took some time to determine which cases benefited the most. Although we did occasionally use epidurals for low abdominal and pelvic surgeries, i.e., hysterectomies, we eventually concluded that the benefit was much less in these cases.

By 1995, using epidurals to manage post-op pain was a well-established and an important part of our overall practice. That year we also opened a small pain clinic that saw eight to ten patients one day a week. Since no one in our group had done a fellowship in pain management, we all took turns staffing the clinic. The most common procedure by far was the injection of steroids into the epidural space to assist in alleviating back pain. This clinic was very tiny and primitive by today's standards. It was not a full service pain clinic; however, it was an important step in the right direction.

Two important events in the practice of surgery and anesthesia occurred in 1993. The first was the creation of a "free standing" surgery center by CMH, connected to the main hospital by long hallway. Prior to this point, the increasing number of outpatients were handled in the main OR suite and they mingled with the sicker inpatients. As the number of outpatient surgeries grew, many physicians and some administrators felt they could be handled more efficiently if they were physically separated in a facility designed to meet the needs of quick turnover cases and patients who entered and left the facility on the same day. Several surgeons had advocated a joint venture with a private company, excluding CMH, to create a privately-owned outpatient facility. These threats motivated the administration to proceed with its own surgery center. A committee of several doctors, Hammonds, Chalfant, Burke, Bobbitt and myself and several administrators, was appointed to assist in the planning. Opening in the summer of '93, the surgery center proved to be a big success. It was so efficient that in 1998 CMH built several more ORs adjacent to those opened in '93. They then moved all surgery cases, inpatient and outpatient, to the new surgery center. Although this partly defeated the original goal of separating the two types of cases, the new arrangement seemed to work out okay for several years.

The second major event in 1993 was the initiation of an open heart surgery service; the first case was done February 15, 1993, the day after Valentine's Day. Rumors about starting an open heart surgery program at CMH had been circulating since at least the late '80s. At first I had my doubts about how realistic and practical such a program would be in Concord. We were only about 25 miles from downtown Charlotte. Perhaps the failed HMO in 1987 had opened some people's eyes to the great revenues being lost as these "outlier" patients were referred to other hospitals. At any rate these rumors of starting an open heart program at CMH gained serious traction in 1990 when Dr. Ralph (Chris) Christy left his general surgery practice with Piedmont Surgery Clinic to do specialized training in heart surgery. By 1992 the plans to do open heart surgery cases at CMH were well under way. It seemed to be a win-win proposition. Patients could have a coronary bypass procedure or a valve replacement without having to leave Cabarrus County. The hospital would gain the extra business as well as the spin off businesses; i.e., ICU, radiology imaging, rehab and other secondary operations. Perhaps the open heart program would serve as a catalyst to further spark growth and vitality of the medical community.

These plans in 1992, however, presented some challenges for the anesthesia department. We were all trained to do open heart cases in our residency, but none of us had done a fellowship in cardiac anesthesia. Furthermore, at that time it had been a good 14 years since I had done an open heart anesthetic case in my residency in Florida. These cases were not necessarily more difficult or risky than many cases we did such as thoracotomies or abdominal aortic aneurysms, however, they did have their own set of distinct challenges related to using the cardiopulmonary bypass machine, "the pump"; especially going on and coming off the pump. Special protocols for anticoagulants, inotropic agents (stimulants) and cooling and rewarming techniques are used. Anesthesia for open heart surgery is very protocol driven; that is, the exact dosage and timing of various drugs and techniques are standardized. Some variations may exist from one big center to the next, but they are remarkably similar throughout the country.

It therefore seemed wise that my partners and myself engage in some continuing education, refresher courses or hands-on experience to prepare for our first open heart cases. I contacted a key physician at CMC (Carolina Medical Center) in downtown Charlotte to arrange a visit to observe some open heart cases downtown. I made one visit and was allowed to closely observe a case at CMC main. I was treated well and garnered some insight on how the cases were managed by anesthesia. One visit, however, was far from adequate. When I called to arrange a follow-up visit, however, I discovered I had stirred up a major controversy. The physician was receiving significant flak from his partners for allowing me to visit. Instead of a fellow physician honing his skills, the Charlotte physicians saw me as a competitor who was attempting to steal business from them by ultimately encouraging them to have their coronary bypass or valve replacement done in Concord, instead of Charlotte. This attitude surprised me because we were actually just trying to keep our own patients in Cabarrus County from having to travel to Charlotte for surgery. Didn't they know that we would begin our open heart program in 1993 with or without their help? What was more important-working as a medical community to improve patient welfare, or drawing battle lines to defend one's financial domain? It seems even more ironic today since in 2007 our two hospitals merged and came under one political-financial umbrella. Of course no one knew that was going to happen in 1992.

After being denied access to CMC, it occurred to me that Duke Medical Center would be a logical place to seek guidance and help starting our new open heart program. Although a two-hour drive away, CMH had a pre-existing relationship with Duke for continuing education in many other departments, so why not anesthesia? With our administrator's blessing, I called the Department of Anesthesia at Duke to arrange a visit. They were quite receptive to the idea. Dr. Chekan and myself spent several days each observing anesthesia techniques for open heart cases. We were treated very well and gained significant confidence for starting our cardiac program. But we still had some concerns.

An idea occurred to me while observing cases at Duke. Why not arrange for an anesthesiologist from Duke to visit and assist us with our first ten or twenty cases at CMH? Duke could bill for and keep the income from those initial cases, but we would be directly involved with the patient care. This put the onus on the Duke anesthesiologist to travel to Concord,—I thought it made good sense. We were in no way competing with Duke for patients, and Duke was already assisting us by allowing us to observe. Perhaps as a world renowned medical center, Duke would feel a noblesse oblige to help a smaller hospital serve its population. I discussed the idea with Bob Conroy, COO at CMH, and several people at Duke. They all seemed willing to participate.

I put the concept in writing: Duke anesthesiologists would administer anesthesia for the first ten open heart cases at CMH and if necessary the first twenty, if ten seemed inadequate. I then forwarded a copy to Duke and CMH administrations. The Duke lawyers put it in contract form. It was signed by several people including Dr. Jerry Reeves, Chairman of the Department of Anesthesia at Duke, Robert Wall, CEO at CMH and myself. I saved the original copy of the contract.

In preparing for our first open heart case we had scheduled several non-cardiac cases in the heart room to make sure that the room was in good working order. Funny, but I noticed an increased tension and a mild tremor in my hands when merely entering the heart room. What was that all about? I am normally a very calm person. Very little upsets me. The anxiety greatly diminished after a few cases.

So, we finally did our first open heart surgery case on February 15, 1993. I remember this date for several reasons; first of all for being the day after Valentine's Day. It also happened to be the day Christy's Nursery landscaped my home on Williamsburg Drive in preparation for my fiancée, Rebecca, and I moving into my old house in July. Christy's Nursery was owned and operated by Dr. Ralph Christy's parents. So the father of the heart surgeon was landscaping my yard the same day the surgeon was doing the first open heart surgery case in Cabarrus County. It makes it easier to remember.

The first open heart surgery, a coronary bypass graft, went well overall. When coming off bypass, however, we had to use several inotropes before we could totally wean from the pump. I am glad that the Duke doctors were present to give us guidance. After ten cases we no longer needed them, but there is no question they played a critical role in getting our cardiac surgery program launched.

I mentioned my fiancée, Rebecca (Becky) and landscaping my old house in February 1993. That deserves some elaboration. After dating a nurse at CMH for several months in '90 and '91, I met Becky at the Sportscenter (where else?) in the summer of '91. Our first date was on the day before Halloween. We went to the Sandwich Construction Company off 49 in the University area. I don't recall too much about our first date except that I told her she had nice veins —something anesthesiologists tend to notice —and she forced me to drink several margaritas. Besides having good veins and being physically attractive, I was intrigued that she was an occupational therapist who specialized in treating hand injuries. Later, when I played my guitar for her I learned that she knew all the verses to "Puff the Magic Dragon."

That was the clincher. I could never remember If "green scales fell like rain" before or after he "slipped into his cave." I was glad to get that straightened out.

In addition Becky had two Children, Amanda Lea (Mandy) born September 19, 1978 and Benjamin Harper born December 11, 1978. Since Becky had experienced multiple miscarriages and Mandy was 6 weeks premature she had elected to adopt their second child. By early 1992 we were going steady and in February of 1993 I gave her an engagement ring. We planned a wedding in August 1993 in Gatlinburg when my family would be present. We didn't desire a big ceremony.

Later I learned some interesting facts about my wife's early childhood. Her life was dramatically and irrevocably changed by Typhoon Wilma, a Category 5 hurricane on October 26, 1952. On that date her father, Captain Donald Baird, departed Andersen Air Force Base on Guam at 3:30 a.m. in a B-29 weather reconnaissance aircraft along with nine other airmen. It was to be a 14 -hour flight to obtain information about the typhoon and would end at Clark Air Force Base in the Philippines. At 8:20 a.m. a message was received from the B-29 three hundred and twenty miles east of Leyte Island stating they were in severe turbulence near the eye of the typhoon. That was the last contact. The crew was officially reported missing at ten p.m., the estimated time the fuel supply would have been exhausted. Local fishermen witnessed a large four engine aircraft crash six to eight miles off the southern tip of Leyte Island that morning. No wreckage or debris were ever recovered to confirm those sightings.

On April 12, 1953 Major General McCormick, USAF, sent Rebecca's mom, Mrs. Leona S. Baird, an official letter noting that his status as missing was terminated. His date of death was noted as October 26, 1952. A plaque honoring her father stated: "In Grateful Memory of Captain Donald Baird, United States Air Force, Who Died in the Service of his Country with the United Nations Forces in Korea," was signed by Dwight D. Eisenhower.

I am in awe of such acts of heroism. I would never question the bravery or dedication of those airmen. I can now also somewhat understand Becky's fascination and concern about storms in general, especially hurricanes. When she decides to cancel plans due to bad weather, I rarely argue with her.

Of interest, 1993 saw the legalization of liquor by the drink in Cabarrus County. Predictably a number of chain restaurants quickly opened in Concord: Applebee's, O'Charley's, Chili's, Longhorns and many more. It was no longer necessary to go to Charlotte to get a decent meal with a drink. We soon had lots of choices. Our most memorable dinner date in '93, however, did not involve any of the new restaurants. One Friday afternoon we decided to see a movie at the GEM theatre in Kannapolis. The GEM was originally constructed in 1936 for mill workers and was rebuilt in 1948 after it burned. We stopped on the way to eat dinner at the K&W in Concord. The price of our dinner was $7.86 for both of us. The GEM tickets were only a dollar a piece at that time. So the total price for a dinner and movie for two was only $9.86. There were no parking fees. I don't think we impressed too many of my fellow physicians with our dining and entertainment. But as a value investment I am pretty sure Warren Buffet would have been pleased. The important thing was that we enjoyed both our meal and the movie playing at the GEM.

So 1993 saw three major events: the opening of the surgery center, the initiation of open heart surgeries and my re-marriage. The '90s had much more in store.

For the most part my three kids had been doing reasonably well in the Florida school system up until 1993. Each one had gravitated toward special interests and hobbies that would ultimately determine their career choice and define them personally. Corey, the youngest, at age ten, was very much into horseback riding. This skill was complimented later by dancing, gymnastics and aerial arts skills. She was also a good student and especially adroit in language arts, eventually gaining fluency in French, Spanish and Portuguese. Dustin gravitated strongly to music and became quite proficient on the keyboard and acoustic guitar and bass. By age twelve he had equaled or surpassed my skill level on both instruments. He was also a good student, level headed and philosophical. Stability was his middle name. The oldest, William (Billy) was a good student and somewhat precocious in math and science. At age ten and eleven he was reading books on quantum mechanics and Einstein's theory of relativity. I am sure that at age thirteen he could ace any reasonable high school senior test in math or physics. It all seemed almost too good to be true. It was.

Significant problems first began in the seventh grade. Since Billy was in school in Gainesville, Florida and I was in North Carolina, these stories are all second-hand, though well corroborated. He was assigned to do a science report on a topic of his choice. He chose quantum physics as his topic and produced a lengthy paper. His teacher gave him an "F" because he didn't believe or understand how he could have done the work himself. This episode reinforced his negative view of the "system," especially public schools. This was also about the time that I got remarried. Some rebellious behavior, including spray painting slogans on school property continued into the eighth grade. His mother was struggling to control him. In January 1994 I enrolled him in Concord Middle School after Christmas, instead of sending him back to Florida. Here too there were a few problems; I got called at the hospital twice for his inappropriate clothing. T-shirts with beer ads. He passed all his courses with mediocre grades. I could see that he was wasting his time attending public schools.

I decided to have an extensive evaluation of his abilities and behavior by a professional psychologist. <u>Ann Carol Price of Educational Consultants </u>in Columbia, South Carolina, did a thorough evaluation of his situation. We then allowed him to return to Gainesville to commence ninth grade, but with some definite back-up plans to use if problems reoccurred. After struggling with the same issues again in Florida, we sent him on a wilderness program for troubled youth in Idaho in February 1995.

The wilderness program consisted of two weeks of camping and hiking in the Wind River Valley of Idaho. It was led by professional counselors who helped the teenagers deal with their angst while learning survival skills. Billy accomplished the physical challenges, but on the last day learned he wasn't going to pass the course because a counselor didn't like his attitude.

All the camper's boots were secured with locks at night. Billy was undeterred. While everyone was asleep he escaped, running 14 miles back to town in his boot liners. Following an unsuccessful attempt to call his grandmother in Florida, he was declared officially missing for about 24 hours until located by local authorities. I spent a fretful night wondering if I should take off from work. When notified the next morning of his retrieval, I arranged, with Ann Carol Price, the educational consultant, for him to be flown by helicopter to a high security school in Provo Utah, "Provo Canyon." He remained in Provo for about ten months. There he eventually decided it was in his best interest, not to mention everyone else's, to go with the flow. It seemed to be a turning point in his early development.

The 14 mile middle-of-the-night run has been retold many times and somewhat embellished. One version increased it to 17 miles. I think that's incorrect; fourteen is enough, thank you.

So by 1995 the department of anesthesia at CMH could claim a number of accomplishments; the development of a labor epidural service, a post-op pain service, a small clinic dedicated to pain management, and the provision of services for the new open heart surgery program and for the new surgery center. Since 1989 we had grown from one to seven full-time anesthesiologists. The surgery and obstetrical services had experienced their first major growth spurt in decades. Business was booming and we had played a major role in the expansion. I was proud of our success.

Unfortunately, there were significant emerging problems in the department. Simply stated, some of the physicians I hired did not like or respect some of the others I had hired. I was aware of this dysfunction and encouraged these individuals to work in harmony.

Occasionally, however, the internal enmity would reveal itself with subtle verbal digs or outbursts. This display of animosity was most often between MDs, but occasionally spilled over into MD-CRNA relationships. I had not personally been present for any of these spats, but apparently they were witnessed by surgeons and at least once by a patient. I don't think these displays of hostility were an everyday occurrence, but even a rare display was unprofessional and embarrassing to me and my department. The hospital administration held me responsible for fixing this dysfunction.

I have saved copies of much of the correspondence between myself and the administration concerning this problem. The earliest written documentation I have is a letter from Bob Conroy dated April 13, 1992, in which he states there have been many verbal confrontations over the past six months between anesthesiologists that have adversely impacted the work environment. He mentioned that problems had come to his attention via the grapevine. He warned me that if my associates and I did not resolve these issues, then my exclusive contract might be in jeopardy. He requested a written response within seven days to assure him that the group and I would fix the problems personally. He was careful not to mention the specific doctors involved or who his grapevine source was.

I responded to him in a letter dated April 28, 1992, acknowledging the existence of sporadic verbal confrontation and the need for improvement in this area and also a need for better esprit de corps within the department. To this concession I added a plea for increased efforts from the hospital to hire more CRNAs. I suggested the hospital offer pay for beeper call for the CRNAs. This letter was accompanied a document signed by all five anesthesiologists expressing a desire to move on to the task ahead with a "higher level of professionalism."

I followed this up with a letter dated May 13, 1992, re-emphasizing the need to be more aggressive in recruiting CRNAs. The new surgery center and open heart surgery program, both slated to start in 1993, would create a need for at least three more CRNAs. I challenged the hospital to be competitive with Charlotte in their reimbursement package. This letter was answered by a letter dated May 18, 1992, stating that the administration was not in favor of paying beeper call for the CRNAs. It also advised me that I should not support the CRNAs on this issue because "it would only create difficulties for both of us."

The next correspondence on this issue that I have is a memorandum dated July 23, 1992, in which the hospital announced the initiation of pay for beeper call for the CRNAs as well as other improvements in benefits. Thus after chiding me for being an advocate for the CRNAs for the ultimate benefit of the department of anesthesia and the medical community, the hospital at last accepted my advice and improved their benefits. This decision was made after a survey of area hospitals revealed that most were already paying a small hourly fee for beeper call. This episode demonstrates the professional, but slightly adversarial relationship, that I was developing with the administration. The rapid expansion of hospital services and increased need for doctors and other personnel was definitely creating some tensions.

I realized that a pending shortage of CRNAs at CMH was not the fundamental problem that had caused the bad blood between MDs and occasionally CRNAs within the department. That issue had multiple causes. But the need to recruit CRNAs rapidly was a particular concern that could potentially aggravate the existing situation if not addressed. I followed up with a letter in November 1992 to the administration pushing them to be more proactive in recruitment. After my dressing down, I was challenging the administration. They may have resented it a little bit. This issue was put to rest in May 1993 when I recruited a chief CRNA, Clem Markarian, who took over the CRNA personnel issues.

My annual review by the hospital dated January 19, 1993, made note of the conflicts between two physicians in my practice, but otherwise was fairly bland and even complimentary on some issues. The anticipated open heart program starting in February and the Surgery Center opening in July were looming. As noted before these programs were launched successfully. It seemed that the discord had taken a back seat to the great demands of our mission to expand services. It seemed they were too busy to fight.

On August 23, 1993, however, I received another letter from Bob Conroy that suggested a crisis of confidence, and a level of dissatisfaction with the leadership in the anesthesia department. He stated there were concerns of competence among some of the anesthesiologists. My clinical competency was not in question, but my perceived leadership capabilities were. He acknowledged some improvement in the unprofessional behavior in our group, but then proceeded with a litany of our deficiencies. Because of the nature and number of these concerns he was considering the termination of our exclusive contract to provide anesthesia services. The plan was to monitor the situation and reconsider the possibility of terminating the contract in 30 to 45 days. On November 5, 1993, we were notified that the exclusive contract would be terminated effective February 7, 1994, a 90-day notice.

The deficiencies noted in August, in addition to my leadership and competency of some of my employees, also included a perception that some physicians were unwilling to work hard; i.e., they were lazy, and that some physicians were more motivated to maximize income than to take care of patients. This pretty much covered the gamut. It was also noted that some members of the corporation had not passed their specialty boards as was required by our contract and hospital by-laws.

My initial reaction to the hospital accusations was one of anger and defensiveness. Their assessments seemed too severe. We had done a lot for the hospital despite some internal dysfunctions. Basically they were saying some, or all, of my partners were greedy, lazy, incompetent and unprofessional in conduct and I was at fault for not fixing the mess. The comment about some physicians not passing their specialty boards was true but irrelevant. They were all still within the time limits allowed by our mutual agreement.

Ultimately, however, I did have to admit there were significant problems within our department, even if they seemed to be exaggerated at times and that I had played a major role in their genesis. It would be hard to describe the major developments in the department over the last five years without acknowledging my role as the leading actor. After all, I had created the professional corporation and developed the guidelines on how it would operate politically and financially. I had allowed new doctors right out of training or from other hospitals to receive full pay for their productivity after just one year. The system of compensation was directly based on how much income the doctors generated. I helped create a practice situation that I believed would be highly desirable. Each doctor I recruited had a better "deal" after one year than I did after ten years when based on their incomes and the volume of calls taken and hours worked. It was difficult for me to understand why they didn't all cherish their employment and strive to work in harmony. It seemed that some people felt they were irreplaceable.

When conflicts began I had a tendency to defend the inexperienced employees. At one time a key administrator recommended that I fire one of the younger MDs to increase the value of my corporation's stock. I disagreed. I thought both the younger doctors deserved the full time allowed by contract to pass their boards. Perhaps this decision was perceived as weakness by some. Perhaps a stronger leader would have kicked butt. I thought I was doing the right thing.

We had fundamental changes in the anesthesia department in a few short years: expansion of services to cover cardiac, obstetrics and post-op pain, the addition of several new doctors and the adoption of a totally new system of administering anesthesia; i.e., supervision of CRNAs. During a supervised case the anesthesiologist has less direct contact with the surgeon. The majority of his time in the OR is during induction and emergence just when the surgeon is arriving or leaving. As a result, my interaction with surgeons, in particular, was lessened. This was mostly unavoidable. Had I been more proactive in the PR department, however, I might have garnered more support from the surgeons.

Giving new doctors so much so soon in our practice was probably not in the best interest of long-term stability. If I could have turned the clock back to 1989 and rewritten the contracts, I would have made some major changes. In part, I was reacting to the situation from which I came. I had underestimated the forces of chaos and over-estimated the goodwill of some and the maturity of others. My mistake.

So my challenge in 1993 was to eradicate the interpersonal difficulties among my employees. And while eradicating away, I'd upgrade their software to new and improved clinical competence and improved protocols for ethical behavior. This seemed to me analogous to the challenge of surgically removing a metastatic cancer that was intricately wound around vital organs and blood vessels. I didn't have the surgical skill to perform the task without seriously risking the life of the patient. I had to resort to palliative treatment.

The termination letter dated November 5, 1993, stated that the official termination of our exclusive contract for anesthesia services would occur Monday February 7, 1994 at 12:01 a.m. Seriously 12:01 a.m., not twelve midnight. That means if I woke up at midnight on Sunday February 6, I could bask in the warm glow knowing that I had one more minute of exclusivity left. We weren't especially happy about the termination of our exclusivity, but we really were not sure what it would mean for us. They still needed anesthesiologist to keep the wheels running, didn't they? What was the overarching goal of this termination, and how would it affect us in the foreseeable future?

The stated purpose of the "exclusivity" clause in the contract from April 1989 was that "more efficient and coordinated anesthesia medical care may be rendered to the general public at a lower cost by utilizing a single provider of anesthesia medical services" and that "management of the hospital will be improved by a unified practice." In light of these noble goals of exclusivity, what then was the goal of canceling exclusivity? If internal discord and greed were problems under the old order, in what manner could we expect to see improvement now that multiple groups may be allowed to provide services? Was this a well-thought out plan to improve health care in Cabarrus County or were we merely being punished for our perceived deficiencies? Or was there something else going on?

Along with the cancelation of our contract in February '94, the administration recommended that Dr. Chekan serve as medical director for the department for a two year term. Under a new "agreement" my corporation would provide a medical director. I continued to serve as president and financial officer for the group. This was not necessarily a bad arrangement. My visibility and duties were reduced. Dr. Chekan seemed to handle the situation satisfactorily. For a while tensions seemed to ease and business went on as usual. Except for this change of medical director, we didn't see any major change in our practice. How long would that last?

One may legitimately ask just how bad was the dysfunction in the anesthesia department in the early nineties that lead to the contract cancelation and how did it affect patient care and satisfaction? If you were a nurse or a doctor who witnessed a verbal spat, you might judge it quite severe. Others might judge it not so bad. I thought the problem was very significant and embarrassing, but overhyped at least a little. Why was it that the biggest critics of the department, from inside and outside, seemed to be fanning the flames? Was there not some semi objective means to evaluate our performance and compare the anesthesia department to other departments in our hospital and to other departments in our peer group of hospitals?

It turns out there was such a mechanism to make some statistical comparisons. In 1993 CMH participated in a standardized patient satisfaction survey with about five hundred other hospitals, including 52 hospitals considered in our peer group. In the first quarter of '93, anesthesia services rated poorly on the satisfaction survey. CMH as a whole was also below average for this quarter. Our ratings significantly improved to somewhat above average for the second and third quarters of 1993. In the last quarter of '93 the anesthesia department performed extremely well on the survey, outperforming our own institution internally and also well enough to be ranked in the top one percent of anesthesia departments in our peer group. Since there were only 52 hospitals in our peer group, this would mean that we outscored all other peer group departments for that quarter.

The date of the memorandum announcing this stellar performance by our department was February 25, 1994, only eighteen days after the termination of our contract. The date of the termination letter was November 5, 1993, the quarter during which our department ranked in the upper 1percent. When I mentioned these results to Bob Conroy, he was nonplussed and seemed uncomfortable. It seems the dye was cast.

Why such an apparent disconnect between the degree of patient satisfaction and the administration's evaluation of our department? Part of it could simply be the timing of the survey results, appearing after the termination date. But, fundamentally, they are based on different metrics. The administration is heavily influenced by a coterie of physicians and board members, insiders, who have their ear; i.e., the grapevine. The patients don't have such an inside connection. They depend on patient surveys and patient advocates for influence.

Nevertheless, that seemed to be quite a paradox; to be rated in the upper one percent of your peers on a patient satisfaction survey, and simultaneously rated so poorly by your administration that your contract is canceled. Could there be something else going on upsetting the equilibrium in an otherwise stable level-headed administration to enhance their perception of our dysfunction? I struggled to comprehend the reasons for this incongruity at that time. I still struggle to bring logical analysis to a time of instability, yet hindsight and reflection have enabled me to offer some plausible explanations.

It so happens the administration of CMH was being destabilized during this time frame. A group of physician activists were calling for a major change in the administration at CMH. By early 1994 it was accepted that Bob Wall, CEO, would be "retiring" soon. He would be replaced by Tom Revels, the young CEO in Florence, South Carolina.

Still uncertain was the fate of Bob Conroy; conceivably he might remain as COO. However, we subsequently learned that Conroy would be leaving also.

These physician activists were mostly the same coterie of physicians referred to before; i.e., the grapevine. I was not among those pushing to make a change in the administration. I am not an activist by nature. I thrive personally and professionally on peace and tranquility and have an aversion for turmoil and instability. I don't even like grapevines. Perhaps this explains why I have never been labeled a mover and a shaker.

So this underlying instability of the administration does help in understanding the interactions between them and the anesthesia department. No, I am not trying to blame the administration for the pre-existing dysfunctions in the department; I must accept a major responsibility for allowing that to develop. However, the evolution of the department of anesthesia cannot be fully understood without appreciating the parallel instability in the administration.

I have to remind myself that these events discussed occurred during the year after I got remarried on August 10, 1993. They were worrisome but not devastating. I was developing a strong immunity to the personal effects of political instability. The wheels of change rarely stop after one revolution. I didn't have the ability to stop the wheel. Meanwhile life goes on. In October 1993, Becky and I went to Bermuda for a brief honeymoon. In June of 1994 we undertook a much more ambitious adventure. We flew to London with all five children: Billy (14), Dustin (12), Corey (10), and Mandy and Harper, both (15), and enjoyed a nine-day Globus bus tour of England and Scotland. The kids loved the Tower of London and the Buckingham Palace. I enjoyed the Lake district and Stratford-on-Avon. I usually make a good effort to study the history and local culture of places I visit. By the end of the trip I was almost fluent in the native language.

There were two important events for the department of anesthesia in the summer of '94. The first was the recruitment of Vernon (Van)

Merchant in July. He had just finished his residency in Charleston, South Carolina and was a former roommate of Mark Ellis. This brought our total number of anesthesiologists to seven. We were happy to have Van.

Also in the summer of '94 Tom Revels took over as CEO of CMH. Young (forty) and vibrant, he projected an image of confidence and ability. He would get things done. Foremost among his priorities was a need to overhaul the system of billing and reimbursing for medical services in the community. He promised that in two years we would have a whole new system in place. It would be a joint venture between CMH and the medical staff and involve reimbursement via capitation payments instead of the traditional fee for service arrangement.— Hmmmmmm—sounded familiar. Didn't he know about the failed attempt just over seven years ago for this very same concept? What would we do differently this time? Maybe he knew some magic tricks.

Under Mr. Revels leadership anesthesia services continued pretty much as usual. We were aware of meetings and efforts going on to initiate a new HMO, but they didn't have any direct effect on our daily practice. Occasionally we felt like we had X's on our heads, good for target practice. Outside groups might come in at any time and set up shop. As the months rolled by and no one challenged us, we gradually grew less paranoid. Who needs an exclusive contract anyway?

The events of 1995 served to further increase our confidence. In May both Dr. Merchant and Dr. Hines found out that they had passed their boards. Unfortunately for Dr. Beach, her time limit would be up soon. As agreed by contract she would be leaving in July. Dr. Frank Schwalbe would be arriving to replace her. I proudly wrote a letter to the administration in May announcing our good news. Someone could still accuse us of being greedy and lazy—very subjective qualities—if they chose, but they could no longer follow that with the derogatory clause, "and your doctors can't even pass their boards." Unlike some other departments that grandfathered in older doctors who had not passed their boards, the department of anesthesia would be 100 percent board certified, just as we had agreed in the original (now canceled) contract.

Therefore, as 1996 rolled around we had reason to feel confident. Once crippled by a canceled contract, we showed we could go with the flow. Adaptability was our middle name. You could hardly detect a limp.

The new year, however, would hold many surprises for our department. How could we have known? In order to understand and appreciate the events, it is helpful to inspect the emotional milieu and atmosphere in which they occurred. This era was in the early phase of the dot com bubble. Most physicians were already beginning to see significant increases in their retirement plans. Since business was booming, this increase was coupled with an additional increase of income or cash flow for many doctors. The result was a feeling of unbridled enthusiasm many felt for their financial future, especially their investments in technology. On December 5, 1996, Alan Greenspan, chairman of the federal reserve, used the term "irrational exuberance" to describe this enthusiasm, suggesting these gains may not be sustainable.

In Cabarrus County another factor may have augmented this sense of financial well-being. Founded in 1937 by Mr. Cannon as a low cost hospital for his mill workers, CMH had traditionally been less expensive than the Charlotte or other urban hospitals. Even after Mr. Cannon died in 1971 the ethos of a low cost medical center extended through the '70s and most of the '80s. By the mid '90s, however, the medical community was considerably different. The mills were fading in importance. Many new doctors felt little allegiance to the concept of a low cost medical center. Whereas in 1980 a physician might feel bound by historical precedence to keep fees a little below average, in 1996 these ideological restraints were broken. There was little to keep us from competing on a parallel basis with the more expensive hospitals in Charlotte, both with services rendered and fee schedules. Prometheus was unbound; not even Zeus could stop him now.

The exuberance of the late '90s helped illustrate the duality in many physicians' characters. Most doctors have a strong altruistic desire to help people. We are humble servants of mankind. I have seen skilled surgeons agonize long hours to save life or limb of patients without health insurance of other means to pay. At other times I have seen physicians near tears in sympathy for a suffering patient. This is an important aspect of who we are. I'll call this the "Mother Teresa" side of our character.

On the other hand most physicians have a strong need for financial and social or political success. We thrive on material rewards and power. I will call this the "masters of the universe" ala Tom Wolfe side of our character. These two qualities inherent in doctors (Mother Teresa and masters of the universe) are in a constant struggle to gain total control of operations. In 1996, the masters of the universe were gaining the upper hand. Mother Teresa was sitting on the beach in Miami, with a tall, cool one by her side.

I personally noticed during this time an increased enthusiasm and interest in unbridled financial success. One of my partners was quite excited about his investments. He fervently informed me that he expected the DOW average to exceed ten thousand by the year 2000. What was he smoking?

So while many people were boarding the train of irrational exuberance, I was hesitant to get on board. Perhaps I had worked too long under the old system of low charges to be capable of mentally grasping the concept of incredible financial gains in this new world of technology. Or perhaps I had suffered actual brain damage while carrying fifty pound bags of limestone for two dollars an hour the summer before medical school. It's not that I had any foreboding that this train was going to be involved in a crash; it's just that I didn't think it was bound for glory.

It was during this time frame that two new problems gained notoriety for our anesthesia corporation. The first had been smoldering for at least a year. Dr. Ellis was growing impatient and worried about our failure to accept him as a partner in our corporation; someone was voting not to accept him as a partner in our group. We required a unanimous vote at the time to become a shareholder. I was sympathetic and reassured him of his value to our group. Law suits were threatened due to different interpretations of the contracts. Although many groups do struggle with internal conflicts, I could see no virtue in blocking his acceptance as a partner. He would eventually play an important role serving as acting chairman for the department of anesthesia and later as chairman of the department of surgery. Of course no one knew this at that time. This issue was soon to take a back seat to other developments.

The second problem our corporation faced was totally out of the blue. Sometime in the mid-summer of '96 I got a call from the FBI. I couldn't have been more surprised. What did they want with me? We arranged a meeting one afternoon when I was off. I greeted them (two agents) at the door and led them downstairs to the basement where we could talk in private. Why the basement? My wife was gone, no one else around. I'm not sure why I opted for the basement. It just felt more appropriate. Maybe this was a clandestine government operation. Top secret.

They asked me a lot of questions about how my corporation functioned internally; especially relating to billing, collections and internal financial operations. I answered honestly in general terms, but was careful not to give specific numbers or financial data on individuals. It soon became apparent what this interrogation was all about. They suspected that one, or possibly two employees of my corporation may possibly be guilty of Medicare fraud. How could that be? We all used the same relative value guide and conversion factor and billed for the same cases. I quickly ruled out any blatant source of fraud such as billing for non-existent services or duplicate billing for cases. The only difference in how we billed as individual doctors was in how each doctor determined the starting and ending time of each case. Some physicians were more liberal in their interpretation of the ending time, frequently adding ten to fifteen minutes to the anesthesia time after entering the PACU. This is totally legitimate if indeed he (she) is actually engaged with caring for the patient during that extra time. If not, however, it could be construed as fraud. Did this difference between individual physicians reach statistical significance? Was fraud being committed under my aegis as corporation president?

Of course I kept my lawyers informed of these developments. Initially they suggested that the investigation may have been triggered merely by a routine audit that may have pegged one or two doctors as statistical outliers in their billing profile with Medicare. Later, however, they suggested that somebody who was aware of their billing practice reported them to the Medicare fraud hotline. Although I believe this is probable, I never discovered the final outcome of the investigation, or who may have reported them. I am aware that it was ongoing for several months. My lawyers said these types of investigations sometimes seem to die out and then reappear months later. Other times they simply die out. Either way, we had two issues or red flags involving our corporation in the first six or seven months of '96. That was two flags too many.

Things really continued to heat up as the summer progressed. By now it was clear that a new system for doing business at CMH (an HMO) was not going to happen as was promised in '94. Unlike the HMO of 1987, it never got off the ground. The administration now turned its attention back to the department of anesthesia. The red flags were easy to spot. They suggested we participate in a reorganization of the department by submitting a proposal for providing anesthesia services for the hospital. Other groups would be allowed to submit proposals with names of doctors who would participate. The hospital would select the best proposal and award an exclusive contract to that group to strengthen and unify the department. What a good idea!

Shortly after this "suggestion," Dr. Bruce Hines and I elected to sever our ties with Dr. Chekan and Caruso, the husband and wife team. Although the political repercussions of such a maneuver were uncertain, Bruce and I felt it would be in our best interest to do so. The stage was therefore set for a free for all. The hospital was in the driver's seat. We were all begging for the right to practice medicine at CMH. We spent considerable time polishing our CVs and putting together a proposal for providing services. At least four other groups would compete including physicians from Duke, Presbyterian and Chekan et al. This was serious business. We knew there was no guarantee that we would be awarded the contract. But we did feel we had a slight inside advantage. The process of responding to the RFP (request for proposal) went on for several months. Tensions were heightened, but business went on as usual.

During the time the RFP process was in full swing, I recall a somewhat unpleasant day that is still vividly etched in my memory. On this day I was supervising the anesthesia for a coronary artery bypass graft and also a laparoscopic general surgery case in the main OR. The heart case was well underway and I was supervising the CRNA as she induced the other surgery patient with IV drugs and then proceeded to intubate the patient. After over eighteen years of private practice, this was surely at least the 10,000th time that I would have personally intubated or directly supervised the intubation of a patient for surgery. The patient had no profound anatomical characteristics to suggest that they would be difficult to intubate. The CRNA, however, was unable to visualize the glottis (tracheal opening) and asked me to try. No problem; that's why I'm there. While this was transpiring I was paged to come to the open heart room. They were preparing to transition the patient from the cardiopulmonary bypass machine to his normal circulation; a process called coming off pump. This is a key phase of the operation and demands the full attention of the CRNA, anesthesiologist, pump technician and all the usual personnel.

Needing to be in two places at once is not an unusual occurrence for a busy anesthesiologist. We quickly learn to prioritize the needs and occasionally request a partner to help out. Assisting in the heart room is extremely important when coming off pump, but few things trump an acute airway problem. I requested for one of my partners to go help in the heart room. I attempted for ten or fifteen minutes to visualize the glottis unsuccessfully. Someone reminded me that the patient had consumed some liquids about four hours previously. This was allowed by our protocol, but was still a little worrisome. I don't believe I panicked, but I was "spooked." "Spooked" is the level on the anxiety scale right below panic. When you get to "spooked" you need to seriously evaluate your situation and take good precautions to avoid going up to the next level. I elected to abort the case. We allowed the patient to awaken. The patient suffered no ill effects from the failed intubation attempts.

Was I a little stressed out by the ongoing RFP process? By the need to be two places at once? By the recent ingestion of liquids? Would we have been more likely to be successful under more normal circumstances? The answer to all of these questions is most likely yes, although you never know for sure. I had never flat out canceled a case due to inability to intubate. Occasionally I had altered the game plan by using another technique, but this was a first. I was embarrassed. I had not anticipated a problem at all. Handling the unexpected difficult airway is an important part of my job. My consolation: the patient was not harmed in any way, and one out of 10,000 is not a high incidence of failure to intubate.

The RFP process came to a head on December 2, 1996, when Mr. Revels sent by certified mail the decision of the hospital's appointed advisory committee. They had selected one of the respondents, Presbyterian Anesthesia Associates, to provide a medical director and at least one other physician to build a new anesthesia group to provide services for CMH under an exclusive agreement. The process would involve a 90-day period starting January 1, 1997, during which two physicians from Presbyterian would work alongside the current physicians to evaluate our clinical performances. On April 1, 1997, the new anesthesia group would begin its exclusive provision of services.

The evaluation of physicians involved not only direct observation of our performance, but also extensive questionnaires and written evaluations from surgeons and CRNAs. An interview with a twelve-member panel from the Presbyterian group was also conducted with each physician candidate individually. The evaluation process was as thorough, objective and professionally done as one could imagine. The physicians chosen by this process to form the new group were myself, Dr. Ellis, Dr. Schwalbe and Dr. Merchant.

The new medical director was Dr. William Goglin from Presbyterian Anesthesia associates. A new recruit from the military, Dr. Tara Chronister, plus the four selected physicians formed the core of our new group. We were soon joined by three more recruits: Dr. John Roper, Dr. John Talbot and Dr. Scott Aumuller in the first few months. Thus three of the first four recruits were from the military. It was truly a new group in every way except for a few remaining familiar faces. In with the new, out with the old.

My old corporation, Concord Kannapolis Anesthesiologists PC ceased to perform services April 1, 1997, exactly eight years after it had first gone into operation. A brief recap seems appropriate. We had facilitated a major growth spurt in surgical and obstetrical services. We had also added a post-op pain service, a small pain clinic, a labor epidural service and had helped launch an open heart surgery program and an outpatient surgery center. We had also made a transition to supervision style anesthesia, in lieu of MD only or CRNA only anesthesia. The type of practice we had in 1988 was worlds apart from that of 1998. I feel we played a useful role in making a bridge between those two worlds.

To what or whom do I attribute the failure of my corporation? No single actor, administrator, anesthesiologist or surgeon could be held responsible. Indeed, I helped create the stage on which the play unfolded. I allowed some dysfunctions to develop past the point of no return. Nor can I honestly attribute our problems to the co-existing mania of the tech bubble which permeated much of our lives and business dealings of the late '90s. No Shakespearean play would attribute such an important role to an invisible actor. Yet, if the difficulties within our department and the aggressive actions of an unstable administration were the gears driving the evolution of our department, the exuberance of the '90s may have been the grease that lubricated those gears.

Interestingly, none of the physicians in my group who were recruited with the help of the hospital-affiliated head hunter were selected to be part of the new group. Likewise, none of the first three physicians recruited in the first twenty months as required by the hospital contract were chosen. All of the physicians I personally recruited independent of the head hunters passed their boards in the required time frame. Additionally, all the physicians I recruited independently of the head hunters were selected to the new group except for Dr. Hines. After leaving CMH Dr. Hines did a fellowship in Pain Management at Wake Forest. Subsequently he was hired by Dr. John Neeld, the head anesthesiologist at Northside in Atlanta, arguably one of the premier anesthesia groups in the Southeast. While employed at Northside, Dr. Hines served as president of the Georgia Society of Anesthesiologist. Of course none of this was known at the time our new group was being formed.

The strengths of the new anesthesia corporation and department were readily apparent. To start with, all the new MDs were already board certified. This created an aura of competence and helped avoid some of the criticism my old group had been subjected to. In addition, our new leader, Dr. Bill Goglin, had worked with Presbyterian Anesthesia Associates, a successful larger physician group, and therefore had a ready made plan on how to handle many of the financial and administrative issues of the corporation. Even such a mundane task as scheduling vacation or time off with a group of twenty or more physicians can be a juggling act unless a well-thought out set of guidelines to ensure fairness is in place. Bill proved to be both an effective leader as an administrator and a clinically stellar physician. He set high standards in both categories. The business operation of the corporation was greatly facilitated by the computer skills of Mel Murray, Dr.

Chronister's husband. To say the business operations were a notch more sophisticated than my old corporation would probably be an understatement.

Many of the new doctors had been in the military. This helped reinforce a sense of structure and hierarchy within the group. The trade off was a four-year time table to become partner and a salary compatible with an entry level position. I could only hope this would be the last upheaval in the workplace that I would have to endure.

The major changes in the department came so fast that it took me a little while to adjust my mindset. Being a somewhat analytical and skeptical person by nature, I looked for any significant flaw or weakness in the new arrangement. I saw none to speak of. My left brain (the reasoning center) was able to comprehend the transition. It was cut and dried. My right brain (the emotional part) was a little slow to catch on. This became apparent to me two or three weeks after the transition took place. I had stopped by the hospital in the early evening to check on the schedule for the next day. This was not a big deal since I lived about a mile away and the hospital was conveniently located between my house, the mall and the Sportscenter. The hospital was the epicenter of my universe and more like a second home than a work destination. I entered the old office I had used since 1978 and sat down at the desk. This was the same office I had used to draft the proposal to have the Duke physicians assist us start our open heart program and where I sat after receiving the news that my father had passed in 1988. As I was sitting, one of the new doctors from downtown who was assisting Dr. Goglin entered the office to check on things. We exchanged brief greetings but it seemed a little strained. Why was he looking at me suspiciously? I felt uncomfortable and left the office to return to my home. But then I got it. I meant no harm, nor did I challenge his authority or right to use the office for the new corporation, but I was the outsider. I was invading his territory. My bad.

In 1998 six more ORs were added to the surgery center and the entire surgery service was moved to the new area. The exception was cardiac surgery, which remained in the old section next to the ACCU or cardiac ICU. The newly-built surgery ORs were bigger and more efficient. They were arranged in a rectangular formation with a large central supply and storage area in the middle. The only disadvantage was that we could no longer look out the window of OR 3 and see what was happening at Shoney's, which was no longer Concord's finest restaurant.

Better staffing and larger pre-op areas in the new surgery suites built in '98 led to a major improvement in the ability to prepare patients for surgery. This was especially helpful for larger cases that needed epidurals for post-op pain control and for placement of invasive monitors like arterial lines or central lines. The more that could be done before the patient went into the OR, the less the surgeon was delayed in starting the operation. The use of pre-op areas for facilitating patient turnover had been ongoing even before '98, but the new facility upped this practice to a new level. Of course, moving the main OR suites next to the outpatient areas meant that inpatients and outpatients were again mingled to some extent. No one seemed to mind too much due to superior quality of the new ORs and the enhancement of patient turnover. The dilemma was ultimately resolved when a joint venture in 2003 create a truly free standing surgery center on Copperfield Boulevard over a mile away.

Our anesthesia group continued to grow in 1999 adding Dr. Catherine Cheung and Dr. James Hancock in the spring. They were joined a few months later by Dr. Albert Ho. Thus by 1999 Act Three of my medical career was well underway. Many new actors would take the stage in the next ten years.

Perhaps the biggest change for our practice as a whole was the growth of the pain clinic. Initially under the direction of Dr. Chronister and later Dr. Hancock, the pain clinic was rapidly morphing into a full service clinic. This included a trend toward invasive procedures such as implantable stimulators and drug pumps for severe pain. Of course it also meant dealing with problems of drug abuse, depression and simply difficult to manage cases. Through it all, pain treatment was a big growth area for our practice in the '90s.

I did not directly participate in the growth of the pain clinic since I was not a "pain doctor" per se. The greatest change I saw was a trend toward doing more blocks such as the interscalene block to decrease post-op pain after shoulder surgery, and an increase in anesthesia services outside of the OR such as for GI procedures (colonoscopies and upper endoscopies) and for MRIs on patients who were too claustrophobic to go into the MRI "tunnel" or were unable to hold still; i.e., small children. In addition we occasionally served as consultants to the emergency department or the ICU, performing emergency intubations or starting urgently needed central lines or IV access of some type on a critically ill patients. Sometimes these procedures were no less than life-saving. Although I understood the need, these consultations compounded the stress of treating an acutely ill patient with the disorientation of working in a hospital area in which we were less familiar. Unlike the OR suite where we knew the location of needed supplies, we now became dependent on unfamiliar faces to provide these pronto. I have discussed the trials of airway management several times; obtaining rapid venous access may be equally challenging and life-saving in certain situations.

One evening in the late '90s I was paged emergently to come to the main ICU to start a central line on a critically ill woman. I recognized a legitimate need for a central line, but there were several co-existing factors working against an easy central line placement thus increasing the risk of failure. She was obese, close to three hundred pounds; she was severely dehydrated and acidotic from her uncontrolled diabetes and she was delirious and uncooperative. Diabetes can trigger a cascade of problems. The serious conundrum presented by such cases is that the more urgently an IV access is needed, either a central line or peripheral, the more difficult the cannulation of the vein will be. That is because, with severe dehydration, the vein will be collapsed. In rare cases this may preclude resuscitation. Obesity and delirium only added to the problem. The risks, in addition to failure to obtain venous access, include a possible pneumothorax due to accidental puncture of the lung and major hemorrhaging due to accidental puncturing of an artery instead of the vein.

After twenty years of practice I was quite experienced with central lines, having placed close to 2000 with a less than one percent complication rate. However, this case, with all its issues, was a different matter. Should I proceed immediately with the central line due to the urgent need, or try another approach? If only I could correct the dehydration and or the delirium before attempting the central line, my odds of success would be bolstered. But this basket of problems was precisely the reason they called me in the first place; no one could start an IV on her anywhere.

I desperately scoured her hands and feet for superficial veins. I found a very small vein on the top of her foot; not very impressive as veins go, but I was able to place a very small "baby IV" —a 24 gauge— the smallest we have available. I then ordered an infusion of lactated ringers solution at 500 ml per hour. That is the maximum setting for the infusion pump. I left the ICU and returned to the OR to check on things.

Three or four hours later I returned to the ICU. Our patient had now received close to two liters of fluid and was a good deal less dehydrated. What's more, I could now safely administer a sedative to make her less agitated and uncooperative. I proceeded then to place the patient in Trendelenburg (head tilted downward) and prepped the right side of the neck with betadine. I now placed the central line into the right internal jugular vein approaching it lateral to the sternoclei-domastoid muscle. The procedure went well and she recovered from the ketoacidosis crisis. Although normal procedure would have been to proceed immediately with the central line, I believe that obtaining the smaller IV first and waiting a few hours for rehydration to occur was safer and ultimately just as successful.

My disposition and outlook in general seemed to be on the rise as the '90s progressed toward the millennial year 2000. It didn't hurt that in 1998 Tee Martin led Tennessee, my alma mater, to the national championship with a perfect 13-0 season. Perhaps more importantly 1999 was the year of my fiftieth birthday, an important psychological milestone. My wife totally stunned me with a surprise birthday party. That evening I accompanied Corey as we entered the unlit Sportscenter to retrieve an item she left there. As we entered the lights came on and at least seventy people gave me the surprise of my life. Red faced but appreciative, I am still not quite sure how she pulled it off without arousing my suspicion. Still am.

At fifty I could safely conclude that both my professional career and my total life span were at least at the halfway mark. I could hope for a more stable and peaceful second half as I set my sights on retirement and life after work. What could I do to commemorate this milestone? Buy a Harley and ride cross-country? Take up skydiving? Go to Africa and hunt big game? I decided to keep it simple. The biggest challenges are always within. Why not compete in a 10K road race as I had done in my thirties. Perhaps I could place well in my new age group. In my early years of practice I had run a 10K in close to forty minutes flat. I picked an arbitrary goal. Why not attempt to run a forty-five minute 10 K at age fifty? That would be a decent time.

I had never quit running routinely as an exercise; but was not pushing myself hard on my workouts. In the fall of '98 I began interval workouts; i.e., four hundred yard runs with a slow jog in between, repeating for a total of eight on some weekends. The best place to do this was on Arbor Street, a flat straight road near the hospital with little traffic. I alternated these workouts with five to six mile runs on other weekends. Midweek I would usually do a shorter less intense run.

The big day was April 10, 1999 at the 22nd annual Charlotte Observer Marathon and 10 K race starting in downtown Charlotte on Tryon Street. I ran a time of 47:12, good enough for 23rd out of 136 in my age group. I failed to meet my goal of forty-five minutes, but I wasn't too disappointed. I had given it a good try. I was happy with my overall effort and result.

As we approached the end of the century my life seemed to be firing on all cylinders. All children and stepchildren were in a good place and doing well in school. In '99 Mandy was starting her last year at UNC Wilmington. Harper was a junior at James Madison in Harrisburg, Virginia. Billy was a sophomore at the University of Chicago. Dustin was a freshman at Florida State in Tallahassee. Corey was a senior in high school in Gainesville, Florida. She would soon start college at New York University in September 2000. So yes, we did have all five in college at one time.

The fact that I could expect to be a partner in our new corporation with a significant increase in total income by the year 2001 was also uplifting. I was in a celebratory mood. During this time frame I finally worked out the chords and finger patterns to a song I had admired for some time, "Here Comes the Sun" by George Harrison. Randy Clay of Music Consultants assisted me with this enjoyable task. The secret is to place the capo on the fifth fret, or higher, and play a D finger position. With a little practice it flowed nicely. Playing this song on my Taylor rarely fails to brighten my outlook even today. It seems appropriate that I picked it up in the late '90s.

It would be wholly appropriate, therefore, to say that the twentieth century was ending on an upbeat note. At the same time there was this co-existing concern called the Y-2K problem that had been looming for several years. The heart of the problem was that many computer programs, especially older ones, had abbreviated years to two digits instead of four to save computer memory. Therefore the year 1999 might be expressed as 99 and the year 2000 might be expressed as 00 in these older systems. Conceivably 00 might be interpreted as the year 1900 instead of the year 2000 creating a serious problem with calculations. Predictions of outcomes from this discrepancy ranged from negligible to catastrophic. This concern was significantly profound that the UN sponsored a global meeting of a 120 countries in New York on December 11, 1998 to develop plans to minimize the possible worldwide effects. An estimated three hundred billion dollars was spent worldwide to upgrade computers and programs to pre-empt possible global computer failures. Computer chips were an integral part of anesthesia monitors as well as most sophisticated medical equipment. It seemed unlikely that the Y-2K problem would have any effect on the normal operations of our department of anesthesia. But did anyone really know for sure? Time would tell.

As fate would have it, I was scheduled to be on call for my anesthesia group on Friday December 31, 1999. If some monitoring equipment began to malfunction at midnight it would be my problem to deal with. Since I was the oldest and most experienced anesthesiologist in the group, I had plenty of experience trouble shooting problems of manifold etiology in the middle of the night. Furthermore, I had practiced for seven or eight years before the oximeter and the capnograph were in general use. If these monitors failed, it would be bad, but not catastrophic. I could survive without them. It was plausible to claim that I was selected to take call on this noteworthy occasion, the last day of the millennium, because of my vast experience. However, that would be a little delusional on my part. It was merely my turn to take call. As a matter of fact, I believe that I volunteered to cover call that date.

We did several cases on December 31, 1999. As you may have guessed, we experienced no equipment failures when the New Year rolled in at midnight. Da nada! No problems. As a matter of fact it was a reasonably quiet night as New Year's Eves go. Perhaps the "doomsday" predictions relating to the new millennium had subdued celebrations and encouraged people to behave. No accidents. No trauma. No emergency surgery.

Around 6:15 a.m. the next morning I arose from my bed in the call room and went to the bathroom to splash water on my face to wake up. I dried my face and then went to the main OR to give the call beeper to the physician coming on call. There was not much to report, it had been a quiet night. It was now Saturday morning; not much was posted since it was a holiday. I then changed clothes and left the hospital by the back entrance. I walked across the doctors' parking lot where my '98 Jeep Sport was waiting to take me home. I unlocked the door, climbed in and turned on the ignition; I then turned the defrost on high to help clear the thin glaze of ice on the windshield.

As I waited for the windshield to clear I struggled to absorb the significance of the moment. A new century was just beginning. The twentieth century was history. As centuries go it wasn't too bad. I would say it was my favorite one so far. But maybe that was because I wasn't born until 1949. I missed the Great Depression, Hitler and two world wars. Vietnam was bad enough. Perhaps it would be more meaningful to ask someone much older what they thought about it.

The ice was beginning to melt on the windshield, but it would take another minute or two until my visibility was acceptable. Meanwhile I reflected. What adventures lay in store for me, my family, my town and country in this new century? Was there anyway I could have predicted the tragedy our country was to endure on 9-11? How could I have known what disasters lay in store for the once proud mill town of Kannapolis? What seer could have foretold the tragedy that occurred within my own professional group of physicians? Furthermore, who would have believed that my immediate family would soon experience the legal battle of a lifetime? Had someone informed me of these events as I sat in my car, I am not sure I would have believed them. If I thought they had any credibility I would have been tempted to turn off the engine and return to the call room where I could lock the door and somehow hide from all this impending doom. Perhaps I could somehow fall into a deep sleep and isolate myself from the rest of the world. Then like Rip Van Winkle I would wake up after twenty years and start life anew.

And yet, maybe that was not such a great idea. If I were in a coma I wouldn't have witnessed the heroic deeds of the rescue workers in New York City. I would have missed the wave of patriotism and unity that swept the country. I would not have seen how the resilient citizens of Kannapolis endured one hardship after another and fearlessly struggled to gain a new identity. I wouldn't have seen the compassion and support of my partners for the family of one of our own whose life was ended too soon. Finally I would not have appreciated the perseverance my own son displayed while undergoing a heart wrenching legal battle and prison sentence; nor the support and empathy from family and friends. If I had missed all these events, I might feel somewhat like Garth Brooks when he sang; "I could have missed the pain, but I would have had to miss the dance."

As the last piece of ice slid down the windshield, I put my Jeep in reverse and slowly backed out of my parking spot. Hopeful, but clueless, I then began the short drive home to begin my life in the twenty-first century. The ice was gone from the windshield. I could see clearly now, but did I really know where I was headed?

The New Millennium

—✦—

The Practice of anesthesia, as did life in general, went on as usual in the twenty-first century devoid of earth shattering changes. There was notable steady growth as we added Dr. Christine Cullen in 2000, Dr. Donald Schmit in 2001, and Dr. Shaun Williams in 2002.

The rest of the world saw some upheaval, however. The stock market began its downward spiral later in the year, wreaking havoc with retirement plans. The election debacle in November between Gore and Bush raised some serious questions about our electoral process and the role of the Supreme Court. But these issues could all be construed as bumps in the road in our democratic and capitalistic system.

The year's major event for Becky and me was a September trip to Germany and Austria. We flew directly into Hamburg and rented a car. Since the Opel we had already paid for was unavailable, we were forced to drive the upgrade, a five speed manual Mercedes coupe. We headed south on the "Romantic Road" through Rothenberg, Innsbruck, Salzburg, Vienna and back to Heidelberg. The homes of Einstein, Mozart, Mad King Ludwig (Neuschwanstein Castle) and the site of the "Sound of Music" were all suitably enchanting. I revived my college German to the level of barely passable, maybe. Near the end of the trip, however, we incurred the wrath of a German motorist by only going 120 kph on the Autobahn thereby slowing his progress. I confess that his frustration filled me with a warm glow of schadenfreude. I knew enough German to understand that. Except for this blip, a delightful time was had by all.

About this same time my baby daughter, Corey, then seventeen, was starting college at New York University (NYU) in Manhattan. She had skipped a grade somewhere around middle school and was therefore quite young to be going away for college. We worried some, but felt she was mature enough physically and socially to handle things okay.

Corey did well academically at NYU, but sometime that fall she decided she did not want to continue there. She would return to Florida to her mom's house to re-evaluate her situation. Perhaps a smaller university would be better. Someone would need to drive to her school in downtown Manhattan to retrieve her mountainous pile of indispensables: clothes, books, artwork, random detritus, and schlep them southward, ultimately to Florida. That someone had a easy to remember name. It's spelled D-A-D.

Sometime in mid-December 2000 I left Concord, North Carolina, and headed north. I started out on I-85 and worked my way over to I-95. This took me eventually to the Lincoln Tunnel and, voila, New York City.

NYU is conveniently located in Greenwich Village in the southern part of the island. I had no trouble finding the school. In fact it's hard to miss. I parked my Jeep exactly where my daughter had advised; a special loading zone only parents, VIPS and CIA agents are allowed to use. I stepped into the dormitory lobby and called the number my daughter had given me. While I was waiting I sat on a sofa and observed the busy students entering and leaving.

After about ten minutes a young attractive female got off the elevator and walked over to where I was seated. She was about the same height and weight of my daughter and had similar facial features. She claimed she was my daughter. Right away I knew I was the victim of a practical joke because this young girl also had a tattoo on her left upper arm and a lip ring. Furthermore her hair color didn't match that of Corey's, much too dark. So I decided to go along with the gag. She knew quite a bit about her past life and had a voice pattern and mannerisms very similar to hers. Holy Smoke! It suddenly hit me. She was my own sweet daughter. She had merely acquired a few superficial adornments. She was the very same loving, intelligent, beautiful daughter I had once known now with a few upgrades. I meant to ask her in which academic class at NYU she had acquired these accoutrements; but I didn't have time. We needed to load all her belongings in my Jeep quickly. It was after 3:30 p.m.; I was hoping to leave before five to beat the rush hour traffic. We loaded my Jeep to the hilt with boxes of who knows what, clothes, books and other paraphernalia. Then I hugged my daughter goodbye.

It was a little after five on this mid-December day when I finally departed NYU. I know my way around the city reasonably well for a Southern boy, but the massive Christmas crowds, the holiday traffic and the glaring late afternoon sun near the horizon conspired to make navigation a bit problematic. The Lincoln Tunnel is reasonably easy to find; you go several blocks north and then head west. However street numbers were hard to read. Which lane do I need to be in? I chugged along slowly and turned when it felt right. After a minute of uncertainty the tunnel appeared.

Once through that gauntlet I knew I had it made. No GPS. Maps were a nice back-up plan. But fortunately, unlike fifth graders today, I actually had studied geography in the fifth grade. I carry a map in my head. All I had to do after heading west out of the tunnel was look for a major thoroughfare heading south. Routes that had an "I" in front of them painted on large green signs were preferable. I needed to traverse the wilds of Newark and then re-enter the conduit continuing dead south. As long as the Atlantic Ocean was somewhere off to my left I knew I would eventually reunite with North Carolina.

In my case, I was headed to Wilmington, North Carolina, right on the coast. This makes it easy to locate. At this time my step-daughter,

Amanda (Mandy), was graduating from UNC Wilmington. I attended the graduation ceremony along with her mom, Becky, and then headed west back to Concord. All the while being sure to keep my Jeep locked at all times to keep Corey's belongings safe. Eventually her stuff made it back to Florida; I don't remember those details.

This little vignette poignantly illustrates how the joys of parenthood continue well after your child leaves home. It's what we signed up for, somewhere in the fine print. Perhaps you failed to see it. In a few years I would learn much more about the vicissitudes of parenthood with my oldest child. Only this time it would be much more serious.

The year 2001 gave no early warning that it would be a momentous time in our country's history. Of course the tech bubble was still imploding with predictable negative effects on our net worth, but we took that in stride. Actually for some of us there was a bright spot. Sometime around April 1, 2001, I along with several others, were accepted as full partners in our corporation, NAPS, Northeast Anesthesia and Pain Associates. This event was celebrated with a wonderful dinner party at the McNich House in downtown Charlotte, arguably Charlotte's finest restaurant located in a gorgeous Victorian house on Church Street. I would highly recommend it to anyone as long as you don't mind the cost.

In the summer of 2001 I received a call from Ann Carol Price, the educational consultant who had assisted me in managing Billy's high school challenges. Did I mind doing a phone interview with a reporter from the *New York Times* about my experience using educational consultants to deal with my son's problems in high school? Of course I said I didn't mind. Sara Rimer, a reporter for the *Times*, called shortly thereafter. I had nothing but praise for the consultant's advice. What would I have done without them? The article she wrote cited examples of parents like myself who had used special educational consultants to deal with special behavior or academic problems in high school. The article was titled "Desperate Measures, Parents of Troubled Youth Are

Seeking Help At Any Cost." It seemed to be mostly complimentary of how the parents had dealt with the problems. The article appeared in the New York Times on September 10, 2001. That's right. Next day, I almost forgot about the article but was able to do a Google search recently and print out the entire article.

On September 11, 2001, I was experiencing a routine day supervising anesthetic cases in the main OR suite at Northeast Medical Center (the named changed from CMH to Northeast Medical Center in 1997). Someone mentioned to me that a bizarre plane crash had occurred in New York City. When I had a free moment about ten minutes later I went to the doctors' lounge to hear what reporters were saying about this quirky incident. I entered the lounge just in time to witness a second plane as it crashed into the South Tower. The surgery schedule continued uninterrupted. But every thirty minutes or so when I had the chance I would dart back into the lounge as the disaster unfolded to learn of the latest developments: an attack on the Pentagon, another plane crashing somewhere. Then I would report to the nurses and other staff what I had learned. For a few hours it seemed the whole world was falling apart.

What effect did the events in New York City on September 11 have on the administration of anesthesia or the surgery schedule that day? The short answer is nothing. We suppressed our anxiety and carried out our duties as if nothing had happened. Isn't that what professionals are supposed to do?

But in the back of my mind, questions were churning. Why did these people hate us? What did they expect to accomplish? What would be their next move? Who were their primary supporters? How could we begin to neutralize the extremists without inciting the moderates of the Islamic world? Didn't they know as users of petroleum that we were a key source of their wealth? I said I had the questions, but never claimed to have the answers? I was, however, thankful that my daughter, Corey, no longer attended NYU. That would have been too close for comfort.

Prior to 9-11 we had arranged a short trip to New York to see some plays in December. No reason to cancel. So we saw Nathan Lane and Mathew Broderick in the *Producers* plus a couple other shows. While in New York, however, we couldn't ignore the obvious recent events. Why not pay our respect to 9/11 victims with a visit to the site? We hailed a taxi and rode silently to the sacred epicenter of the catastrophe, However, when we reached Canal Street the cab driver stopped. He was spooked; that was as close as he was willing to drive us. So we got out and walked the last few blocks. The disaster area was well demarcated by barricades and chain link fences. It had been a good three months since the calamity occurred. The smoke, ashes and stench had vanished, but the aura of unspeakable suffering and tragedy was not diminished. We gazed in reverent silence for about ten or fifteen minutes. There was a vast array of memorials; flowers, plaques and various written tributes. One such plaque caught my eye. It was from the students of Rowan Cabarrus Community college back home. Who would have expected that?

The events in the mill town of Kannapolis in the early years of the millennium also bore some elements of tragedy. In the year 2000 the company had filed for bankruptcy as the Pillowtex CEO Tony Williams replaced Hanson. What more could happen in the foreseeable future to totally demoralize the citizens of Kannapolis? The final death toll of its primary industry and raison d'etre? The sudden loss of its iconic hero and most famous citizen in a horrific accident? Unfortunately, both of these would contribute to a portentous start for the new era.

It was the final lap of the Daytona 500 on February 18, 2001, when his car was tapped from behind. He spun out of control and hit the wall at about 160 mph. He was pronounced dead at 5:16 p.m. at Halifax Hospital, but it was believed he died on impact. Recognized as one of the greatest NASCAR drivers of all times, Dale Earnhardt was the Michael Jordan and Tiger Woods of Kannapolis. The loss was a heavy blow for the people of that beleaguered town.

Pillowtex emerged from bankruptcy briefly in 2002 with a new line of products; however the company filed for bankruptcy July 30, 2003, and shut its doors for good. This tragic event caused a sudden loss of 4,800 jobs in North Carolina of which 3,984 were in Kannapolis. That was the largest layoff in the state's history. A combined effort of local charities and social services helped ease the pain by assisting with job relocation or with job training. However, two years later less than half of the 3894 were employed. The jobless rate went from 6.9 percent to 9.6 percent in Rowan County, despite the good efforts of many.

Concord attorney and state senator, Fletcher Hartsell, had an idea to turn around the economic demise of Kannapolis. Why not encourage billionaire David Murdock to repurchase the property of the now defunct Pillowtex and use the site to bring new industry and economic revival to Kannapolis? This was accomplished through Lynne Scott Safrit, the head of Murdock's real estate holdings in North Carolina. He purchased the Pillowtex property for 6.4 million in December 2004.

Murdock's plan for the property? A biotechnology research center. The new entity was to be called the North Carolina Research Campus. It was to be formed in collaboration with private biotechnology firms, Duke University, North Carolina State, North Carolina Central University, North Carolina AT&T University, UNC Chapel Hill, UNC Greensboro, UNC Charlotte and Rowan Cabarrus Community College. The research campus was projected to create 5,000 technology jobs and 35,000 ancillary jobs. The creation of the research campus would fulfill two goals for Murdock: promoting health through improved nutrition due to research at the campus, and provide jobs and economic growth for Kannapolis. Unfortunately, the real estate bubble of 2008 greatly stymied the fulfillment of these projections. Murdock is well in his nineties. Who will write the next chapter in the saga of Kannapolis' economic development?

The demolition of the remaining mill buildings from November 2005 to November 2006 is a noteworthy story in its own right. Five and a half million square footage of buildings were demolished by

D.H. Griffin of Greensboro. This was the third largest demolition project in American history.

One may ask if this book is a story of my profession and related adventures as an anesthesiologist, why such an interest and concern for a depressed town, once the home of a vibrant textile industry and now the home of unfulfilled promises for a biotechnology research campus? The town's future has little immediate relevance to my job or life in the foreseeable future.

Part of my interest in Kannapolis is merely historical curiosity. Once the primary industry in the area, the fate of the mills was closely linked to the well-being of the community. The original hospital, as noted before, was created through the efforts of Charles Cannon in 1937. I was fortunate to have worked with two of the doctors on the original medical staff. The history of how the hospital was created and later evolved is a fascinating story. Of course I'm motivated by an altruistic concern for the citizens of Kannapolis. It's disconcerting to watch anyone struggle, even more so your neighbor. I certainly have a strong desire to see the former mill workers do well.

And yet, it would be misleading, even dishonest, not to admit that a major part of my concern and interest in the fate of Kannapolis has been self-serving. I do have a selfish interest in the welfare of its citizens. In the delicate ecosystem of the economic world, how can the whole survive in harmony for long if a major sector is ailing? Can the professional class thrive indefinitely if the working class is chronically ailing? I believe we all have a vested interest in a well-balanced economy. If one cylinder is misfiring, the whole engine is affected. The $1.5 billion, 350-acre research campus has enormous potential to transform Kannapolis. I can only hope it will succeed, not only for its citizens but for myself and future generations.

Despite the misfortunes of the early millennium; 9-11, the demise of the textile industry and the bursting of the tech bubble, my personal life was buoyed by a couple of noteworthy events. On May 5, 2002, Dustin married his high school sweetheart, Adrienne Wise, at Grace

United Methodist Church in Gainesville, Florida where Adrienne's father was serving as youth minister. The wedding was large by most standards, well planned and traditional except for one important component. When it came time for the special music preceding the nuptial vows, Dustin stepped aside, picked up his acoustic Takamine guitar and played "My One and Only Love" a classic love ballad first released by Frank Sinatra in 1953. He sang and played beautifully without a glitch. Finishing the song, he gently set his guitar down on the stand and returned center stage to complete the ceremony. How cool was that? Few people could give such a smooth performance anytime, much less on their wedding day.

Dustin and Adrienne were both students at Florida State in Tallahassee where Dustin was a music major and Adrienne a music and history major. Adrienne went on to get a master's degree in Religions of Western Antiquity. Both were excellent students and well grounded. Our family is enriched by their joint musical talents and strengthened by their stability and reliability. As a side job Dustin worked for "Signs Unlimited" making commercial signs for businesses in the Tallahassee area. In 2005 they moved to the Sandy Springs-Marietta area just north of Atlanta where they have been making music and thriving ever since.

In June of the same year, Billy graduated from the University of Chicago. He did so in grand style by winning the Cohen math award and the John Haeseler Lewis Physics award; top honors in both math and physics. Thus after floundering academically in his early teens, he had made a complete turnaround in this department. The highbrow, slightly rarified atmosphere at the University of Chicago was exactly what he needed to flourish scholastically. He even requested, and was granted the right to take graduate courses in physics. He was perhaps somewhat fortunate to be accepted at all because of his spotty performance record in high school; he proved he was where he belonged. In addition to academic success, he joined the track and cross country team as a walk on. He became a competitive member of both teams as a distance runner under coach and former Olympian Jim Spivey.

Accepted at Cal Tech with a full scholarship for graduate studies in physics, Billy travelled cross-country in the 2001 Camry I bought for him in Chicago at the end of his junior year. A short stop at Yosemite National Park where he and a friend climbed the face of El Capitan, then on to Pasadena; never a dull moment. At Cal Tech he made the highest grade in physics that year (and for several years) on the entrance exam. It seemed great things might happen.

By the summer of 2003 my career and life in general seemed to be in good shape. I was 54 and in good health. All five of my kids and step-kids were college graduates or almost so—Dustin was finishing up at Florida State and Corey was a junior at Mills College in Oakland. I had experienced several major changes in the workplace, a divorce and remarriage and some challenges with raising teenagers. I could reasonably hope for ten more tranquil years of medical practice before full retirement. The possibilities of a second home in the mountains and trips out of the country were enticing. I felt I had paid my dues both at the professional level and in the domestic arena as well.

Unfortunately, my plans to sail smoothly into the safe harbor of senior citizenship and respectable retirement was not to be realized. My boat was viciously rocked by a storm I could never have foreseen. I was in for a rough ride.

My first awareness of the approaching storm came in early October 2003 when my ex-wife, Heidi, called to tell me about some issues our son Billy was facing. She suggested I sit down before she informed me of the developments. I immediately felt uneasy. Had I heard anything about a fire that had destroyed a number of cars at a Humvee dealership in the Los Angeles area? No! What could that possibly have to do with me or our son?

It seems that in the late evening of August 21 he was recruited on the spur of the moment by "friends" to assist in a spray painting endeavor at car dealerships in the area. Indeed he had previously agreed to a campaign to place bumper stickers on SUVs stating "My SUV supports terrorism"; a reference to America's dependence on Middle Eastern oil. There was a glitch in obtaining the bumper stickers. So of course he now agreed to spray painting environmental slogans on SUVs. They suggested using his car for the evening's activities.

The details of what happened in the wee hours of August 22, 2003, are beyond the scope of this treatise. Indeed I don't know most of them. I would most likely put my own biased spin in them if I did. An overview, however, is helpful to understand the ensuing controversial developments and the wider consequences for the family.

In the early hours of August 22, 2003 over a hundred cars were spray painted with environmental slogans at car dealerships in the Los Angeles area. In addition 12 or 13 SUVs were partly or totally destroyed by an arson-caused blaze. Billy was involved in the spray painting spree with at least two other people. In addition he also witnessed some of the arson.

In the week or two following the arsons several noteworthy developments took place. A local environmentalist, Josh Connole, was arrested and jailed without trial for the arsons. He was later released with an apology and a payment of $100,000. The two people who had recruited my son in the middle of the night at some point left the country before they could be apprehended. They were gone. Unfortunately, Billy elected to inform several friends at Cal Tech about the activities of August 22. It was an act of pure braggadocio. He also sent several emails to the *LA Times* chiding the FBI for their mistakes.

Without knowing the details, one can make several valid assessments concerning these events. First of all, Billy used poor judgment on August 22. He was slow to distance himself from the arsonist. He furthermore showed poor judgment by emailing the *LA Times* and boasting to friends. Politically and socially naïve to say the least, he seemed to have little grasp of the probable serious legal repercussions. Furthermore, it seems very likely that he was recruited on August 21 to be the designated patsy for the evening's events. He seemed oblivious to that concept.

The reaction of the judicial system to these developments was predictable. A grand jury on October 26, 2003. An arrest on March 9, 2004. An arraignment. A trial in November 2004. A sentencing in April 2005. He was found not guilty of the most serious charge: using a Molotov cocktail. That could have led to a thirty-year sentence. Yet, in the absence of any other defendants, he encountered the full brunt of the prosecution's wrath. The sentence: 100 months of incarceration and a fine of over three and a half million dollars.

It isn't my intention that the story of my son's troubles hijack the story of my career. But I couldn't do justice to the severity of the situation or its impact on me personally without some elaboration and vignettes about his legal battle and incarceration. As a parent, the only thing that could have surpassed this trauma would have been Billy's death. Fortunately, I was at a stage in my professional career that was stable. I was sufficiently grounded to absorb most of the shock. The storm caused severe listing, but my boat never capsized.

The tribulation of having a child in prison was multifaceted. It was personally painful to watch a child suffer, however stoic he may have been. It was embarrassing to have to acknowledge this failure to others. Of course there was the financial burden associated with the legal defense. It was a burden on me personally, but also on my wife and children who saw my time and energy diverted from them. In my experience, most misfortunes we endure have some redeeming feature, some sort of upside. The loss of one thing is followed by a gain somewhere else. I struggled to see any upside associated with my son's incarceration. It seemed like a lose-lose situation. I could see no redemption for the price I was paying. Perhaps that would come later.

The one hundred months of incarceration translated into almost seven years of actual prison time and six months in a halfway house. During this time he was incarcerated in six different locations. The logic behind and timing of the transfers was difficult to understand. One transfer occurred on Christmas Eve. Prisoners have very few rights or means to address grievances. Simple chores like moving his books from one location to another were problematic. The FBP (Federal Bureau of Prisons) is a veritable bureaucratic behemoth replete with numerous rules and regulations. This is an obvious necessity given the difficulty of their mission. My intent is to relate what it felt like as a parent of a prisoner to interact with that entity.

At one point in the year 2005 he was transferred from the San Bernardino Jail (a county jail that frequently held the overflow of federal prisoners) to the MDC (Metropolitan Detention Center) in LA. When that occurred I received a large box of his personal books. This was necessary since federal regulations limit the number of books that can be sent with prisoners on transfers. These books were his most valued physical possessions. Included were: *Introduction to Plasma Physics*, Gurnett and Bhattacharjee; The *Road to Reality,* Penrose; *The Fabric of the Cosmos*, Brian Greene; *The Millennium Problems*, Devlon; and *The five Biggest Unsolved Problems in Science*, Wiggins Wynn; as well as a number of books on philosophy, history and classic literature, about fifty in all. I estimate they were worth close to two thousand dollars. Without thinking, I repackaged the books and forwarded them all to his new address at the MDC in LA using our local UPS.

After a week or so the books were nowhere to be found. Apparently it was illegal to get that many books in one shipment, a possible security risk. It wasn't my role to question the rules, but what happened to the books? In the ensuing weeks I called the MDC every three or four days. They repeatedly denied having the books. Billy informed me that the guards or other prison workers sometimes take prisoners possessions if they think they won't be missed. How could that be? I became obsessed with locating the books. UPS verified to me that the books were shipped and received by the MDC. They gave me a photocopy of the receipt with the date, time and a signature, "Montoya." Armed with this proof of delivery, I again called the MDC. When they again denied having the books I suggested I may have UPS investigated for fraud since they claimed they had been sent there. Three days later the books arrived at my house. No apology or explanation was ever given.

As his prison time elapsed, I adapted by developing a double identity. The majority of the time I was the mild mannered anesthesiologist and citizen of Concord everyone knew. About once every six months I would make a trip to California—later it was Arizona— to visit my son in federal prison. I kept a low profile and learned how to blend in with other inmate families; empathizing with the plight of their loved one. I call this my prison mode. When hotel clerks asked me the reason for my visit to the coast, I would say to visit family, even though it was none of their business. "How nice!" Perhaps they wondered why I was so solemn.

Back in Concord on Sunday evenings, I would resume my usual role. Except for a small circle of friends, I generally avoided discussing my children in public during this time. Too complicated, too painful. "So the younger two are doing well; what about your oldest child?" "We are very proud of his progress; he just got moved from a medium security to a low security prison. He has become fluent in Chinese and Spanish and is teaching cosmology and physics. Unfortunately, the salary that he earns for these services is not very competitive."

Fortunately my ability to function as an anesthesiologist didn't seem to be affected significantly. These were busy times. The Gateway Surgery Center that opened in 2003 grew steadily in business each year, as did our overall practice. It was helpful that I could sleep at night. I believe my energy release through my guitar and my dedication to routine exercise were key to deflecting stress. At any rate I survived these times better than you might think. I am grateful for my partners who covered for me in November 2004 so I could attend the trial. Otherwise my ordeal had little effect on my vocation.

As time progressed, my visits to California became more routine and less stressful. One noteworthy visit in March 2006, however, stands out as a reminder of the harshness of the bureaucracy with which I was dealing and the implications for the families of prisoners. In telling this story, I am not attempting to criticize the FBP (Federal Bureau of Prisons), how it operates, or the need for strict rules concerning inmates and family. There are good reasons for their existence. Neither do I wish to patty-cake issues I had to deal with. Why not just tell it exactly as I remember it? Perhaps someone may benefit. The times included are approximations

On a Saturday afternoon in late March 2006 I flew direct from Charlotte to Los Angeles on a USAir flight. I rented a car at LAX and drove about three hours north on US 101 to the town of Lompoc, a town of about 40,000 near the coast. I estimate it to be about one third of the way from LA to San Francisco. I would describe the town as pleasant, but the weight of my mission overshadowed my appreciation of the surroundings. There I got an inexpensive hotel room on the main strip, a Holiday Inn Express I believe.

Sunday morning I arose at 4 a.m. My biological clock was still functioning on Eastern Standard Time. I tried to keep my system tuned to the East Coast to avoid readjustment problems when returning home. I donned my T-shirt, shorts and jogging shoes; by 4:30 a.m. I was jogging down the main street of Lompoc. I headed west on W. Central Avenue and jogged away from the town center into rural farmland. It was still quite dark and my mind drifted between thoughts of my upcoming visit with my son and the natural habitat and nocturnal hunting patterns of the California mountain lion. That is why I carried several nice sized stones in each fist. Mountain lions hate stones. I had a brisk five mile run.

Back in my hotel room I showered and shaved and then had a nice breakfast at the breakfast bar on the main floor. By 7:35 a.m. I was in my rental car driving down the main street. I turned west on W. Central Avenue where I had jogged earlier in the morning except now I turned north on Floradale Avenue toward the Federal Correctional Institution of Lompoc. We used to call them prisons.

Around 7:45 a.m. I pulled up to the guard station at the prison to be allowed admission as a visitor. After verifying that I carried no guns or other weapons, the guard informed me that I was too early. Visitors were not allowed in until 8 a.m. and he did not want me to wait outside the prison. He advised that I leave and return in fifteen minutes. This seemed foolish to me, but I wisely elected not to argue with an armed guard. No future in it. Thus my plan to be first in line and get my visit off to a good start was foiled. Strike one.

I drove back to the edge of town, made a U-turn in a shopping center parking lot, and then headed back to the prison. I arrived at 8:01 a.m. There were now at least twenty visitors in line ahead of me. It takes a minute or two to check visitors in so it was about 8:30 a.m. by the time I reached the check-in point. Strike two.

But now a new problem arose. The guard who checks visitors in told me I wouldn't be allowed in the prison because of the pants I was wearing. That's right, my pants were illegal. They were a pair of size 34 x 32 Hagar khaki pants purchased at Belk for $29.90 on sale less than a year prior. The problem was the color. The light brown or khaki was similar to the shade of the pants that inmates wore. I would be a security risk if admitted because I could be mistaken for an inmate or vice versa. I had to leave. Strike three, but who's counting?

The guards were helpful enough to tell me that if I could find some pants of another color, I would still be allowed in. So I left the prison around 8:45 a.m. pondering my plight. I had flown two thousand miles to visit my son and was being turned away because I was a security risk. Stores would not be open till much later. In my hotel room I had a pair of colored shorts and another pair of pants, also brown, but a little darker. I took a chance; I changed into the slightly darker pair of pants. I then drove back to the prison. They allowed me to enter. *Gracias a Dios!*

By this time it was close to 9:30 a.m. I had missed an hour and a half of visitation time. I was tense and a little frazzled. The atmosphere at this medium security prison seemed darker and less welcoming than other prisons I had visited. Perhaps that was simply my own personal spin based on my misfortunes of the morning. I only had one more small hurdle to negotiate before being allowed inside. I must lock my billfold and other valuables in a locker and then go through a metal detector, similar to those used at the airport. Understandably, I was a little flustered and unfamiliar with the layout of the check-in area. So I asked the guard where the lockers were located.

At this point I experienced a significant cognitive dysfunction that is difficult to explain. I would very much like to omit relating the details because it is quite embarrassing. However, it would be difficult to understand what happened afterwards if I didn't mention it. Perhaps my brain was a little rattled from the stressful morning and the stern environment. Or perhaps it was just a routine senior moment. That's as close as I can get.

The guard pointed to a wall of lockers about fifty feet off to my right. Unfortunately, directly in between his finger and the wall was a small cart of some type with a locked metal cabinet on top. I saw the cart before I saw the row of lockers off to the right. It didn't look like a normal locker, but I attempted to insert the key he had just given me into the key hole. After ten or fifteen seconds of fumbling, I realized my folly. Guards snickering, I retreated to the wall of lockers twenty feet away. I chose a locker that would be easy to find on the way out; top row in the middle section, next to the last on the left. Red faced, and feeling lower than a worm's belly, I handed the guard the key in exchange for a wooden token with the locker number on it. On the way out, of course, I would exchange the token for the key to retrieve my valuables and then make my escape to my normal environment; the land of McDonald's, churches, schools and friendly people.

After going through the metal detector, I was finally allowed into the big room where families can meet with inmates. Billy had been patiently waiting, unaware of my morning adventures. Visiting a child in prison is always bittersweet. You are always glad you came, but you long for better days. We talk about everything under the sun: philosophy, religion, history, the education system, exercising and, of course, family. The only nutrition available is from vending machines; so families are allowed to bring quarters into the room. The inmates considered machine food to be superior to their normal meals. A scary thought! I found it to be adequate; I have no complaints. Just one piece of advice. Stay away from the cheeseburgers.

Time always passes swiftly; It's three o'clock before you know it. Time for some awkward goodbyes. It was well worth it, despite all the hassles involved.

Leaving the visitors hall at 3 p.m., I had only one thing on my mind. That was to retrieve my valuables as quickly and gracefully as possible, and then make my retreat in my rental car. I handed the guard the token and he gave me the key to the locker. I went straight to the locker I had chosen; it was easy to locate. I attempted to put the key in the key hole. It wouldn't fit! I tried both ways multiple times. Unbelievable! I knew I had the correct locker. What could the problem be? Then it hit me. I was the target of a nefarious prank. Humiliated, but resolved to appear calm, I returned the key the guard had given me and requested the correct key. Grinning from ear to ear and acting smug, as if he had pulled off an ingenious Houdini stunt, the guard handed me the correct key. I retrieved my belongings and quickly left the building.

Obviously, I was fair game for the guard's entertainment. My senior moment on arrival had merely whetted their appetite for a little fun. It appears to me that some of the guards—certainly not all of them—see themselves as the overseers of the flawed masses of reprobates. The families and other visitors are merely extensions of those miscreants, certainly not on the same level as themselves. Was there anything I could do about my experience with the guards? Not really. I had suffered no physical injury. There was nothing I could prove. Write a letter? To whom? I did make a mental note of my ordeal. Perhaps someday I would have an opportunity to relate it to someone.

I returned to Lompoc for a second visit on Saturday October 7, 2006. This visit was somewhat less onerous despite the same disagreeable atmosphere.

The time Billy spent at the medium security prison in Lompoc, California, was the low point of the entire legal battle and incarceration experience from several points of view. As a parent it was the most uninviting and formal institution that I would visit. Fortunately he was there for only one year. But he also experienced significant problems in this prison.

At one point he was forced to share a cell with an inmate who was mentally unstable. Whether this placement was intentional or merely bad luck is unknown. They had little in common and predictably didn't get along well. This cellmate had a low threshold for anger. One day he decided to destroy some of Billy's books following a verbal disagreement. The confrontation escalated and a scuffle ensued. The cellmate wound up with some significant facial injuries, requiring hospitalization. Fortunately Billy was unharmed. Surprisingly, he didn't get reprimanded for this conflict. Most likely this was because the video confirmed his version of the confrontation that his cellmate had been the aggressor.

As an intellectual Billy was an outlier in the federal prison system. A misfit. An aberration. We were aware that his credentials as an academic superstar were not considered an asset in the legal prosecution and sentencing phase nor in the actual incarceration process itself. However, it seemed at times that just the opposite was true; that his treatment was harsher than typical. A skid row drunk who shot a man in a bar, or a back alley drug dealer who stabbed a competitor might expect a lesser sentence and better treatment in many instances. What is the meaning of justice?

We were in over our head. We had good lawyers—an appeal process was in place, but the prison system was a rough row to hoe and the legal system moves at a deliberate pace. Could we do anything in the meantime? A prisoner's advocate, Bruce Kates, who appeared in the early phase of the legal battle had a suggestion: contact the well-known scientists at Cal Tech and Chicago to sign a letter of support for Billy to help improve his treatment. In September 2006 he spearheaded this process by composing a letter and coordinating the significant effort to obtain the signatures. The letter noted that "Billy's treatment in prison, far from being rehabilitative, is nothing less than night-marish". It ended with the plea "In the interest of both justice and science, we ask for the amelioration of Billy's treatment." It was signed by a number of noteworthy scientist, Stephen Hawkins (University of Cambridge), Hirosi Ooguri (Cal Tech), Kip S Thorne (Cal Tech), Savdeep Sethi (University of Chicago), Jeffrey Harvey (University of Chicago), David Kutasov (University of Chicago) and Peter Freund (University of Chicago). I have several copies of the letter.

It is difficult to know who actually read the letter or what goes on behind closed doors, but the letter did appear to have a beneficial effect. Shortly after the letter was issued, he was moved to the Federal Correctional Institute of Victorville, California; though still consid-ered a medium security prison, it was a notch less severe and visitor friendly. After a year at Victorville he was transferred to the low secu-rity facility in Safford, Arizona for his last few years.

He was able to collect and read a number science-related books and literature in prison. I arranged to have *Physical Review Letters* sent to him to stay current in the physics world. Additionally he taught classes in a number of scientific fields and simultaneously intensely studied Mandarin Chinese, memorizing close to two thousand symbols to become fluent. Because he never gave in to passivity he was able to rejoin his academic career, seemingly without missing a beat upon release in 2011.

I learned more about the prison system than I ever cared to know or would have ever thought likely. Most prisoners affiliate with an ethnic gang; i.e., Hispanic, Black, Asian or White for security and protection. The gangs control much of what goes on inside the prison. The guards generally give them an allotment of space as long as fights don't erupt. Billy was able to get by without being affiliated with a gang and eventually he became prison savvy. Discipline rules vary with the security ranking, but similar protocols are used for handling meals, recreations and visitation. They also must all use the same external designers and landscapers. Tall chain-linked fences with barbed wire on top are all the rage.

When I reviewed the statistics for the prison population in this country I made a number of interesting discoveries. The number of people incarcerated in the U.S.A. roughly quadrupled between 1980 and 2003. Our country has the largest prison population in the world and the second highest per capita rate of incarceration, behind only tiny Seychelles with a population of about 90,000. In 2012 0.94 percent of the population was incarcerated, including federal, state and county systems. If you also include those on probation and parole, this jumps to 2.9 percent. The breakdown by race is startling; 2.2 percent for Caucasians, 3.7 percent for Hispanics and 9.2 percent for African Americans. These numbers were quite surprising to me. Is our system treating all ethnic divisions equally? If this trend for increased incarceration continues, how can we afford it as a country? Are we truly an incarceration nation as some have suggested? These are important questions for our politicians.

So far I have avoided the most obvious and important question. Why would a person with such high academic achievements become involved in activities that were of no obvious benefit to himself, but carried a high risk of punitive repercussions? Why didn't he distance himself from the arsonist earlier? Why did he brag about his involvement? Human behavior is very complex and difficult to understand; it is almost impossible to predict and even tough to explain in retrospect. I am unable to offer definite answers; but perhaps I can shed some light on them.

It was suggested by one of Billy's lawyers, Marvin Rudnick, that he seemed to display some qualities of Asperger's Syndrome (AS); also known as high functioning autism or autistic personality disorder. The hallmark of this syndrome is a delay in social reasoning or maturity, often accompanied by an increased intellectual capacity in a specialized subject such as mathematics. If true, this condition might help explain his actions on the night of August 22, 2003, and in the weeks following. It could be part of the defense.

I was skeptical at first. I had heard of the term "Asperger's", but tended to associate it with more profound autism. I wasn't aware of the "spectrum" concept or its prevalence in successful people. This encouraged me to research the topic. I consulted *The Complete Guide to Asperger's Syndrome* by Tony Atwood.

In 1944 Dr. Hans Asperger, a Viennese pediatrician described a number of children referred to his clinic that shared some interesting personality characteristics. He was intrigued that this subset of patients showed not only a delay in social maturity, but impairment in conversational aspects of language. On the other hand their grammar and vocabulary tended to be relatively advanced. He noted a general lessening of empathy among these subjects. These children also had an intense preoccupation with a specific topic or interest that would dominate their thoughts and time.

According to Dr. Atwood, the best way to describe individuals with Asperger's Syndrome is that they have different priorities and ways of thinking. "The brain is wired differently, not defectively. The person prioritizes the pursuit of knowledge, perfection, truth and understanding of the physical world, above feelings and interpersonal experience."

Some classic examples of individuals with AS may be Albert Einstein, James Taylor and Isaac Asimov. At the same it's important to appreciate that AS is a continuum of personalities that merges with the normal. Therefore there is no such thing as a typical person with Asperger's.

Dr. Attwood further states that the rate of conviction of people with AS for criminal offences is the same as the general public. The incidence of violent crimes is remarkably low. He also recommends that when a person with AS is recognized by the criminal justice system, an examination should ideally be made by a clinician knowledgeable about AS to help determine what role the condition may have played in the crime and how it should affect sentencing.

The defense hired Dr. Gary Mesibov of the University of North

Carolina, Chapel Hill, to evaluate Billy for AS. This involved a personal interview and lengthy questionnaire about early development to which both Heidi and I honestly responded. The results? Billy did indeed meet the criteria for AS by the standardized test. We underwent a cross examination by the prosecutions expert, also a psychologist. The diagnosis of AS was confirmed.

During the initial trial in November 2004, however, the judge rejected the findings of the experts. The condition of AS was not allowed as evidence. After a long, tedious and draining appeal process, the evidence was eventually accepted and was instrumental in greatly reducing his convictions. More about this later.

Of interest, the cause of AS is not always obvious, but seems to be more due to genetic factors than environmental or "parenting" issues according to Attwood. Dr. Asperger noted a shadow of the syndrome in parents of children with AS. Twenty percent of fathers and five percent of mothers of the children have the syndrome itself. So first degree relatives are at high risk for displaying some qualities of AS. Could this explain why I frequently prefer to read a good book, or to work on finger picking on my guitar as opposed to more social inter-action? Is this why I stay in my car to hear the end of a favorite song when parking my car? I'm really not sure. But just in case, I would like to reiterate the words of one of Dr. Atwood's patients with AS; "Asperger's is the next stage of human evolution."

The year 2006 was not only the low point in my son's legal battle and incarceration, but also saw the decline of my mother's health. On December 10, 2005, she turned eighty-two and was in reasonable health for her age. A hip fracture several years prior caused her to ambulate cautiously and with a slight limp. Also she had acquired the condition of atrial fibrillation. This necessitated the use of the blood thinner, Coumadin, to decrease the risk of blood clots and emboli. Since the untimely death of my father over seventeen years prior, she had struggled valiantly to create a new life as a single woman. By stay-ing active in Concord United Methodist, serving as church librarian, and staying connected with a wide circle of friends, not to mention five children, multiple grandkids and a few great-grandkids she was mostly successful. On the outside she was a shining example of resilience. But on the inside I'm not sure she ever totally recovered from the death of my father.

Unfortunately in May of 2006 she tripped on a carpet at a bridge party in a friend's house and fell flat, fracturing her second cervical vertebrae (C2). This required hospitalization and a neck brace to stabilize her neck. Unfortunately, she could not tolerate the heavy halo neck brace very well. It seemed too massive and burdensome for her small frame. Neither were we eager for her to undergo a major spine surgery. This left us with no good treatment options. I know she feared becoming a burden to the family and being viewed as an invalid. She became depressed and ate very little. This led to a weakened immune system resulting in pneumonia and heart failure. She died at 10 p.m. on Thursday August 3, 2006 during my watch at Park West Hospital in Knoxville; the same hospital that my dad had spent his last few days. Although the death certificate listed heart failure as the cause of death we all knew better. She merely was ready to join my dad.

The funeral service was held Sunday, August 6, at Concord United Methodist Church. Since she had lived in the area since 1953 and was well-connected through church and community affairs she had many friends and acquaintances. Four hundred guests signed the register. There were many uncounted guest in attendance, but the book had room for only four hundred. We may have come close to filling another book had one been available.

My mother was born Jeannette Elizabeth Milnes December 10, 1923, in Lackawanna, New York, just outside of Buffalo. Her father, Benjamin Milnes, was a dentist and her mother, Mary Ashdown Milnes, worked as his assistant. Unfortunately, Mary died of leukemia during my mother's first year of college at Alfred University.

After marrying my father at Alfred during the war, she dropped out of school when they moved to Oak Ridge. In her forties, however, after raising five children, she returned to get her bachelor's degree in library science at the University of Tennessee. Later she worked for ten years as the head librarian at Bearden High School in Knoxville.

My mother was well read and worldly, having traveled with my father to Geneva and other European cities for conferences on nuclear energy. But the mom I knew was humble and frugal.

In December two or three years before she died, I came to visit her in Knoxville, Tennessee, to take her on our annual Christmas shopping trip. She had indicated that this year she would like to get a new winter's coat. I came prepared to fork over some major dinero. I knew what a nice winter coat might cost and was happy to make the purchase. Don't moms deserve the best? So I allowed her to direct me to the retailer of her choice. Strange! Her directions led us right into the parking lot of the Cracker Barrel on the Cedar Bluff exit of I-40. Inside was the coat of her dreams. A speckled brown waist length faux fur coat for $39.90. At eighty she wore it well.

My mother's death was not as tragic as my father's. Hers was more timely. Still her passing left a big hole. Occasionally I would call her to discuss some minor personal or family issue. She was always available to discuss these simple homely matters in a thoughtful objective manner. That's a void difficult to fill.

Anesthesia Practice in the New Millennium

—∞∞∞—

Although we saw very little change in our anesthesia practice in the first few years after 2000, the new millennium would soon usher in a myriad of refinements for us, including new sites of practice, important new equipment, evolutionary anesthesia techniques and perhaps most significantly, a paradigm shift in hospital ownership and management. In hindsight, all of this was inevitable, but we didn't necessarily foresee the entire range of oncoming events.

Earlier, I alluded to the truly freestanding ambulatory surgery facility, "Gateway Surgery Center" off Copperfield Boulevard which opened in 2003. The facility was a joint venture between my hospital, Northeast Medical Center, members of the medical staff and an outside company. Specializing in medium to short surgeries, the center was an immediate success. It quickly gained a reputation for being user-friendly for both patients and surgeons. Anesthesia played a major role in its implementation. Since physicians were part owners, they had a vested interest in its productivity and success. By avoiding long complicated cases and extremely sick patients (except for very minor procedures) we achieved profitability. "Get the job done" was the catch phrase for its operation.

I enjoyed working at the Gateway Surgery center because it reminded me of the atmosphere of practice in the '70s and early '80s. Red tape and paperwork (or computer work) were minimized. Of course we did see an increased use of regional blocks to assist with pain control for surgery on the hands, arms, shoulders, ankles and feet. This added to the challenge and interest of the anesthesia services rendered which greatly diminished the complaints of pain after surgery.

Given the choice, most surgeons would prefer to do cases in the Gateway Surgery Center as opposed to the main hospital due to its inherent efficiencies. Unfortunately, special post-operative needs, such as prolonged stay or mechanical ventilation or the need for blood products precluded its use in many cases. Scheduling problems could also occasionally be a factor. But overall the center was a big success story.

The early nineties saw the introduction of the laryngeal mask airway or LMA into daily practice. This device, first available in the United Kingdom in 1987, consists of an airway tube connected to a "mask" which covered the glottis or tracheal opening with a tight seal. This is in contrast to the traditional endotracheal tube which enters the trachea via the glottis. The LMA, also called a supraglottic airway device, may substitute for the endotracheal tube in many situations. Many cases that might have been a difficult intubation may be easily handled with an LMA. Though not a panacea for airway challenges, by the mid-nineties, the LMA was an integral part of our daily practice.

The year 2001 saw the introduction of the Glidescope, the first commercially available video laryngoscope. Invented by a general surgeon, John Allen Pacey, the Glidescope consisted of a more or less traditional shaped handheld laryngoscope with a high resolution digital camera tucked away in the blade. The camera was connected by a video cable to an LCD monitor. The net result was that the normal view of the larynx seen by the laryngoscopist, either the CRNA or the MD, was now projected in high resolution on a larger than life video screen. This technique had at least two fundamental benefits. The CRNA or MD performing the intubation could see the laryngeal anatomy in more detail, usually including the vocal cords and glottis, making intubation easier. Likewise the anesthesia personnel standing by, typically the anesthesiologist, would see the same view of the larynx. If the larynx and glottis were slightly off center or anterior, he could assist by gently nudging the larynx externally with a free hand, right or left or downward to improve the view of the glottis.

The introduction of the video laryngoscope into our practice at Northeast Medical Center in 2005 was especially appropriate for our system of supervising CRNAs. When a CRNA struggled with a difficult intubation in the past, we could only imagine what he or she was viewing and make suggestions. With the new scopes, we could have the exact same view as the CRNA and frequently improve the view with gentle manipulation of the trachea. It seemed a match made in heaven.

The video laryngoscopes were a big hit. Other commercial variations of the Glidescope soon appeared on the market including the C-Mac by Storz, Pentax-AWS, McGrath and the Video MacIntosh system. They soon metastasized from the main OR suites to the Gateway Surgery Center, the OB suite and the cardiac surgery suite. I personally championed their use. From their original use only on difficult cases, maybe two percent of all cases, I have expanded the use to at least ten percent (and growing) of all cases. There is little reason not to use them. Perhaps someday they will be a standard of care for all cases.

So in 1986 the anesthetist had a single easy question to answer when giving a general anesthetic, should I intubate the patient, or should I do him with a mask? In 2006 the anesthetist must ask, should I use a mask, an LMA or an endotracheal tube? If I do use an endotracheal tube, should I use the regular scope or a video laryngoscope? The complexity of options had had increased, but it was generally all for the good. When considering the video laryngoscope, the question I ask myself is not why this option was introduced into our anesthesia practice, but what took us so long? Videoscopes of various types had been used in gynecological and general surgical procedures for years. The technology was really not new. Like many "breakthroughs" in medicine we merely used an old technology in a new way.

If one took a snapshot of our anesthesia practice in the year 2007, one would see a vibrant well-run department counting fifteen anesthesiologists. Dr. Karlon Young joined us that year, Dr. Sara Arnold and Dr. Jason Ravanbakt would join us in 2008. The tangible changes mentioned, new sites of operation and equipment upgrades added spice and vitality to our daily routine of "putting people down and waking them up." But there were concurrent intangible changes in the medical community, perhaps easy to sense, but a little difficult to characterize. For starters the medical staff was much larger and diverse. From a homogeneous staff of 68 mostly white males in 1978, it was now a racially diverse and mixed gender collection of about 400 physicians. We seemed, however, to lack focus and unity. Most physicians had no roots or strong historical ties to the community. The hospital administration, on the other hand, seemed better organized and in control of their destiny. The strong political leadership of a few selected physicians was always diluted by their demanding clinical obligations to patients. It seemed the administration was gaining the upper hand in the struggle to define the evolution of health care in the county.

Of course by 2007 the textile industry had shrunk dramatically in Cabarrus County. The anticipated biotechnology industry had yet to become a reality. Furthermore, that same year Phillip Morris, the largest cigarette manufacturer in the United States, announced it would close its large plant in Cabarrus County and shift jobs back to Richmond, Virginia, in about two years. In short, there seemed to be a shortage of politico-economic driving forces in the county. As we all know nature and medical communities abhor vacuums.

Nevertheless, few doctors were prepared for the announcement in late February 2007: Northeast Medical Center would be merging with CHS, Carolinas HealthCare System on June 1 of that year. Many physicians were stunned and unhappy with this revelation. It seemed to be the ultimate betrayal, selling out to our life-long rival. The chief of staff at Northeast, Dr. Tom Trahey, was so upset he resigned his position and left to work at the VA hospital in Salisbury.

Northeast Medical Center was not a small entity with around 400 doctors on staff and a budget measured in hundreds of millions of dollars. It was no match for CHS, however, with thousands of doctors on staff and a budget measured in billions (with a "b") of dollars. It seemed the word merger may have been a euphemism. We would be gobbled up. Northeast would be just another entry on the long list of CHS's conquests.

On Thursday March 8, 2007, the Cabarrus Neighbors section of the *Charlotte Observer* had a lengthy article on its front page noting the resignation of our chief of staff and some unrest and displeasure among a number of physicians. But it also noted that the administration of CHS had no plans to disrupt practices or to shift physicians from Charlotte to Concord. In other words business would continue as usual. This was somewhat reassuring to hear to some of us older physicians who didn't know what to expect. As hospital-based physicians perhaps we could be pressured to "merge" with the larger group of anesthesiologists in Charlotte. Nothing like that ever happened, although we did get an informal invitation to consider a merger with Southeast Anesthesia. We respectfully declined them.

What was initially viewed with alarm was soon accepted as a matter of fact. It was simply a business deal between major players in the health care industry. In a sense it was inevitable. The "merger" as it was called had little to do with the quality of medical practice or patient satisfaction in Cabarrus County. We could rail against it, but that really made little sense. We might as well fight against the computerization of medicine or the trend toward high tech equipment and procedures. Better to go with the flow and focus on what we do best: taking care of patients as we have always done.

Indeed, as part of a mega-healthcare system we could expect better leverage when bargaining with pharmaceuticals and medical supply companies to decrease operating expenses. The crucial questions were: how would the merger effect the medical cost to patients in

Cabarrus County in years to come? How would the quality of healthcare be affected? Would patient satisfaction improve or decline? And who would make these assessments? This was the crux of the matter.

Included in any detailed snapshot of our anesthesia practice in 2007 would be a description of our interview clinic for preoperative patients. Initiated in 1997 with the formation of our new group, the interview clinic was the primary mechanism by which we evaluated patients for their upcoming surgery and anesthesia. The clinic allowed the anesthesiologist the opportunity to order any needed blood work or other preoperative testing. Options for the type of anesthesia, the possible use of invasive monitors and the use of special techniques to deal with postoperative pain (such as epidurals) were discussed. Additionally, any potential problem, like a difficult intubation, could frequently (but not always) be discovered so we could be better prepared on the day of surgery.

A major goal of the interview clinic was to help assure that any underlying medical problem, like hypertension, asthma or diabetes was under reasonable control by the time of surgery. Occasionally we would encounter a patient whose blood pressure was extremely high, who was actively wheezing or with some other medical problem needing attention. When this occurred we would refer the patient back to the family doctor or internist to fine tune the medical problems before surgery. This really didn't happen often. That's because most patients had been under the care of a primary physician; these conditions were already being addressed. In a real sense we were a safety net for patients undergoing surgery. Sometimes we would wind up investigating problems that had already been adequately addressed. But can you really have too many safety nets? Of course occasionally we would get patients who had no preoperative medical care or who were from another state with no medical records available. This put the ball totally in our court. Dealing with these patients could present some real problems.

By far, the medical condition that caused the most concern for us in the clinic was heart disease, due to the blockages of the coronary arteries. The fear was that the stress of surgery and anesthesia may cause additional demands on the myocardium or heart muscle. If blood flow to the myocardium was limited by coronary artery disease (CAD) or blockages, the heart muscle could get ischemic. That is, the muscle's need for oxygen outstrips the supply via the coronary arteries. If the ischemia is severe, or prolonged, some heart muscle may suffer permanent damage. This is called an MI (myocardial infarction) or simply a heart attack. The word heart attack is frequently misused by laymen to refer to chest pain, ischemia or even arrhythmias or irregular heart beat. This may sometimes be the physician's fault for not elucidating these issues.

Since coronary artery disease is fairly common in the general population, many people come to the interview clinic with a known diagnosis of this condition. When this happened we would diligently question the patient to determine if he has had any new symptoms such as chest pains on exertion or change in his activity level due to heart function, or worsening of old symptoms. We would also do an ECG or heart tracing to make sure there were no changes in the electrical pattern to suggest ischemia or new infarction or worrisome rhythm patterns. If any red flags were discovered we would refer the patient to the cardiologist for "cardiac clearance." The cardiologist might recommend a stress test to see if the heart was indeed experiencing new or increased ischemia. Occasionally he may recommend the patient undergo a catheterization and a coronary stent placement before surgery. This was actually quite rare, however. Most of the times we would proceed with surgery after the cardiologist saw the patient and gave his approval to proceed. We would instruct the patient to continue all heart and blood pressure medicines conscientiously. It's also a no-brainer to keep a close eye on his cardiac function during surgery and frequently do a twelve lead ECG and also draw blood to check cardiac enzymes in the PACU to look for early signs of ischemia or infarction.

An equal or greater concern was that a patient may present to the interview with undiagnosed CAD. The disease lurks in his coronaries, but no physician has made the diagnosis. Sometimes the disease is present at a subclinical level; the blockages are causing a reduction in blood flow to the myocardium, but not quite enough to produce exertional chest pain. Or the patient may have actual chest pains but denies this news to himself and the primary doctor. It's a "fear of the consequences" thing. On the other hand many people have complaints of chest pain due to acid reflux or costochondritis or even purely due to anxiety. The correlation between the severity of actual CAD and complaints of chest pains is not especially strong. Inevitably many people undergo surgery with undiagnosed CAD, usually without major problems.

How can we identify those patients that are most likely to decompensate; i.e., develop problems related to ischemia in the perioperative period? There are a number of well recognized risk factors that make it more likely for a person to develop CAD. The main ones are hypertension, high blood cholesterol, diabetes, tobacco use and obesity. We could add to this inactivity, family history, age and poor diet. People with more than two risk factors are certainly at significant risk for having some CAD, even if they deny the symptoms. How do we handle these patients who have a significant risk for heart disease but are asymptomatic? We try to do things to avoid major stress on the myocardium such as severe pain or elevated blood pressure and pulse. In some cases we may use special drugs called beta blockers to decrease the heart's demand for oxygen. Sometimes these maneuvers can prevent the development of ischemia and occasionally even myocardial infarction.

The early beta blockers were developed by James Black, a Scottish pharmacologist with Imperial Chemical Industries (ICI). The first one developed was pronethelol (Alderlin) in 1963. Unwanted side effects prompted its replacement by propranolol (Inderal) in 1965. Their primary function initially was to decrease pain from ischemic heart disease, called angina pectoris, by decreasing the myocardium's need for oxygen and hence for blood flow through the coronary arteries. They were the first drugs introduced that successfully treated angina since nitroglycerin was introduced in the previous century. In 1988 James Black won the Nobel Prize in medicine for his early work with beta blockers.

When I entered medical school in 1971, beta blockers were still relatively new but starting to gain in popularity. My first clinical exposure to the use of these drugs was in October 1973 during my medicine rotation at Grady. An aggressive internal medicine resident was demonstrating how to treat a patient in the ICU with CAD who had a rapid heart rate and hypertension. He gave the patient one mg of propranolol intravenously. The patient's heart stopped beating totally for about ten seconds, then slowly resumed beating at a much slower rate. That was the longest ten seconds of my life, but fortunately CPR wasn't necessary. What did I learn from this case? Dosing is very critical. Many substances are life-saving at one dose and life threatening at another. The resident should have used a smaller dose to start with. Still, it was fascinating to watch as beta blocker usage soared in the '70s and '80s. They were truly helpful in managing many patients with CAD and in subjects with hypertensive cardiovascular disease, plus some types of heart failure.

The VA cooperative study, published in the early '70s, conclusively showed that cardiovascular mortality could be decreased by controlling blood pressure with multi-drug therapy. A logical extrapolation of this finding was to use beta blockers in the perioperative period to achieve a similar decrease in mortality. Numerous studies in the '80s and '90s suggested that beta blocker use before and after surgery might decrease the risk of a perioperative myocardial infarction. By the late '90s the cardio-protective beneficial effects of these drugs seemed undeniable. Protocols were developed to delineate which patients might benefit from starting these drugs preoperatively and on which surgeries. The greater number of risk factors for CAD, and the larger and more stressful the surgery, the greater the need was for this type of drug. Patients with no risk factors did not need them regardless of the surgery. Likewise patients undergoing very minor surgery, like a carpal tunnel release or a cataract extraction, would not need a beta blocker, even if he had multiple risk factors for CAD. Patients who were already taking beta blockers, of course, were instructed to continue them before and after surgery as usual. Around 2000 we began the use of beta blockers, pre and post-operatively, on certain patients as a matter of standard protocol, as did many major surgical centers. We seemed to be on solid ground. I even heard one physician say that a failure to use beta blockers according to protocol might constitute malpractice.

So the anesthesiologist in the interview clinic in 2007 had a number of challenges to deal with when confronted with a cardiac patient: has there been a recent increase in symptoms; i.e., chest pain on exertion? Did any patients with multiple risk factors for CAD need to be placed on beta blockers before surgery? Has there been a significant change in the ECG tracing? Which, if any, of these patients, should be referred to the cardiologist for cardiac clearance before surgery? Even with guidelines and plenty of clinical experience, the anesthesiologist was occasionally left with some tough choices to make.

I was in the interview clinic one day in 2007 after the announcement of the big merger with CHS. The morning had gone quite smoothly with no difficult decisions; but in the early afternoon I had a patient who caused some concern. The man was middle-aged and was scheduled to have surgery the next morning. The exact surgery is irrelevant to this tale, but it was a general surgery case of intermediate severity. At first glance I saw a healthy appearing middle-aged man, well tanned and physically fit. I quickly learned that he was an avid exerciser with no significant limitations or complaints such as chest pain. My first impression suggested little reason for alarm. But a review of his history revealed that he did indeed have some coronary artery disease that required interventional therapy a few years ago.

Since that time he had been symptom free and quite active. On the whole, it still did not seem to be a huge problem. We could just do an ECG and verify no major changes or indications of ischemia on the tracing.

Unfortunately, this gentleman was new to our system. His cardiac workup and treatment were in another hospital system. It would be next to impossible to get a full report before surgery in the morning. I would have to make my decision based on the information I had. An ECG is easy to do and helpful in evaluating such patients.

The twelve lead ECG we did in the interview clinic showed a moderate shift in the baseline electrical pattern known as ST changes. This ECG abnormality is fairly non-specific. Although it can be caused by ischemia, it is also not uncommon in patients with hypertension. The critical question is whether or not this ECG abnormality was new. If it was present in previous tracings, there would be no need to worry. We would go ahead with the surgery. If the abnormality on the ECG was new, however, we would consider referring him to a cardiologist for clearance. Unfortunately, we had no old tracing to compare it with. Very likely the ST changes were pre-existing, but I could not prove this at that time. Should I approve the patient for surgery based on his lack of symptoms and my overall favorable impression, or refer him to a cardiologist in an excess of caution?

This situation illustrates a common dilemma that all physicians face at times in their clinical practice. Should you order a consultation or test of some kind that's very unlikely to change treatment in order to protect yourself from improbable events and possible criticism? Or should you choose the option that is most cost effective but causes a slight exposure to liability? There is no right or wrong answer. Each physician makes their decision based on the specific details of the case, their clinical confidence in that particular area and their philosophy of management. In my early years of practice I was prone, as were many, to request consults or tests to minimize my liability. This practice is referred to as the CYA (cover your ass) policy among doctors.

It is a ubiquitous phenomenon. As I became more experienced, I became less likely to refer patients for consults unless I thought there was a real concern. Obviously I did so at my own risk, but practicing cost-effective medicine was a high priority for me.

This particular case was a fence sitter. In my early years of practice, I would surely have referred him to a cardiologist for clearance. The result would be a delay in surgery and a heftier medical bill; and it would also help diminish my liability if he developed heart problems during or after surgery. After almost thirty years of practice, I put much more emphasis on the patient's clinical status; i.e., active life style and lack of chest pains, and on my overall impression than I did on mild ECG abnormalities. On this occasion I needed to make a decision quickly. The clinic was busy and patients were stacking up in other rooms for me to interview. Despite his history of CAD I gave the green light to go ahead with surgery, then proceeded to my next patient.

The rest of the afternoon was uneventful in the clinic. Two or three times that day the case abruptly popped into my consciousness. Was I sure I did the right thing? Each time I confirmed the judgment I had made based on my favorable clinical impression and my concern for practicing cost-effective medicine. It's good to feel you are doing the right thing for your patients.

After work I went to the Sportscenter for a brief workout, as was my usual custom, and was home by six in time for dinner. It was a Wednesday evening and we were starting to get excited about an upcoming vacation. My good friend and partner, Dr. Catherine (Cathy) Cheung had invited Becky and me to join her and Osbert and Mimi at their time share condominium in a nice resort in Cancun, Mexico. We would all fly out of Charlotte together on Saturday. Margaritaville was a flight away.

I was in bed that evening by nine. Since my alarm went off at 4:45 a.m. at that time, this was necessary if I wanted to get at least seven hours of sleep. A good night's sleep made all the difference in the world in my attitude and capacity to work. I was somewhat obsessed with the subject. That evening, however, I tossed and turned more than normal. Something prevented from falling to sleep right away. Had I consumed too much iced tea? Did I eat the wrong kind of mushrooms? What was the problem? I rested some but there was no REM sleep to be had. At 10:45 I stared at the alarm clock and became depressed. If I didn't fall asleep soon, I would be a zombie the next day. But then it struck me. My concerns about the man with the CAD for surgery in the morning had been well suppressed, but never totally vanquished. I had a small element of doubt. If the patient did well as I hoped and expected, no one would thank me for lowering his medical expenses or for not delaying the case. I would get no reward or acknowledge-ment for practicing cost-effective medicine and accepting increased liability for the patient's welfare. It would be a fait accompli. No one would care or even notice. On the other hand, if this went south, and the patient did indeed suffer a perioperative MI, I would be first in line to be held responsible. I thought an MI was quite unlikely, but no one, not even a savvy world renowned cardiologist can predict which patient will be the next one to have an infarction. My strategy had very little upside for me personally and a very small risk of a major down-side. Why didn't I practice defensive medicine like most physicians? If the worst happened how could I defend my decision to proceed? If the prosecutor came at me with verbal machetes and switch blades where would I run to? Where would I hide?

I regretted my earlier decision, but what could I do now, surgery was scheduled for around nine in the morning. It seemed the dye was cast. But then an idea struck me like a lightning bolt. It wasn't too late! I could arrive early at the pre-op area and discuss the case with the anesthesiologist assigned to his case. I could claim I had a moment of temporary insanity the day before and suggest we cancel the case. It would be awkward and embarrassing, but preferable to facing the slings and arrows of outrageous prosecutors. Having developed a plausible game plan in my head, I finally drifted into a deeper sleep.

It was midnight almost exactly when my phone rang. I tried to ignore it, probably a wrong number. But it wouldn't stop. Disgustedly, I picked up the phone to inform the caller of their error. However, it wasn't what I thought. A familiar, but frantic female voice was trying to tell me something. In my sleep befuddled mind I finally realized it was my partner, Cathy Cheung. In between sobs I recognized a few key words and phrases—on call—emergency room— massive MI—John Roper—cardiac arrest—didn't make it. But what did they all mean? John Roper was one of our partners; young (44), athletic, recently married with a new baby girl only six and a half weeks old. A massive MI with cardiac arrest is something that happens to unhealthy older people who have a lot of risk factors. My mind couldn't accept what she was saying. I had seen John just twelve hours prior in the hospital. I had played golf with him a few months ago. He was as vigorous and alive in my mind as anyone. But unfortunately, it was all too true. My colleague and good friend John Roper had experienced some chest discomfort and arrhythmias that evening at home. His wife, Missy, called 911. He was taken to the emergency room at Northeast Medical Center where Cathy was on call for our group. Unfortunately, he went downhill rapidly; all the usual attempts at resuscitation were unsuccessful.

News travels rapidly in the hospital arena. When I arrived in the OR, shortly before six, it seemed the whole hospital was in mourning. I made no attempt to hide my grief. However, we still had a surgery schedule to run. Drained, both by lack of sleep and the weight of the tragedy, I went about the process of getting patients ready for surgery though somewhat dazed and only marginally functional. The experience felt surreal.

At some point I recalled the patient I had interviewed who had known CAD. I discussed my concerns about a need for cardiac clearance with the physician handling the case. He felt the patient would be fine. Perhaps he thought I was over-reacting due to the tragic events of the evening.

A funeral service was held that weekend at Concord Presbyterian

Church. John's parents lived in nearby Charlotte. His father was an orthopedic surgeon. He also had a brother and sister who lived nearby. We were all in a state of shock. None of us could believe we were burying such a dear friend, husband, father, son, brother and colleague so prematurely. I don't remember the details of the service; it's all sort of a blur. What I do remember is that for weeks afterwards, many people both within and outside the medical community would approach me to express their sympathy and compassion for our loss. The hospital administration was so moved they dedicated a portion of the hospital to him. The meeting area right outside of the Hamrick Theatre is now known as the "Roper Commons."

John Tracy Roper was born May 29, 1962, in Charlotte, North Carolina and there he grew up. He received his MD degree from the University of North Carolina School of Medicine in 1990. He did a year of internship in Roanoke, Virginia, and then came back to Chapel Hill to complete his residency in Anesthesiology in 1994. He joined our group in July 1997 after working a few years in Charleston, South Carolina, to become our sixth full-time physician. With a strong interest in treating chronic pain, he soon became an active part of our growing pain clinic. His marriage to Missy McKibbens in Asheville, (where Missy was the director at Camp Hollymont for girls) in 2005 was a major event for our department. The wedding ceremony was held at First Baptist Church of Asheville. The rehearsal dinner was held at the Grove Park Inn (we were all invited) and the reception and party afterward was at the Biltmore House. I vividly remember seeing John briefly on that Wednesday while on lunch break from the interview clinic. Had I known it was the last time I would see him, I would have told him how much I enjoyed working with him.

What about the man with a history of CAD I had interviewed that afternoon and then obsessed about my decision? My partner, along with the CRNA, proceeded with the case. The surgery and anesthesia were uneventful. The patient had no complaints of chest pain or other indication of heart problems. No surprises there. Just as I indicated earlier, an overall favorable clinical impression is more important than minor abnormalities on the ECG tracing.

So what have I learned about evaluating patients for surgery in the interview clinic who have concerns about heart disease? Humility. There are red flags we can never ignore. What we know about the body and heart disease fills massive books. But it is dwarfed in comparison with what we have yet to learn. There is no simple test that can reliably foresee how a patient will do. We see through a glass darkly. The Great Physician will call us Home when he is good and ready.

It took quite a while after this misfortune for things to get back to normal in our department. The vacation trip to Cancun with the Cheungs was canceled. Several months later we did manage to find a time we could all get off from work. It turned out to be just what we needed. Beautiful beaches, sun and water therapy are all good for the soul. We owe much to the Cheungs for their hospitality and friendship. We returned in good spirits.

Dealing with cardiac patients in the interview clinic continued pretty much the same after these events. Occasionally patients were still sent to the cardiologist for clearance before surgery when red flags appeared, and selected patients were still placed on beta blockers before and after surgery as indicated by protocol. Large studies had verified their cardio-protective virtues, no one doubted that. In May 2008, however, *Lancet* published the results of the PeriOperative Ischemia Evaluation (POISE) trial. In this study over 8,000 patients from a 190 institutions were given either a beta blocker or a placebo before surgery. The details of how this was done are very important, but not the focus of this story. This study confirmed the beneficial effect of these drugs in reducing the incidence of MIs; however, there was a significant trade off. The group receiving beta blockers had a greater incidence of strokes, presumably due to causing a lower blood pressure. The beta blocker dose used in this trial, 100 mg of metoprolol, was quite large. Conceivably the risk of stroke might be much less at lower doses. Nevertheless, the POISE study took the wind out of the sails of aggressive perioperative beta blocker usage. In 2009 the American College of Cardiologist and the American Heart Association toned down their recommendations for their use. We followed suit. Keep in mind that these guidelines for beta blockers were based on large national or international trials. We could not likely draw meaningful statistically-derived conclusions from our limited number of cases.

Is this the end of the beta blocker story? I doubt it. Refined recommendations of doses and indications are more likely. Nevertheless, like most other drugs and medical treatments, they have a downside as well as an upside.

The first decade of the millennium saw several more important medical issues and innovations in our practice. I will get to those soon. But first I want to catch up on some important events on the home front. I have already discussed some critical issues of my son's incarceration and my mother's unfortunate demise in 2006. It amazes me in retrospect that so much was going on that year. Some of it was actually good.

In late September Becky and I undertook enjoyed a nine-day trip to South America to visit Corey in Salvador, Brazil, where she was a graduate student at the Federal University of Bahia. We stayed four days with Corey in Salvador where we met her boyfriend and future husband, Victor, a native of Salvador. Victor showed us the highlights of the city including the Largo do Pelourinho or restored colonial square in the historic district and the Church of Nosso Senhor Bonfim. We learned that Salvador was founded in 1549 and was the first capital of colonial Brazil. With about three million people it is the third largest city in Brazil. It is also the home of the world's largest Carnival.

From Salvador we flew to Buenos Aires for a four-day visit. Of course we saw the Eva Peron museum and tomb in La Recoleta Cemetery, and also the Colon Opera House, rated third best in the world according to National Geographic. We had signed up for a "Tango Package." Each evening we had lessons to master this popular and passionate Latin dance. The final evening we were directed to a local hot spot or *Milonga* to display our skills. It was our first *Milonga* in Argentina and our last tango in Buenos Aires.

In late October 2006, we celebrated another big event. My stepson, Harper, tied the knot with his long time girlfriend and Charlotte native, Lindsey Becker. They had never planned a huge wedding, but several weeks before the actual date they announced their plans to have the ceremony in Las Vegas. It worked out well. The MGM has package deals that save on stress and planning details. It was a whirlwind trip for Rebecca and I. Harper and Lindsey now own a nice home in Concord's Zemosa Acres. They had their first baby, a girl, (Pressley Harper) in December 2015.

In addition to all these noteworthy events, 2006, also saw the completion of our mountain cabin house outside of Gatlinburg near the Little Pigeon River and the Great Smoky Mountain National Park. We had discovered a four acre tract of land for sale in August 2004 while at my family reunion at the Brookside Cottages. The land was convenient for river access but well hidden from tourists and nearby campers. With the help of Heritage Log Homes and a local builder, Verlis Williams and his two sons, we were able to construct a 2,950 square foot log cabin on three levels by the summer of 2006. We rented a small apartment nearby so Becky could make frequent trips to assist with the design and construction details. There were plenty of decisions that required our input. Thank goodness Rebecca had retired from her position as hand therapist with Ortho Carolina in Concord.

If this sounds like poor financial planning due to the simultaneous financial demands of significant legal fees for my son along with the construction of a new house, it was. We were greatly aided by the sale of Becky's original hand therapy building and Ken Yelton of Cabarrus Bank who was more than happy to give us a construction loan. Of course this meant that retirement was not imminent.

Speaking about banks loaning money; there seemed to be a lot of that going around. In 2006 I read articles warning of a possible housing bubble. It didn't seem likely to affect me significantly. In the summer of 2007, however, we noted with some alarm the rapid drop of house values and word of troubled financial institutions. By 2008 we again watched as our retirement plans and other investments plummeted. As Yogi Bera would say, "It's déjà vu all over again." It was fortunate that I enjoyed my profession.

Another concern for anesthesiologists that gained the spotlight during this time frame was the concern for possible awareness while under general anesthesia. This was really not a new issue. We learned in residency that a true general anesthetic, as opposed to just heavy sedation, has at least three basic components: a lack of awareness, an adequate blockage of pain sensation and related reflexes and adequate muscle relaxation for the surgery. The relaxation needs of course vary greatly depending on the case. So the state of general anesthesia; i.e., lack of awareness, did not seem to be too difficult to achieve. Just give the patient x milligrams per kilogram of an induction agent and then follow this with an adequate concentration of an anesthetic gas to maintain a stable level of anesthesia. Mathematical models of pharmacokinetics, uptake and distribution, drug metabolism and excretion and associated chemistry are helpful, but probably over-rated as a clinical guide. More helpful is a vigilant technically adept anesthetist who can administer anesthetic drugs and gases and observe patient responses to these agents and to surgical stimuli. If the patient displays no pain reactions, such as increased pulse, blood pressure, tearing or movement of any kind after a standard dose appropriate induction and with adequate time for equilibration with the anesthetic gas, then it is reasonable to assume that he is in a state of general anesthesia and therefore has no awareness. This is how we achieve and verify an adequate level of anesthesia traditionally. All things considered, not a bad system. Vigilance is the key element.

In my early years of practice, 'round about 1980, one of the CRNAs had a noteworthy case. In those days you recall we didn't work directly on the same case as the CRNA, but rather side by side with our own cases. A well-known citizen of the community claimed he had awareness of events while he was "under." The patient's reputation and character were beyond reproach, so this gave his claim great credibility. So why did this case of awareness occur? There were no obvious equipment problems or competency issues with the CRNA. I wasn't directly involved with the case, I really don't know. It may have been related to using more of an intravenous anesthetic rather than an anesthetic gas technique. Needless to say this case induced us to be more vigilante and focused on the possibility of awareness. It did, however, seem to be an outlier case. We did not find evidence to give cause to make a major change in our equipment or approach to giving anesthesia.

Through the years, thirty-eight and counting, I have had a handful of cases with credible claims of some awareness under general anesthesia. All of these were either emergency Cesarean sections or open heart surgery cases. Both of these types of surgery are well known to have an inevitable increased risk for awareness. With emergency Cesareans, the focus is on speed. If the fetus is distressed, usually ascertained by a low heart rate, his well-being is dependent on how rapidly the obstetrician can deliver him/her. If it takes over ten to twelve minutes to deliver the baby from the time of induction, he is more likely to be depressed and have low Apgar scores than if he is delivered in four or five minutes. Therefore, in these emergency cases, we don't have the luxury of allowing eight or ten minutes for the anesthetic gas to equilibrate in the patient. There is some recognized risk of awareness. Even so, the risk in these cases is in the vicinity of one percent. Furthermore, in my limited experience of awareness, these patients did not report extreme pain or undue suffering.

Open heart surgery patients also have an increased risk of awareness. This is related to the use if the cardiopulmonary bypass technique. After surgery is completed the patient must be rewarmed and transitioned back to his normal circulation, a process referred to as "coming off pump." Optimal cardiac function is essential to this transition, so depressant anesthetic drugs are minimized. The patient may be light. I had one such cardiac patient that had a credible story of recall during this time. As with the Cesarean section patients, he did not report extreme pain or suffer unduly.

Other than these special cases, the occurrence of awareness seemed to be quite rare. I would give an educated guess of one in five to 10.000 that came to our attention. Perhaps if we aggressively questioned patients for possible awareness, we might elicit some more cases.

In 2007 the movie *Awake* was released. The film was produced by Joana Vicente and stared Hayden Christensen. The plot is built around a man who remains awake after supposedly being put to sleep for a critical heart operation. During the surgery he overhears the surgeon talk about murdering him to collect insurance money in collusion with his girlfriend. Never mind that the plot was stupid, as were the OR scenes, and the movie was not a great commercial success, it still had major repercussions. The essence of the controversy was contained in the trailer: "Every year 21 million are put under anesthesia. One in 700 remain awake." The producer Vincente claimed this movie would do to surgery with general anesthesia what *Jaws* did to swimming in the ocean. Not quite! But it did stir up anxieties for a while.

The number of one in 700 does have some legitimacy. But this would include people in high risk categories such as Cesarean sections, open heart and trauma patients in shock. These are cases in which it may be dangerous to the fetus or patient to give the usual full dose or concentration of anesthesia. If you are a reasonably healthy non-alcoholic and non-drug addict patient undergoing elective surgery, your risk of awareness is much lower. The incidence in studies varies widely depending on the patient population surveyed and whether or not you include patients who say they "might have had some awareness". One study put the incidence at .0068 percent or about one in 14,000. That is even lower than I would expect.

In the months after the movie was released in April 2007, I noticed a spike in patient concerns about the possibility of remaining awake when they are supposedly under general anesthesia. Indeed, quite a few patients came to me in the interview clinic and elsewhere claiming that they had woken up in the middle of an anesthetic. When possible, I investigated these claims by reviewing old records. The vast majority of these cases involved sedation other than with a general anesthetic. For example, the patient may have had sedation along with a spinal anesthetic for surgery on his prostate or sedation for a carpal tunnel release along with a local injection at the wrist by the surgeon. Some awareness would be expected. Sometimes the anesthesiologist or the CRNA may contribute to the confusion by informing the patient that we will give enough sedation along with the spinal or local so he won't know what's going on. Some confusion on the patient's part is understandable.

On the other hand, there are occasionally credible patients who have had real episodes of awareness. We don't take that lightly. When a patient presents for surgery with a valid history of awareness, we increase our vigilance to assure it doesn't happen again. This is quite rare, however.

A simple question is frequently asked by people concerned about awareness: how can you tell if I am asleep? The short answer is because I am an anesthesiologist, it's how I make my living. I can observe if you have any increase in sympathetic nervous system activity with the incision. I look for evidence of tearing, any movement or distress. Other than the special cases I mentioned earlier, I haven't had a known case of awareness in over 30,000 anesthetics. I say "known" because conceivably someone may have had awareness but not communicated it to us. These types of questions increased after the movie release.

Despite my clinical experience and favorable record on this issue, I must acknowledge that this is a good question. Awareness is related to neurological activity within the brain. I can only observe the body's physiological reaction to a stressful stimulus. I can't actually measure awareness during anesthesia.

While in medical school, I found two facets of anesthesia as a specialty that were alluring. The first was a heavy dependence on principles of physiology, chemistry and pharmacology. It was a specialty well-immersed in the basic sciences. But the second was equally alluring; that is the actual mechanism by which the brain becomes anesthetized is not known. Or at least it's a little fuzzy. We can describe in some details the pharmacokinetics of how intravenous drugs or gases are taken up by the body and distributed. We can talk about solubility coefficients, metabolism and excretion. We can write elaborate chemistry equations and name a myriad of drug receptors. But just what causes a state of anesthesia? Where is the on-off switch or switches? Is it limited to just one part of the brain? Are there multiple pathways to achieve this state? Do they all converge through a central gateway or control panel? Apparently it's a little complicated. Otherwise I would offer some simple answers.

There have been noteworthy attempts to supplement the anesthesiologist's clinical skills to detect if a patient is at risk of awareness while supposedly under a general anesthetic. The most significant tool developed is the Bispectral Index or BIS monitor introduced by Aspect Medical in 1994 and FDA approved in 1996. The BIS monitor is imperfect and controversial. It deserves credit for attempting to accomplish what no one else has been able to do; measure awareness. It is a noble attempt, but falls short of its goal.

The BIS monitor is a modified EEG, electroencephalogram or brain wave monitor. It will read a number between zero and one hundred based on a complex statistical analysis of the brain waves or EEG. Zero represents no activity and one hundred indicates a fully awake state. The normal reading for general anesthesia is between sixty and forty. If the BIS reading is over sixty, a real concern for awareness exist. If it is under forty the patient is unnecessarily deep.

The important thing to remember about the BIS monitor and its readings is that they are based on empirical data. There is no sound underlying scientific principle that guarantees no awareness with a number under sixty. The BIS is not an awareness monitor per se, but rather a gauge that measures the effects of certain drugs on an EEG derivative. Furthermore, several anesthetic drugs, like ketamine and nitrous oxide, do not affect the BIS reading at all.

Nevertheless, a number of studies seemed to show that the use of the BIS monitor resulted in a lower incidence of awareness. This seemed to justify its use. More recently, however, several large controlled studies showed that when the BIS monitor was used compared to the technique of meticulously measuring the concentration of anesthetic gas from the patient at the end of a breath, or ETAG (end tidal anesthetic gas), there was no difference in the incidence of awareness. The BIS remains a controversial monitor. I would advocate its use only among those who understand its limitations.

So when a patient ask me how I can tell if they are asleep, I answer; "Because I'm an anesthesiologist."

So what will the solution be to the challenge of detecting awareness under general anesthesia? The BIS was a noble attempt, but fell short. Perhaps someone will develop a smarter EEG derived measurement that will be more useful. Or perhaps the best solution would be just to meticulously measure all drugs and gas concentrations to assure adequacy of anesthesia. Lastly, the clinical skill and vigilance of the anesthetist can't be minimized as an important component of the solution. Perhaps all three approaches will someday combine to make awareness under anesthesia a problem of the past.

So what guiding principle or unified theory can I offer to assist in determining the correct level of anesthesia? How would I teach new residents to make sure they gave enough anesthetic to avoid awareness, but not so much to cause unnecessary depression and prolonged awakening? I have read quite a few books and researched the literature on this subject. The following is the best I can do at this time to offer some universal guidance.

Some time ago there were three anthropomorphic bears who lived in a cottage in the woods somewhere in England. The largest was a male weighing about 150 kg. The next in size was a female weighing about 100 kg. The smallest was a younger male weighing 50 kg.

The weights are estimates. They are referred to as Papa Bear, Mama Bear and Baby Bear. One morning they decided to take a short walk to allow their porridge to cool. While they were away an intruder entered their cottage and sampled the three bowls of porridge. The original account by Robert Southey in 1837 described her as an ugly older female. In 1849 Joseph Cundall change her description to that of a young girl with locks of golden hair. For this teaching purpose, it's irrelevant, but we will go with the later version. Sampling the porridge "Goldie Locks" noted that the first bowl was too hot. The second bowl of porridge was too cool. However, she found that the third bowl was just right; neither too hot nor too cold. This happened to be the bowl of Baby Bear. Simple stated, by analogy, we need to place the patient in a state of anesthesia that is neither too deep nor too light, but just right. We need to give Baby Bear anesthesia. This would be the best advice I could offer at this time.

There was much more going on in the world in 2008. The collapse of the housing market was followed by the bankruptcy of Lehman Brothers and the historic seven hundred billion dollar bailout out of several financial institutions. Other noteworthy events included the election of Barack Obama on November 4, the resignation of Fidel Castro and the selection of Vladimir Putin as Prime Minister of Russia. On a lighter note, Taylor Swift won the CMT award and Usain Bolt set a world record in the one hundred meter dash at the Beijing Olympics in 9.69 seconds.

This year also saw a number of important events for me personally; most all of them for the good. Billy was transferred to a low security federal prison in Safford, Arizona. We were still waiting for the appeal process to come to a conclusion. We felt we were at the beginning of the end of the long ordeal. Dustin and Adrienne, in addition to teaching piano and guitar and performing together and with various bands, began creating their own music and producing their own CDs. The first was *Tortoise and Hair* released September 9, 2008 and the second was *A Front Row Seat* released January 26, 2010. Anyone who likes creative and original folk music and love ballads may find them surprisingly enjoyable and are available on Amazon.

Harper and Lindsey were renting a small house in Kannnapolis to save money. Harper was working as a loan officer and Lindsey was pursuing her occupational therapy degree. Mandy had obtained her RN from Duke and was working as a chemotherapy infusionist in the Batte Cancer Center at Northeast. She lived nearby.

By far the biggest and most important event for us in 2008 was Corey's marriage to Victor on November 1 in Williston, Florida, about twenty-five minutes south of Gainesville. The ceremony was held outside on the farm of Heidi and Ken Schweibert, her mom and stepdad. The atmosphere was informal with horses, chickens, donkeys and emus visible beyond the huge gnarled live oak draped with Spanish moss. The men, Victor, myself and Lucius (the best man) wore white lightweight tropical clothes. Corey wore a long blue silk dress that she designed herself. Victor, of course, was from Brazil and Lucius was from Italy; therefore there was sort of an international flare to the festivities.

At twenty-five Corey had just received her master's in Brazilian arts at the Federal University of Bahia. She would soon be accepted into the University of Florida PhD program in anthropology with a focus in Latin arts. I would describe her as confident and opinionated but also focused and dedicated to her goals. She was physically fit and unusually strong due to her workouts in aerial arts, dancing and horseback riding. At the same time she was feminine and attractive.

Victor initially spent much time back in Brazil helping his son Raua apply for U.S. citizenship. This took some time; apparently the Brazilian bureaucracy moves even slower than ours. But he also began developing contacts and forming a band focused on Brazilian style music. Eventually he would serve as a liaison for Brazilian artist seeking opportunities in this country. And yes, Raua did eventually join his dad and stepmom in Florida. He rapidly became a good student and a voracious reader. Obviously learning a new language was no barrier. I was proud of all of them.

August 1, 2008 marked the thirtieth anniversary of my private practice career. With this milestone came a growing sense of calm and satisfaction that my career had been successful. My personal expenses along with the market crash meant a good five or six more years of work. At some point, however, the group would allow me to stop taking call and work only days. It was beginning to look like retirement might be a gradual process, as opposed to an abrupt cessation. But that was a good thing.

It was tempting at the pinnacle of my career to feel that I could more or less coast on my laurels for the remainder of my working years. One can never decrease vigilance or take cases for granted in my specialty. But it seemed reasonable to hope that my major professional challenges were behind me. My considerable experience and consistency in basic skills were assets that would see me through. I wasn't actively seeking new clinical challenges, nor did I expect I would need to develop a totally new set of skills. The increased use of regional anesthesia, or blocks, especially for post-op pain, however, would change all that. I still had a few things to learn. My career was far from over.

If the use of regional anesthesia to help control post-op pain gained a strong foot hold in the nineties, in the new millennium it was skyrocketing. The use of epidurals to control pain for abdominal surgery was well established, but now we saw a dramatic increase in the use of peripheral nerve blocks; i.e., giving shots to block nerves that go to the extremities for various operations. A driving force for this trend was the aging baby boomer generation. My generation, now middle-aged, was very demanding; we wanted it all. We thought we could continue all the athletic activities of our youth; cycling, mountain climbing, extreme workouts, and still enjoy our beer and gourmet food. We didn't always use good sense. Advertisers led us to believe we were not growing older, just more experienced. Knees, hips, shoulders and ankles were being injured or just wearing out. We wanted it all fixed; and we didn't particularly want to pay a pain premium after surgery.

Of course, to meet this demand, surgery techniques improved and expanded along with better equipment and prosthesis. In 1980, a patient with a mild to moderate rotator cuff tear would frequently avoid surgery. It was very painful and patients remained debilitated for weeks afterward. In 2008 such a patient would likely seek out a surgeon for repair. The procedure was generally done arthroscopically; i.e., via a small incision with a scope. An interscalene block would be given to decrease pain and therefore recovery was generally much quicker.

Total joint replacements were becoming quite common; most noteworthy was the total knee arthroplasty or TKA. Knees were wearing out by the thousands and many orthopedic surgeons became proficient at replacing knee joints. While many people chose this route, the procedure did have one significant drawback. It was fairly painful unless special techniques were used to decrease pain. In the '90s epidurals were frequently used for this purpose with some success. Unfortunately, the increasing use of blood thinners, like heparin or Coumadin, to prevent blood clots after surgery made epidurals unsafe. There was a risk that bleeding might occur around the epidural catheter.

In the early 2000s many anesthesiologists began doing selective nerve blocks, instead of epidurals to diminish post-op pain. Since there are three major nerves with sensory fibers from the knee, the anesthesiologist was required to do three separate nerve blocks before putting the patient under for surgery. This was fairly labor intensive and required a significant degree of skill and dedication. It was generally successful in blocking or at least greatly diminishing the pain after a total knee arthroplasty. There was little risk of bleeding problems with these blocks.

Likewise peripheral nerve blocks became more common for foot and ankle, shoulder, arm, hand and hip surgeries. In short, the need for performing multiple nerve blocks quickly and proficiently dramatically increased. Doctors were looking for ways to improve their success rate and speed in doing blocks to avoid surgery delays and to minimize the pain due to an unsuccessful block. Nerve stimulators were of some help. By placing a small current on the injection needle, a muscle contraction could usually be elicited when the needle was appropriately placed adjacent to the nerve. This was helpful, but not foolproof.

In the early 2000s some physicians began using an ultrasound device to help locate the nerves that they were planning to block. This device was based on the principles of echolation used by dolphins and bats for navigation. A high frequency sound wave (above the audible range) is emitted. The reflection is analyzed to delineate the underlying structures. Since soft tissues, nerves and bones reflect sound waves differently, an image of the nerve, or sonogram picture can be obtained. Success with this technique required the use of appropriate ultrasound probes, wavelength, depth and intensity parameters, as well as a fair degree of skill and practice. There is a significant learning curve to gain proficiency, and as usual some people become proficient quickly.

By 2008, ultrasound technology was well-established in most anesthetic departments as an adjunctive tool to assist performing peripheral nerve blocks. In our department, Dr. Karlon Young was the ultrasound guru and the strongest advocate of its use. He was the go-to person for advice or assistance with this technique. I had observed him a number of times using the ultrasound (US) device or sonogram to find a nerve image and then inject the local anesthetic around the nerve. I had actually done a handful of blocks myself with US guidance. But I could not claim to have a high degree of proficiency. I thought the use of US technology to perform nerve blocks was very interesting and held great promise for the future, but I wasn't sure if it was necessary for me to become highly proficient with its use. As the oldest physician in the group, I had the most years of experience doing these blocks without US technology. Furthermore, I expected to retire in five or six years. The return on my investment of learning a new skill would be limited. Did it make sense for a physician to make a major change in his modus operandi for his last few years of practice? I wasn't sure.

During the next year I had a case that helped me decide. A young patient needed a brachial plexus block to help with pain control on an upper extremity. The brachial plexus is a network of nerves derived from the lower cervical and upper thoracic nerves. They ultimately innervate the shoulder, arm and hand. Therefore blocking the brachial plexus is a common procedure done before surgery on these body parts. I had done at least a thousand such blocks with good results and without the help of US technology. On this particular case I cleaned the neck and shoulder area with chlorprep, and then proceeded to place the 22 gauge needle into the side of the neck using the neck muscles as anatomic guides. The needle was attached to an electrical stimulator; so when appropriately placed I would expect to see contractions in the arm and hand muscles. It took longer than normal to obtain the desired contractions, but in about ten minutes I had completed the block. It seemed to go okay; i.e., the arm was starting to get numb. But the patient also experienced some anxiety and unexpected blood pressure changes. The patient returned to baseline in less than an hour and his block was successful, but my confidence was a little shaken.

At this point I began to see the writing on the wall. I may have been reasonably proficient at peripheral nerve blocks, but I wasn't perfect and occasional failed blocks or unexpected side effects were inevitable. The first question a colleague would ask of someone with concerns about a block would be, did you use the ultrasound? If not, why not? At that time using the ultrasound for guidance was prevalent, but not necessarily a standard of care. There was some conflicting data on its efficacy. However, evidence seemed to be growing in support of its routine use. In a short time it would be considered a standard of care.

A failure to become proficient with ultrasound technology could cause me to be labeled as a dinosaur doctor; someone who was unable or unwilling to make the effort to stay current. I searched the web for a good workshop teaching ultrasound technology for blocks. I chose one directed by Dr. Vincent W.S. Chan of Western Toronto Hospital in January 2010. Dr. Chan was the rising president of the ASRA, the American Society of Regional Anesthesia and a recognized leader in ultrasound technology. His workshop was limited to fifty people so each participant received ample attention and guidance. Live models were available for demonstration and practice. It was a turning point in my attitude and confidence in ultrasound. This technology was totally safe, noninvasive and truly helpful in some situations. Besides that it was fun. This meeting was followed with the larger ASRA meeting and workshop in the spring of 2011 at Caesars Palace in Las Vegas. Unfortunately, Caesars was booked, we were forced to find accommodations at the Bellagio next door. The sacrifices we make for our profession.

Interestingly, modern day ultrasound technology has its roots in nautical communication developments. In 1901 the Submarine Signal Company of Boston (SSC) developed a system of communicating using under water sound waves. These vibrations were detected by underwater receptors or hydrophones. The sound waves acted as warning bells for dangerous rocks or shoals: they were like an underwater lighthouse, but were not useful in detecting floating objects, like icebergs or boats. After the *Titanic* disaster in 1912 there was increased interest in this technology. A noted Canadian radio pioneer, Reginald Fessenden, proposed installing a device on ships, not just to detect vibrations, but to emit its own sound and then listen for the echoes, much as dolphins use echolocation to navigate. When World War I began, Fessenden pleaded with the Royal Navy of Great Britain to consider using his device to detect the deadly German U-Boats. The Navy was unimpressed. It is estimated that close to 10.000 lives were lost due to U-Boats by the wars end in 1918. Eventually, of course the principles of echo detection would be useful not only in warfare (World War II) but to help fishermen detect their catch, and to map the ocean's floor. Ironically, it was this same technology that was used to discover the *Titanic*, eighty years after it sank.

From its naval uses the ultrasound devices found uses in medicine. Most notably in the late 1950s Dr. Ian MacDonald introduced the technology into the OB-GYN arena. Mothers and physicians could now see into the womb to examine the baby well before birth. Examining the heart and gallbladder and other vital areas was possible. The use of ultrasound or echolocation was a natural tool for anesthesiologist to use for guidance in blocks.

After my workshops in ultrasound in Toronto and Las Vegas I totally embraced its routine use for peripheral nerve blocks. I would find it somewhat more stressful now to do a block today without US guidance. I was a little slow to adopt the technology, but at least I didn't wait for a world war to make my course correction.

As a spinoff benefit from my ultrasound meeting in Toronto in January 2010, Becky and I developed a love affair with Canadian cities and culture. We stayed at the Hyatt Regency in the entertainment district making access to the many fine restaurants on King Street easy. Attractions such as the Canadian Hockey Hall of Fame and Casa Loma, the home of financier Sir Henry Petlat added greatly to our enjoyment. While enjoying a meal at the Kit Kat Bar on King Street, however, a local patron recommended a visit to Montreal. If it was culture we wanted, Toronto was just a tease.

In September 2011 we flew to Montreal and stayed six days at the Fairmont Queen Elizabeth in the downtown area. The hotel was conveniently located about halfway between the "Old City" on the St. Lawrence Seaway and the classy shopping district at the top of the hillside where McGill University and Mount Royal Park are located. The City is a pleasant mix of old world French culture and more contemporary North American influences. The diversity of gastronomic experiences makes it a world ranked foodie city. We found much to like about Montreal.

Again, in September 2012 we returned to Canada, this time to Quebec with Becky's sister and husband, Lissa and John Henner. We stayed at the Manoir Victoria in the old section not far from the well-known Chateau de Frontenac. The Ursuline Convent (1634) and the Seminar of Quebec (1663) are among the oldest schools in North America. There was very little contemporary in the area around our hotel. It seemed as if we had visited Europe without even crossing the Atlantic. For a change of pace that's convenient and affordable, it's hard to beat Quebec City.

During this time frame some critical legal developments took place in the lengthy appeal process that Billy was undergoing. I am not intimately familiar with the legal process and the technical terminology involved, but I think I understood enough to get a good feel of what went on. The following is my take on things as a legally naive parent whose child was once the top student at a prestigious college and now was struggling to regain his life and career.

On October 18, 2006, W. Michael Mayock argued the case for appeal to the United States Court of Appeals for the Ninth Circuit. He was heard by a panel of three judges. A key part of the argument was the failure of the judge to allow the evidence for Asperger's Syndrome (AS) to be heard by the jury at the original trial in November 2004. On February 25, 2009, the trio of circuit judges responded: they upheld the original decision. The appeal was denied. This denial was noteworthy for several reasons according to Mayock. First, it took almost thirty months for a panel of three judges to reach a conclusion. Why so long for a simple denial? Secondly, the denial was announced in the form of a memorandum instead of a published legal opinion. Memorandum decisions are typically drafted after oral arguments when there is no dispute over the facts and the law. The memorandum for denial was clearly labeled "not appropriate for publication and not a precedent except as provided by 9th Cir R 36-3." It seemed the judges did not want to be held culpable for denying Asperger's Syndrome as a defense. As Mayock suggested in a letter to Billy on the date of denial; "Clearly something else is afoot here. This is what we need to figure out."

In response to the denial. Mayock suggested challenging the panel's decision by asking for a rehearing "en banc" by the Ninth Circuit. The term "en banc" means all the judges in the Ninth Circuit would come to a collective decision on the Asperger's question; not just a panel of three. He also suggested filing a Petition for Certiorari to the Supreme Court in case the Ninth Circuit denied a hearing. That is simply a request for the Supreme Court to review the decision of a lower court.

The Ninth Circuit did, however, agree to a rehearing en banc, shortly thereafter. This time there was a totally different result. The appeal was upheld. As a result of this all seven counts of arson were overthrown. This left a single count of conspiracy to arson. His sentence of 100 months and fine of over $3.5 million was vacated; that means it was done away with. In light of this development he would need to be resentenced by the judge based on the single conviction. It wasn't a complete victory, but seven out of eight wasn't too bad. It was a legal victory for the defense; time to break out the champagne. In view of the fact that he had already served over five years, it seemed reasonable to expect his release was imminent.

The resentencing procedure sounded simple in concept. In light of the dramatic reduction in convictions, he would merely appear before the judge to learn how an 87.5 percent decrease in convictions would effect his sentence. In reality, not so simple. Billy was first transferred to a holding cell several hours away. On the hearing date he was given a meager breakfast in the wee hours and then shackled and brought before the judge, the same one who presided at the 2004 trial. It was a momentous occasion; an opportunity to finally reap the benefit of the tedious drawn out appeal process. The Judge's decision: "I need more time to think about it." Therefore he was returned to his cell. Several days later he was re-shackled and brought before the judge. This time the judge announced his decision; the new sentence would be 100 months plus the same fine. In other words the dramatic decrease in convictions would have no effect on his sentence. Billy would return to prison to complete the original sentence.

What did I learn from my son's conviction and legal battle? The first lesson would be to avoid the actions that precipitated the charges to begin with. Legal battles are taxing emotionally physically and financially. There are usually better ways to direct one's energy.

The second is that legal knowledge and theory are important, even critical to success. But the legal nuances and practical problems are equally so. Prisoners have very few rights. The judge has a lot of authority and leeway to interpret sentencing guidelines. The system is far from immune to emotional bias. Victory or defeat may have as much to do with attrition as it does with the virtue of one's legal argument.

Nevertheless, I refrain from making any professional or moral judgment on the judicial system that incarcerated Billy for seven and a half years. For the most part they are honest hard working servants of the government interpreting events through the prism of the federal judicial system. Their own actions have defined themselves far more accurately than my poor power to add or detract. I do feel grateful for our lawyers, Marvin Rudnick and W. Michael Mayock, both from Pasadena, for their stellar legal and personal support.

In February 2011, Billy was transferred to a halfway house in Ocala, Florida. In August 2011 he was released for good. Immediately he began the process of rehabilitating his career by applying to graduate school in theoretical physics. In September 2012 he moved to Madison, Wisconsin to re-enter the world of academia at the University of Wisconsin.

The Last Years

Our practice continued to evolve in the first decade of the new millennium, driven by technology and the political structure of the hospital. These changes were integrated smoothly enough into our daily routines, but just around this time I noticed another change that was gradually exerting its influence. I was aging. I turned 61 in the year 2010. I was considered an "older doctor" by many. Although I remained quite healthy and active, with no serious mental or physical disabilities, I know I was not the same physician I had been twenty years ago. I was acutely self-aware and constantly monitoring myself for any kind of dysfunction. I felt my technical skills were still strong and my ability to focus more than adequate. Perhaps my greatest concern was recuperating after a busy call, especially the twenty four hour calls on the weekends. It seemed to take longer to get back to normal. By my own assessment I was in the early stages of the inevitable overall decline associated with old age, but hanging in there pretty well.

The term senior citizen, or just senior, is a euphemism for old age. The exact year this begins is subject to debate and interpretation. People surveyed in their thirties viewed old age as sixty and up. People over sixty-five thought old age begins around seventy-four. A common interpretation is that seniors are retired people, and therefore at the age of sixty-five or over; some use the age fifty-five. AARP allows people to join at the tender age of fifty. My local movie theatre started giving me a senior discount at age sixty-two. The concept of old age or senior citizenship has multiple connotations. Hence to avoid any unattended implications, I refer to my years of practice after 2010 as the last years of practice. Bob Dylan said it best; "I might look like Robert Frost, but I feel just like Jesse James."

A byproduct of my advancing age was a change in perspective on my life and career. I was more philosophical and less prone to follow rigid guidelines. "Whatever works" was my motto. Whereas many older physicians tend to ossify into rigid routines I tended to be more improvisatory, perhaps like a jazz musician. In my early years I saw myself as a clinical scientist using the laws of chemistry and physiology to produce a desired result. As I matured I saw myself more as a true professional; someone who worked on patients using standardized protocols and techniques while adhering to high standards of conduct. In my later years, however, I began to view myself as an artisan; someone who learned a trade to assist people in the community. Yes, it was a trade well rooted in the sciences and with many professional guidelines and protocols, but my ultimate goal was merely to be of some use to the patient. When I saw an OB patient after delivery who had an epidural I would ask; "Did it relieve most of your pain? Did you get a backache or a headache?" My focus was on patient satisfaction. In this sense I was like the village cobbler who asked, Do you like your new shoes? Do your feet hurt?

Fortunately, there were also some benefits to longevity. In 2010 I had practiced 32 years in the Concord area. Likewise Becky had been a hand therapist for over twenty years. That makes for a lot of patient interactions and social connections in the medical community. Whether going to a movie, eating at O'Charley's or just going to the grocery store, we would frequently run into prior patients or nurses and other hospital personnel. These encounters would reinforce our sense of community and bring a degree of personal satisfaction. Growing old could be a pain at times, but the good seemed to outweigh the bad.

We also found our life in Concord enhanced by our affiliation with All Saints Episcopal Church where Becky had been a member. Although I was leery of becoming overcommitted after my experience with church membership in the late 80s and 90s, I found that being part of this church community complemented our professional and personal lives. I had much to be thankful for; Becky above all.

No story about my medical career would be complete without a close look at obstetrical anesthesia. Since I played role in starting a labor epidural service in 1990, I have always had a keen interest and bond with obstetrical anesthesia. For years I attended the obstetrical department meetings as a representative from my department. I also taught classes for expectant mothers on pain relief for labor every other month in conjunction with Dr. John Talbot and the hospital.

In 1990 the hospital did about 1200 deliveries. This grew rapidly to almost 3,000 in the next ten to twelve years. The Cesarean section rate was about 15 percent when I first entered practice. By 2010 it was over 30 percent. Roughly 75 percent of laboring patients were requesting an epidural for pain control. Therefore anesthesia services in 2010 consisted primarily of providing epidurals for labor and delivery, and providing anesthesia (usually a spinal block) for Cesarean sections. Occasionally we would also do post-partum tubal ligations, either in conjunction with a section, or as a separate procedure.

The most common procedure we do in obstetrics by far is the epidural for labor and delivery. It is the most common mode of pain relief used for laboring women in our hospital. The essence of the technique is to sterilely place an epidural needle in the lower back between two lumbar vertebrae, frequently at the L3-4 interspace but sometimes L2-3 or L4-5. The needle is carefully inserted through the skin and subcutaneous fat, the supraspinous and interspinous ligaments and finally the rubbery ligamentum flavum until it reaches the space right outside the dural sac which contains the spinal cord and spinal fluid. The goal is to deposit the local anesthetic, usually bupivacaine or ropivacaine, right outside the dural sac where it can block the conduction in nerves emanating from the spinal cord. The physician performing the epidural block must assure the needle is in far enough to reach the epidural space, otherwise it will not work. At the same time he must be sure it doesn't go too far that it punctures the dural sac. This could lead to major leakage of spinal fluid and very likely a spinal headache. It could also lead to a major drop in blood pressure and a higher level of nerve blockade than desired. The difference in depth between a needle that goes in too far and one not in far enough may be three or four millimeters or even less in some patients.

A key to success in performing epidurals is a good sense of feel and good motor control of the hands and fingers. Advancing a needle through the ligamentum flavum requires a small steady force. It feels like pushing a needle through a piece of bubble gum or rubber. When the needle tip comes out the other side into the epidural space, the force needed to advance the needle normally drops dramatically. That's how we know we have reached the desired space. By placing a syringe with air and a little saline on the proximal end of the needle and gently pushing the plunger as we advance, we can get added feed-back on the needle placement by detecting a sudden loss of resistance with the plunger. This is called the loss of resistance technique.

After the epidural needle is placed, a small test dose followed by a loading dose of local anesthetic is given. After that a small bore cath-eter of Teflon or nylon is inserted through the needle three or four centimeters past the needle tip. Next the needle is removed over the catheter taking care not to pull the catheter out along with it. The catheter is then connected to a pump and used to infuse a local anes-thetic for hours as needed for the control of labor pain. This is essen-tially the same technique used when placing an epidural to help with pain control associated with a major operation.

I estimate I have placed at least 10,000 epidurals, many of them for obstetrical patients. The routine placement of a labor epidural in a normal-sized patient who is cooperative and has no major back deformity is fairly easy with a low stress factor and a nice reward; the patient becomes pain free, or almost pain free. The risk of the needle puncturing the dural sac and causing a headache is still there, but quite low. Perhaps as low as one in four hundred in skilled hands.

Unfortunately, women in labor frequently do not meet all these criteria. She may be hysterical with pain. This may be due to severe contractions and an abnormal fetal position. Or the patient may just have a low pain threshold. Through no fault of her own the mother may have scoliosis or spinal stenosis, spine abnormalities that make epidural placement difficult. Mild to moderate obesity does not seem to cause much problem, but extreme obesity understandably can make placement more difficult. For these reasons epidural placements vary from quite easy to fairly difficult. The risk of failure and spinal headache or wet tap is still low, but obviously somewhat greater in these more challenging cases.

So when I get called for an epidural placement in a laboring mother, whether at ten a.m. or three a.m. on call, I never know what to expect. Secretly, I hope the patient is calm and relaxed, has a normal symmetrical back and looks like Taylor Swift. But I am resolved to help the patient regardless of the circumstances. Usually ten to fifteen minutes after placing the epidural, the mother experiences a great decrease in contraction pains and is very grateful. I have actually had a number of women propose to me when this happens. We always get a good laugh out of that.

The flip side is that if the epidural doesn't work well, or if the mother gets a spinal headache, she may be very upset. This is fortunately not very often. All things considered I have enjoyed providing labor epidurals and making women feel better. It is one of the most rewarding aspects of my practice.

The key to successfully covering OB is to adopt a policy of flexibility and adaptability. One has little control over the volume of cases or the timing. You may do very little for a couple of hours and then get three requests for labor epidurals and an emergency Cesarean section within a thirty-minute period. Learning to prioritize tasks and keeping your cool are essential. I made notes of a "typical" busy day in OB during my last years, although there really is no such thing as a typical day.

I arrived one weekday morning a little before 6 a.m. and went to the main OR desk to check the master schedule. I noticed that there were two elective Cesarean sections scheduled in the obstetrical suite that day. I then went across the hall to OB and wrote my name on the blackboard so the RNs would know who was covering for OB, and then checked their schedule. There were now four elective sections scheduled. The OB Cesarean section schedule is a work in progress, cases being frequently added as needed and occasionally dropped when it is learned that they delivered early. By the afternoon we had two more sections added for a total of six.

The first patient for Cesarean section was very short, only about four feet tall. This meant that the normal dose of agent used in the spinal block, usually about 1.8cc of 0.75 percent bupivacaine for an average-sized patient with the technique I use, would need to be adjusted downward. But how much? If I reduced the dose too much she might not get an adequate level of anesthesia. Moreover, she might start feeling pain in her upper abdomen during the case and require a general anesthetic to be induced to get her through the operation. This would undermine most of the advantages of the spinal anesthetic. If I failed to reduce the dose sufficiently, she might get a spinal block that rose too high causing respirations to be diminished and causing the blood pressure to drop. This might require intubation to assist the patient's breathing. I elected to give a dose of 1.4cc of bupivacaine. This calculation was based on a proportionate drop in volume of drug based on her height compared to an average person; about a twenty percent decrease. She actually did quite well with the surgery at that dosage.

The rest of the Cesarean sections were more normal in size and were handled in the usual manner without problem. In addition, however, I also did four labor epidurals. They were all routine until I got to my last case of the day.

The patient in question was quite large, average in height but weighing almost three hundred and fifty pounds. I discussed the procedure with the patient and then palpated her back to search for the space between two vertebrae in her lower back where the epidural needle would be inserted. It was very difficult for me to feel her vertebrae due to the folds of adipose tissue that overlapped the midline of her back. I needed help exposing her back. So I placed several long pieces of four inch adhesive tape on both sides of her midline and stretched them tightly circumferentially around her trunk to somewhere on her abdomen. In this high tech world of medicine adhesive tape is still irreplaceable; I have used it several times in similar situations. The midline now was exposed nicely; I could more easily feel her vertebrae. I then prepped the skin with betadine and placed the epidural in the L3-4 interspace. The procedure took about ten minutes but went well; in a few minutes she was feeling much less pain. Apparently her previous epidurals had required multiple attempts.

So I had two patients that day who were outliers due to their unusual size. This made management more challenging. It was, however, very rewarding to assist these pleasant patients with childbirth as well as the more normal-sized patients. Unfortunately, Taylor Swift didn't show up that day, ha, ha.

Good communication between a physician and his patient is important in general, but especially when placing an epidural or spinal. It is critical to the procedure's success that the patient not make sudden movements or jerks during placement and that she correctly position her back by bowing it outward. When the back is correctly arched outward like a Halloween cat the interstices between the vertebrae will widen, making epidural placement easier. When the lower back is concave or swayback, it can be nearly impossible to insert the epidural needle correctly. Paradoxically, those patients most nervous and fearful may worsen their plight by failing to understand these essentials. Not infrequently, when I ask a patient writhing in pain to push her lower back out, she will do just the opposite. Good patient rapport and communication will help minimize these problems. So by calming and reassuring the patient, the anesthesiologist not only decreases her fear, but makes the task easier for himself. Technical skill is great but an empathetic bedside manner can make a crucial difference.

As our labor epidural service grew and flourished in the '90s and early 2000s, the need for good communication skills became increasingly obvious. One night on call in the early 2000s I had requests for five epidurals in laboring patients. This was more than average, but not an unheard of number for one night. The hook was that all five were non-English speaking Hispanic mothers. I struggled through. Everything turned out well, but communication was a challenge.

To its credit the hospital provided interpreters to deal with this challenge. The number of Spanish-speaking people in Cabarrus County was steadily rising. Many were women of reproductive age. More and more women were showing up in labor and delivery who spoke very little English. But using interpreters had two associated disadvantages. Though very helpful and normally readily available, you may have to wait a few minutes for them to arrive. The patient's anxiety is directly proportional to the length of waiting. Furthermore, telling a patient you will be very gentle and careful can be done via a third person. They hear the words. But sometimes the trust and confidence would be lost in translation.

So around 2000 the hospital offered a ten-week course in medical Spanish. For two hours every Wednesday evening for ten weeks I attended this crash course. I studied a fair amount and bought some additional study guides on my own. I can't claim now that I am fluent in Spanish. Some physicians tease me for speaking Spanish with a Southern accent. To add interest I occasionally throw in a few French words. But I can now handle most medical situations okay without having to wait for the interpreter. It makes for a happier patient; a better assured, more trusting patient. Frankly, I didn't know learning a few hundred words in Spanish would be so helpful until I did it.

It seems that communication challenges have plagued the practice of medicine, especially in obstetrics, since the early days. Dr. Lance Monroe, an OB-GYN physician on the original medical staff in 1937 described some of the communication techniques of yesteryear. In those days the hospital was adjacent to the Cabarrus Country Club with its golf course (all fourteen holes I am told). With no beepers or cell phones he had to keep in touch with land phones if he left the hospital. If he wanted to play golf, however, they developed a special system. He would keep an eye on the OB wing as he played. When the OB nurse thought he needed to come in for a delivery, she would hang a white sheet out the window. Easier than lighting a signal fire I suppose. To my knowledge it worked well.

In 1968 the country club moved to its current location on Weddington Road making this system inoperable. By then beepers were becoming commonplace.

In 1974 Motorola developed a beeper called the "pageboy." This is what I first used in 1978 at the beginning of private practice. When the beeper went off the physician would call the operator to learn who was paging him. Later beepers provided the phone number of the party calling him. In the '80s and '90s the beepers became smaller and lighter. In 1992 I got my first personal cell phone. Several years later we began to use in-house Cisco cell phones for communication among ourselves. This really did facilitate intra physician and nursing communication.

So when I took call during my last years, I carried four different communication devices: my personal beeper, a special beeper for the call doctor, the in house Cisco cell phone and my own personal cell phone. It certainly seemed excessive, but there were valid reasons for each device. I won't argue the need, but some days I felt like a walking tele-communications center. Maybe we should bring back the white sheet in the window?

The dramatic increase in the number of non-English speaking

patients put a new twist on the challenges of doctor-patient communication and rapport. The interpreters were excellent but not always immediately available. A recent concept called the video interpreter seems to be helping to solve this problem. A wireless video connection, similar to Skype, can put us in touch almost immediately with a professional interpreter. There can be a three-way conversation between the doctor, or nurse, the patient and the interpreter. Not only Spanish, but Chinese, Vietnamese, French, German, etc. The hospital reimburses the company at x dollars per minute of actual use. This would seem to be more cost-effective and expedient than the old system of hiring in-house interpreters. Though not in wide use yet, the "video interpreters" may be the wave of the future and the answer to our translation problems. Estimates of the number of languages in the world vary between five and seven thousand. I wonder though; does anyone still speak Inuit?

Another assignment I frequently had during my last years was that of "out doctor," also simply referred to as the "out doc." This consisted of anesthesia cases outside the main OR suite such as GI cases, upper endoscopies and colonoscopies, and of patients having MRIs who were claustrophobic or unable to lie still such as babies and small children. Occasionally we might be asked to cover a case in the cath lab such as a pacemaker placement or a procedure in the interventional radiology room. We might occasionally cover up to four sites, but normally it was only two or three. This assignment required a good bit of flexibility and shoe leather. Seriously, it was important to have good walking shoes, or as we jokingly would say to "bring our roller skates."

These were not the macho cases in our department. A quadruple bypass, a craniotomy for brain tumor or even a total knee replacement would seem to be much more demanding and rewarding. However this assignment had its own unique set of challenges. We did a greater number of smaller cases scattered throughout the hospital. Furthermore, someone may be occasionally too frail or sick to have a total knee replacement. But is anyone ever too sick to be put out for a colonoscopy? Almost never. Especially if he has an acute problem of pain or bleeding that needs investigation. We therefore had a lot of interactions with patients as the out doc. Many of them were very sick. The best way to illustrate what this experience was like is to describe an unusually busy day I had once in recent years.

My initial assignment was to cover three cases for MRIs and several endoscopies and colonoscopies in GI. This is the usual for the out doc. GI was actually very light so it looked like an easy day. But the MD coordinator told me I might also need to help out in the cath lab since the anesthesiologist covering the heart cases was tied up doing a ruptured thoracic aneurysm, a very demanding case. When I stopped by the cath lab at 6:30 a.m., however, he informed me that he had things under control. He was able to cover both the aneurysm and the cath lab concurrently. If things changed he would call me.

So I focused on the GI and MRI cases. Around 9:30, however, the coordinator requested that I now cover a case in interventional radiology. The Patient was an elderly male with multiple medical problems who needed a kyphoplasty, a minor surgical procedure on his back. While discussing the anesthetic with him I noticed he had a class three airway. This meant would be at least a little difficult to intubate. To help deal with that challenge I asked the CRNA to make sure and bring the C-Mac or video laryngoscope to the radiology suite. The videoscope was our usual go-to technique for difficult intubations. Anticipating and preparing for a problem is at least half the battle.

Before this case began, however, I received an urgent call to assist in the cath lab with an ASA four (very sick) patient who needed a pacemaker insertion. This was the first time I was informed that I was needed for this case. Apparently the other anesthesiologist was totally tied up managing the ruptured aneurysm. No big surprise. The patient had come from the cardiac intensive care unit with a single small IV (#22) in her left forearm. She was lying supine with arms closely tucked to her side on the small procedure table in the cath lab. The small room was crowded with fluoroscopy equipment, cardiac monitors and the anesthesia cart with supplies. But our mission was simple; all we had to do was administer a slow infusion of propofol to cause a state of light sleep and closely track her vital signs and oxygenation.

There was one minor glitch. The small IV catheter had infiltrated; it was worthless. Theoretically its function should have been verified before she left the ICU and certainly before her arms were tucked. Now it was my job to deal with it. I untucked her arms and legs and scoured each extremity in search of a usable vein. Her hands arms and feet were pale and swollen. I saw no veins. I was tempted to remove the patient from the cath lab to an open area where I had more room and better access to the patient. But this would be a big hassle and delay the case. My last resort, short of a central line, was to use the external jugular vein. By placing the patient in steep trendelenburg (head down), I could frequently cause the vein to "pop up" enough to insert a sizable intravenous catheter. Unfortunately, this particular procedure table did not perform that maneuver. Therefore I requested that her legs be elevated by placing a pile of blankets under them. I noticed that her external jugular veins were now slightly bulging. With good assistance from the CRNA and a little bit of luck I was able to insert an 18-gauge catheter into the vein. The case could proceed as usual.

Just as I finished up in the cath lab, I was paged to come to radiology to help induce the anesthesia for the kyphoplasty. As I swiftly high-tailed it down the hall to the interventional radiology room, I thought of the elderly man we would be inducing. I was thankful I had noticed his neck anatomy and anticipated a possible difficult intubation.

In the radiology suite the CRNA had connected the patient to the usual monitors and was pre-oxygenating the patient with the mask; making sure his lungs were full of oxygen before we gave the propofol and the anectine to facilitate intubation. She was all set to start, but where was the C-Mac? I didn't see it anywhere. She had simply forgotten to bring it. I asked the CRNA to hold up. We called the anesthesia tech to bring us the scope. In three or four minutes it rolled through the door. We plugged it into an outlet and then proceeded. Even with the video scope the intubation proved difficult requiring three attempts. I suspect it would have been much worse without it. Once we secured the endotracheal tube with tape the patient was turned prone (on his stomach) and the case proceeded uneventfully.

I returned to the GI suite to help out with three more cases. The rest of the day was uneventful.

The last years offered ample opportunity for me to reflect on my career and try to put things in perspective. I recall one senior resident advising me in residency: "Make sure you have a good airway and good intravenous access, everything else is secondary." Time had shown this to be good advice even if it wasn't 100 percent correct. We learned in medical school that when we hear hoof beats we should think of horses, not zebras. We also learned the principle of Occam's razor: given the option of multiple theories to explain a phenomenon, the simplest is most likely to be correct. I've found these guiding principles to be helpful in dealing with challenges in anesthesia. It is interesting and educational to learn about zebras. I have actually seen two or three. But year in and year out I prefer to bet on the horses.

Even though many aspects of my anesthetic practice had evolved significantly since 1978, the basic principles that I learned in residency still rang true. Airway and venous access challenges were still the major foci of concern and angst they had always been. Certain types of clinical challenges seemed to pop up over and over again despite improved drugs, equipment and techniques.

I had a case in my last year of residency I described earlier that made a big impression on me. I had to re-intubate a patient in the PACU due to the prolonged effects of the muscle relaxant. In that case it was due to a sudden decrease in kidney function which delayed the normal excretion of the drug from the body. I have always therefore been sensitive to the possibility of a prolonged weakness after surgery due to these drugs. Frequently I will question the CRNA about the status of the muscle relaxant in the patient. Has the muscle relaxant been adequately countered with the reversal drugs? Does he have any residual weakness? Normally the CRNA will assure me the reversal drugs were given and no significant weakness is present. Most of the time they are correct. But occasionally we had cases that caused concern.

The CRNA and I put a middle-aged man to sleep for abdominal surgery. Unfortunately, the patient had cancer with the strong possibility of metastasis. Nevertheless he appeared fairly healthy despite his diagnosis. The cardiovascular, renal, pulmonary and neurological systems seemed to be unimpaired. The anesthetic consisted of suprane, dilaudid and an intermediate acting muscle relaxant, rocuronium. At the end of the case the CRNA gave a standard dose of neostigmine to reverse the muscle relaxant. When the twitch monitor indicated that muscle strength was at, or close to baseline, the CRNA extubated the patient and transported him to the PACU for emergence and recovery from the anesthetic. I came by to check the patient as he was wheeled into bay number nine and the experienced RN connected him up to the usual monitors.

Right away I noticed something was a little bit off. His respirations were slightly labored and rapid. Blood pressure and pulse were also slightly elevated and his O2 saturation was 90 percent, a little lower than expected. He was not crashing, but he did have mild respiratory distress. The most likely source of the problem was either residual muscle weakness from the rocuronium or increased airway resistance due to bronchospasm. I asked the CRNA to give a repeat dose of neostigmine and the PACU nurse to give an albuterol bronchodilator treatment with the nebulizer. Thus I was covering both possible causes. In five minutes I saw a possible mild improvement, but his situation was still worrisome. At this point I asked the RN to bring the crash cart to his bedside in case he deteriorated rapidly. I continued to watch him closely, debating whether or not to re-intubate. It was a close call. But instead of re-intubating, I requested the CRNA to give yet another dose of reversal drug. In another five minutes I saw a definite improvement in his situation. His respirations became slower and less labored. His oxygen increased to the upper 90s and he lost the appearance of being distressed. The rest of his recovery was uneventful.

Apparently this patient had prolonged weakness from the muscle relaxant, despite a reasonable dose of reversal drug. Why would that be? The doses of muscle relaxant and reversal drugs were appropriate. The patient's renal function was normal so it was unlikely that excessive blood levels of the muscle relaxant was to blame. It seemed as if the patient was hypersensitive to a normal dose of the muscle relaxant. What could cause that?

Myasthenia gravis is a rare neuromuscular disease affecting between 14 and 20 people per 100,000. It is an auto-immune disease caused by antibodies in the blood attacking the post synaptic membrane in the neuromuscular junction. The patient's primary presenting complaint is one of weakness. Occasionally the weakness occurs only in the eye muscles, but in most cases it involves muscles of the trunk and extremities. It commonly occurs in women under thirty and men over sixty. Its onset and course are quite variable but is usually progressive in the early years. Such people afflicted would be very sensitive to neuromuscular blocking drugs. However, this patient had no such diagnosis or symptomatology before surgery.

Lambert-Eaton or Eaton-Lambert myasthenia syndrome is a rare autonomic disease that resembles myasthenia gravis. It is distinct, however, from that entity in that the antibodies attack the presynaptic area of the neuromuscular junction. It is often (50 -70 percent) associated with lung cancer, but may also be associated with other malignancies. It is therefore considered a paraneoplastic syndrome. It is also noted that these patients have an unusual sensitivity to neuromuscular blocking drugs; i.e., muscle relaxants. I have seen this hypersensitivity to muscle relaxants several times in my career in patients with various neoplasms. Despite no prior diagnosis of weakness, this patient discussed almost certainly had Lambert-Eaton syndrome. He was an outlier in terms of how he responded to our drugs. Very rarely does it take three doses of reversal to be successful in achieving adequate muscle strength. But in this case at least, it was preferable to re-intubating the patient. This particular case in my last years re-affirmed my sense that despite major advances in my specialty, certain types of problems reappear periodically.

A retrospective review of almost 50,000 patients receiving intermediate acting muscle relaxants for surgery at Massachusetts General, reported June, 2015 in Anesthesiology, showed there was an increased risk of postoperative respiratory complications when high, versus low doses of neuromuscular blocking agents were used. The implication is that some residual weakness may contribute to respiratory problems after surgery. It doesn't prove cause and effect. However, adequate reversal of muscle relaxants is a universal concern now as it has been for the last seventy years. I believe we are considerably better today, but diligence in monitoring neuromuscular blockade is a critical component of a good anesthetic.

On August 1, 2012 I was granted the right to stop taking call by my colleagues. With this privilege I surrendered my partnership status and accepted a two-year limitation on my right to practice medicine. Fortunately, by August 1, 2014, Dr. Goglin had negotiated a contract with CHS for our group to take over anesthesia services for University Hospital including its small surgery center in Huntersville. We were entering a new phase of our practice. Therefore, the group still had need of my services. I happily agreed to extend my practice a year or two. On October 1, 2014 I became the primary anesthesiologist at Huntersville.

Also of note, our group had expanded to twenty physicians by August 2014. This included Dr. Jin Kwak (2009), Dr. Jason Rowling (2010), Dr. Wes Hudson (2012) and Dr. Kyle Branham (2014). Thus my last years of practice were enriched with both new practice opportunities and new colleagues. I would hang around a little longer than previously anticipated. After I quit taking call in 2012, my stress level dropped significantly. I was generally less fatigued. This allowed me to view my career from a fresh perspective.

In 2013 the hospital celebrated its history by creating a timeline wall mural with actual photographs beginning with its opening in 1937 and continuing through 2013. The mural is located in the main hallway connecting the surgery suite and family center with the rest of the hospital, so therefore I walk by it frequently. There is a picture of Mr. Charles Cannon and the original Board of Trustees of the hospital at one end including Joe Glass, W.W. Flowe, George McCallister, George Batte, Douglass Kincaid, Zeb B Bradford, Eric G Flannigan and Jo Nolan. A set of triplets born in 1937 is included. Major building additions in 1952, 1970 and 1993 are displayed along with ground breaking ceremonies with noted administrators and physicians. There is a picture in 2006 of Jeff Gordon of NASCAR fame cutting the ribbon for the new children's hospital named in his honor.

To add cultural mile markers, the mid 1950s includes a picture of Elvis Presley singing while doing his pelvic gyrations. The late 1970s is represented by John Travolta from *Saturday Night Fever*. I smile when I see a picture of three attractive nurses from the mid-'70s attired in white slacks and tops. The caption reads, "Nurses are allowed to wear pants." Oh really! What took so long?

One of my favorite pictures is a 1960 photograph of the medical staff, all thirty of them. Included are familiar names such as George Liles, Vincent Arey, Clayton Jones, John Ashe, Tommy Tomlin, Russel Floyd and Lance Monroe to name a few. Another favorite is a picture of Nancy Burrage when she graduated from nursing school in 1950. Nancy served as OB supervisor for years before serving as a volunteer, a job she just recently relinquished. She still thinks of me as a young doctor.

Many group photos and candid shots of various hospital employees are displayed including kitchen staff, maintenance men, orderlies, nurses and nursing assistants, physical therapist, respiratory therapist,

CRNAs, PAs, IT experts, telephone operators, lab technicians, secretaries, administrators, housekeepers, purchasing agents and Chaplin to name a few.

The mural includes noted hospital administrators such as Robert Wall, Larry Hinsdale, Mark Nantz and Phyllis Wingate and also noted executive committee leaders; George Batte, Bub Coltrane, Derwood Bost and Ralph Barnhardt. The medical staff is well represented by noted surgeons, pediatricians, OB-GYNs, internists, family practitioners, radiologists, pathologists and ophthalmologists. The mural is a well-done, fact-filled, chronological documentation of the hospitals growth and evolution. Each time I pass by I stop to admire it. Frequently I will notice some new tidbit of history. I have noticed one small deficiency, however. There are no anesthesiologists pictured or named in the mural. Not as individuals or in any group picture starting from 1937 through the whole gamut. Not one. It is as if we didn't exist. Those physicians who perform the greatest number of the most basic resuscitative and therapeutic techniques in medicine; i.e., intravenous access and airway control, are not included in this otherwise excellent and comprehensive pictorial history of the medical community.

At first I was a little resentful of this omission. Was this a political ploy by the powers that be to humiliate us? Did somebody have it in for us?

But then it all became more clear. This is just our legacy. It's what we signed up for. Our work is mostly behind the scenes to facilitate surgery, childbirth and other procedures and to treat acute and chronic pain. On most days we prefer not to draw too much attention to ourselves. That usually implies we have done our job well. (okay, but one little picture would have been nice!)

The last years helped me appreciate the idiosyncrasies and perversity of my specialty. What kind of professional prefers oblivion to notoriety? Who else constantly observes someone's neck and facial anatomy in public to look for possible difficult intubations? How many people when given a baby to hold will immediately check the hands and feet to look for veins? We focus on airways and venous access because it's our raison d'etre. When I said I was enamored with my future wife on our first date due to her wonderful veins, I was only half joking.

We are also the drug dealers of the medical world. We administer sedatives, anxiolytics, pain killers and muscle relaxants intravenously to obtain desired effects. The drugs we administer on a daily basis would be lethal in many cases if not followed by timely and skillful maneuvers to support breathing and the circulatory system. We can never forget this basic reality; but we strive to avoid drama.

Just like drug dealers we get paid for our services. In a complex series of bureaucratic maneuvers, money gets transferred through third parties and is eventually deposited in our bank account. Due to complicated insurance plans and contractual arrangements the original payment may get whittled down a bit. Unlike "El Chapo", however, we are totally legitimate. The government gets its fair share out of the transaction; everybody is happy. It's a living.

As the drug experts in the medical field, we are acutely aware of the widespread abuse of drugs in the population at large. Many illegal and abused drugs are closely related to our own legitimate drugs. Sometimes they are the same drugs but are used without the benefit of medical direction. We are a nation obsessed with drugs for better or worse. We both vilify and idolize drug abusers. We love to trash Robert Downey Jr. for his alleged cocaine and heroin addictions. But when he successfully battles these demons and stars in another action flick we treat him like a superhero. Is this logical? Why did he get addicted to start with? The story of drug abuse in this country is too pervasive and convoluted to broach in a comprehensive manner, but I think it deserves a few comments.

The mere definition of the word drug is complicated. The most general definition is found in the Oxford Dictionary: a medicine or substance which has a physiological effect when ingested or otherwise introduced into the body. The term "or other substance" leaves it wide open. By this standard water, salt and even foods qualify as drugs.

Other definitions limit a drug to medications or substances specifically taken to treat, prevent or diagnose a disease; a commonly accepted meaning. Yet some definitions clearly point to drugs as chemicals taken illegally to obtain a "high" of some type. You can take your pick; each definition has some legitimacy.

As a physician with a chemistry background, I prefer the first definition. I believe it is the most universally valid. Foods contain chemicals that interact with the body's metabolism and neurological system. Historically most medicines were derived from plants. The point is the body doesn't care if caffeine is ingested in the form of a pill or in the drink derived from the coffee bean. It's the same chemical.

Interestingly, coffee has been periodically condemned as dangerous and unhealthy from the women of London in 1674 who thought it made their men impotent, to C.W. Post (think Post Cereals) who claimed it attacked the "pneumogastric nerve" in the early 1900s. As late as 1978 Sanford Miller of the FDA waffled "We're not saying caffeine is unsafe. We're just not saying it's safe." okay then; drink coffee at your own risk.

In this context it's not too surprising that the legalization of marijuana in Colorado recently stirred up so much controversy and vitriol from some parties. The mild euphoria and feeling of relaxation seems fairly harmless to many. Nevertheless, it's not too hard to find examples of teens and young adults who seem to lose motivation and focus with routine smoking. It is highly preferable that we direct our youth to higher grounds.

Yet it is also worth noting that all three of our most recent presidents (Obama, Bush and Clinton) have confessed to smoking marijuana in their younger days. Who knows what other nefarious activities they may have undertaken. But somehow they muddled through. It's interesting to speculate how their lives might have turned out if they had just said "no" like Nancy Reagan suggested. They might have actually amounted to something. The slackards!

I mention these ironies, not to minimize the risk or concerns about illegal drugs, but merely to put them in perspective. "Legal" drugs may be equally harmful to the body if used inappropriately. Our physiology is legally naïve. Therefore, treat your body with respect. Do what's right.

One more example helps illustrate the hypocrisy and ambiguity surrounding drug abuse. In the 1960s my generation was labeled as irresponsible for its experimentation with various drugs. Undoubtedly, quite a few indulged. We were labeled the generation of drugs, sex and rock and roll. The theory is that some of my contemporaries consumed chemicals (ingested, smoked, etcetera) that made them feel good. Aided by the suggestive lyrics and heavy beat of rock and roll or reggae they then began sexual interactions with members of the opposite sex. While many can verify the validity of this theory, it's difficult to know if these activities were really more egregious in my generation than in preceding generations or those ensuing. Nevertheless, the label stuck. We wear it like a scarlet letter emblazoned on our shirts.

Now enter the age of Viagra and Cialis. These are drugs specifically developed and promoted to facilitate sexual intercourse. For procreation? No! To combat disease? No! Unabashedly these are drugs for sex. What was once taboo is now aggressively marketed. Pfizer spends over two billion annually for advertising much of it for Viagra.

So, on the one hand, we bear the burden of guilt for the perceived indiscretions of our youth. On the other hand we must watch on prime time TV as an attractive female explains how our erections can be improved by using drugs. Not to worry. It's all FDA approved.

I offer one last caveat on the use/abuse of drugs, especially psychotropic ones to improve one's mental status. All drugs, legal or illegal, have a ceiling effect. You can only feel so good. Furthermore, repeated use of drugs will cause the threshold for satisfaction to be edged ever higher. Addiction occurs. What once seemed pleasurable is now a monkey on one's back.

Unfortunately, many people with chronic pain become tolerant to the effects of opiates. Their threshold for effectiveness is now abnormally high. If they have an acute injury with severe pain, management is a real problem. Nothing seems to help.

A wise policy would be to use our most potent drugs sparingly; for occasions of extreme pain. At some point most of us will have a need for strong drugs. John Dryden, the seventeenth century English poet put it this way; "For all the happiness mankind can gain, is not in pleasure but in rest from pain." I can't explain it any better than that.

The last years were especially busy and rewarding for Becky and I in our personal life, especially concerning our children. In October 2013 Dustin and Adrienne gave us a grandchild, Jude Ryan Nurseged Cottrell. Born February 23, 2013, in Addis Ababa Ethiopia, he was seven months old when the adoption agency finally allowed his parents to transport him from Ethiopia to Marietta, Georgia. If there was a small concern that he was a little developmentally delayed upon arrival, it was short lived. Jude is a well-adjusted, well-behaved three year old; well ahead of the curve by most standards. I watched in amazement recently as he rapidly solved puzzles for five to six year olds. He is a real joy and treasure to his parents and grandparents. Good parenting makes a world of difference.

On May 25, 2014, Mandy and her fiancée Robbie Hill blessed us with Meriel Tara-Elizabeth. Arriving a few weeks early and weighing six lbs. and four ounces at birth, she is now an active toddler. It didn't take long for her to win our hearts. She draws a crowd wherever she goes. With two sets of doting grandparents, she will not want for much. But on August 7, 2015, Meriel's brother, Weylin William arrived, also a few weeks early and weighing six lbs. seven ounces. Weylin is very laid back so far; taking everything in stride. We know the stage is set for some tough competition with Meriel.

Not to be outdone Harper and Lindsey recently blessed us with a new grandbaby, Pressley Harper, December 21, 2015. They have an ideal home and neighborhood for raising babies. No doubt they will be great parents. It looks like the Holidays will be especially blessed. We can hardly believe our good fortune; four new grandchildren in a little over two years. Where will it all end?

During this same timeframe Corey became the first member of our immediate family (not counting Rebecca's brother Thane) to earn a PhD when the University of Florida awarded her a doctorate in anthropology in June 2015. How she managed to do that while running and expanding her school of dance and aerial arts in Gainesville as well as keeping Victor and Raua in line is beyond me. But it must have a lot to do with drive and determination.

Not to be left out of the domestic happenings, Billy informed me in May 2015 that he and Manni had just gotten married in Wisconsin. He was afraid we might be upset for not letting us know earlier. Not so! We were delighted. Manni had recently earned her degree in industrial engineering and was now working on her masters. We had met her the previous summer and were delighted to have her in the family. She is smart, congenial, attractive and fashionable. She helps keep Billy focused.

Perfect! Now all five children were married. Grandchildren galore and the possibility of even more. What more could we want?

Amid all this activity was a noteworthy trip to the Amalfi Coast of Italy in September 2014. The trip was a package deal sponsored by Country Walkers. Our travel group included the Keippers, Harpers, Stegmans and Andrews. The trip began in Naples and proceeded to Ravello, Capri and Sorrento. Highlights included the ruins of Pompei, the Path of the Gods on the Amalfi Coast, the Blue Grotto and Mount Solaro in Capri. Becky and I extended the tour with three days on our own in Rome. The usual historic sites were impressive, but my favorite activity was a walking dinner tour in Travestere. As a side attraction we were allowed to enter the Farmacia Santa Maria della Scala. Opened in 1597 by the Carmelitani Scalzi (Carmelites Without Shoes) who were masters of herbal medicine, it is one of the world's oldest pharmacies still intact, though not in operation.

Back in North Carolina I began my new assignment of supervising anesthesia at the Huntersville Surgery Center affiliated with CHS on October 1, 2014. Most weeks I work four days in Huntersville and one day at Northeast back in Concord. This allows me to keep in touch with my former colleagues in addition to providing new services.

In the summer of 2015 I signed a contract to extend my services through December 2016. Surely that should do it. I love my work, but getting up at 4:30 a.m. is getting to be more and more a challenge. I am entering the final scene of the final act of my career. My desire is to transition smoothly into retirement in 2017, avoiding any major problems clinically or otherwise. In addition I am asking myself how will I be remembered as a physician? What will be my legacy? How can I make sense of a career full of unexpected twists and turns? What was my underlying guiding principle for each major decision? Was I too naïve and gullible? Or was I too self-righteous and condescending? If I could start all over again, what would I do differently? Was I so busy dealing with the trees that I forgot I was in a forest?

As the end was drawing nigh, I was searching for peace of mind. I wanted to put my career in perspective with the rest of my life. I wanted to put my life in perspective with my community. I was looking for closure.

Closure

As it turned out, the Huntersville assignment was a nice way to spend the last few years of my career. Slower paced and a good bit smaller than the Gateway Surgery Center in Concord, there I was able to provide a useful service for my group without obtaining the normal high level of stress. The only significant disadvantage was the location; a twenty-five minute drive in the morning, sometimes more in the afternoon. But I got used to it quickly.

Since it became my primary home for over two years, it deserves a brief description. The surgery center itself was on the ground floor of a four-story medical building containing multiple doctors' offices, a pain clinic, an endoscopy suite, an emergency department, a pharmacy and a radiology department. The surgery suite itself consisted of four good sized operating rooms arranged circumferentially around a central supply room. The most common cases were cataracts, ENT, dental, OB GYN, general surgery and urology cases. Occasionally we would do an orthopedic case requiring a nerve block. Typically we ran only two rooms and did five to ten cases except on cataract day which added ten to fifteen cases. I was the only anesthesiologist present; so if we had a difficult intubation or a resistant IV start, there was no back up help. With over thirty-seven years experience, nothing about this exceeded my comfort zone.

Guidelines had been established to limit surgery complexity and patient risk. For example, patients with BMIs greater than forty were not permitted as a rule to be done there. I was comfortable with occasionally bending that rule for select cases. The nurses were excellent in their pre and post-operative care. RNs pre-screened patients over the phone. Naturally I consulted with them during this process.

The surgery center made a meager profit on its operations. Its primary function was to capture market share in the Huntersville-Birkdale area for the CHS system instead of its competitors. The patient demographics were favorable (patients were well-insured) and the area was in the middle of a population explosion.

On the one hand the work demands at Huntersville rarely tested my limits. I sometimes itched for a bigger challenge. On the other hand I felt fortunate to have a position without call; it wasn't guaranteed by my original contract. Overall, I viewed it in a positive light. In a sense it served as a slowing mechanism for exiting a train at full-throttle. I would ride the train at a reduced speed before jumping off. It was perfectly suited for the end of a career.

This allowed more time and energy for other activities. I continued my twice weekly Nautilus workouts at the Sportscenter interspersed with swimming laps and occasional elliptical workouts. I felt fortunate that I could still run three miles on the weekend, if somewhat slower, as I had been doing for years. Picking up my guitar in the evening remained an important part of my stress relief. Even if mediocre in quality, the resonance of a classic Gordon Lightfoot or Jim Croce ballad from my Martin was the best salve for the soul I knew of. In August my friend Gerry Dionne took my guitar to luthier Carl McIntyre in Charlotte to adjust the bridge and the bridge saddle to lower the action slightly. This subtle change improved the playability dramatically. Funny how little things can make a big difference.

But most importantly I could now view my career in hindsight more objectively. My missteps now stood out in sharp relief. I had failed to go with the flow at times. I didn't always defer to those in power. I wasn't a rabble rouser by nature, but I might justifiably be labeled a contrarian at times. Even so, if mistakes are the condiment that give success its flavor, I knew that my career had been well-seasoned. But was there an underlying logic to my mistakes, or was I like a blind rat in a maze randomly running into walls in search of the cheese?

The death of my father in October 1988 at age sixty-four was quickly followed by the implosion of Cabarrus Anesthesiologist PA and the failure of my marriage to Heidi. We all viewed my father's death as tragic due to the missed diagnosis of cancer and his relative youth. Now that I was several years older than he was at the time of his death, his misfortune looms even larger in my consciousness. Compounding this humiliation was a series of personal and political challenges that diverted my time and energy. I didn't have the time and desire to ruminate on the tragedy; rather I duly noted the events and stored them in my memory bank in a file labeled "open at your own risk." Perhaps it was time to revisit that file.

Reviewing the events of my father's life illustrates the serendipity of our family's fortune. If not for World War II and the Manhattan Project he would most likely have remained in New York. Instead, he left Brooklyn for good in 1944. A tentative move from Oak Ridge northward to Ithaca in 1946 to accept a teaching position at Cornell was thwarted by a fire which burned down the graduate student housing. After a brief stent with the Glenn L. Martin Company in Baltimore working on guided missile development, he returned to Oak Ridge in 1947 when Eastman Kodak offered a research position with his former colleagues. Thus our family was destined to develop Southern roots.

In my early years I viewed my father's career and accomplishments with unfettered admiration and envy. Unsure exactly what a nuclear physicist did, by all accounts it was a noble profession garnering respect from all. He was an unimpeachable source of wisdom and authority. Perhaps he had always been so.

Without diminishing my respect or admiration, I can now see him in a new light. He was a young man with only a BS in math and physics competing in the world of nuclear physics. At times he must have been frustrated. In the 1970s he took a stand against the AEC on safety issues in the face of harsh criticism. He did what he thought was right. Beyond doubt he was occasionally uncertain and insecure. Aren't we all? True courage is facing one's fear, and punching through without dwelling on it.

Such a shift in thinking about one's parents is surely more common as we reach old age ourselves. We want to understand how our parents handled their struggle for success, even as we struggle ourselves and even as we prepare our children and grandchildren to do the same. We try to visualize what it was like to be in their shoes.

In my case, the visualization process was hampered by one glaring deficiency. In my memory bank under the heading "fond memories of grandparent's and parent's childhood home" there is a nearly blank slate. This is primarily because all four of my grandparents were deceased by the time I turned four. Distance also guaranteed that I would have only the vaguest memory of my paternal grandfather. His home on 209 Greene Avenue in Brooklyn, where my father lived as a child did not stay in the family. I have no recollection of the home itself.

When I was very young we traveled through Brooklyn several times on the way to visit my aunt Angie Foster in Baldwin, Long Island. She was the much younger sister of my father's deceased mother, Helen. As an adult I have travelled at least a half dozen times through Brooklyn on the way to Manhattan from La Guardia. The landscape was a tedium of row houses, factories, non-descript retailors, restaurants and hotels. But the lackluster scenery belies a vibrant culturally diverse metropolitan area with a rich history. Founded in the 1640s by the Dutch, it took its name from Breuckelen in Holland. When the English prevailed twenty years later, New Amsterdam became New York and Breuckelen was anglicized to Brooklyn. The historic Battle of Brooklyn, a.k.a., the Battle of Long Island, in August 1776 was the first major clash of the Revolutionary War and also the bloodiest. Had Washington failed to withdraw his troops over the East River in a timely manner, our losses may have been unsurmountable. The Civil War gunboat *U.S.S. Monitor* was built in Brooklyn, and Brooklyn Navy yard made such famous ships as *U.S.S. Maine, U.S.S. Missouri and U.S.S. North Carolina.* In World War II the shipyard employed seventy thousand workers. Today it is the new home to 230 or so small businesses.

My interest in Brooklyn, however, was focused on more mundane and contemporary issues. Why was it making a comeback as a desirable place to live and work? What was it like to attend school there as a child? What is so good about its pizza? Why do many people from Brooklyn still ardently follow the Dodgers years after they defected to Los Angeles? To answer these questions and to view my father's childhood home at 209 Greene Avenue, I would need to personally visit the area.

So I proposed a trip for Becky and myself. Why not visit New York in September (2015) when I had a few days off? In addition to visiting Brooklyn we could see a couple plays and visit the Neue Gallery to view the newly acquired painting by Gustav Klimpt, Adele Bloch-Bauer. Becky was almost as excited as I was.

I got reservations at the historic Warwick Hotel on 54th Street and tickets on-line for *"Hamilton"* and *"The King and I"*. I made reservations for a flight with an ETA of 2:51 p.m. at LaGuardia on Thursday. The play started at seven. The theory was to allow plenty of time to transition from airport to hotel and dinner before the play without undue pressure to rush. But the reality was something else. Our plane landed at LaGuardia three hours late due to bad weather. We still had hopes of checking into our hotel and then going directly to the theater on 46th Street. We could always grab a bite later in the evening. But our cabdriver dashed all hopes of carrying out this plan. Communicating through a combination of broken English, frantic hand signs and pig-Latin, I tried to ask him why we were now on 97th Street if our hotel was on 54th. It seemed we had gone forty-three blocks too far north. I'm not sure but I think he tried to blame it on road construction.

Driving slowly south on Fifth Avenue we encountered horrific traffic. It was now clear we didn't have time to check into the hotel before the play. So we instructed the driver to take us straight to the Richard Rodgers Theatre on 46th. However, traffic on Sixth Avenue was no better. Somewhere around 50th Street we elected to exit the cab and walk the last four blocks; it was that bad. It was like a scene from the film, "*Out of Towners.*" Pulling our suitcases through puddles and over curbs in a steady rain we made it to the play at 7:25 p.m. Our first meal in New York was a "gourmet" McDonalds hamburger at eleven p.m. Thus an evening well planned in theory was quite different in reality. Sometimes reality sucks, and you may quote me on that.

Despite a rocky start, we kept an optimistic attitude. The play was actually a well-done parody on the life of Alexander Hamilton done in rap style. Our getting-to-the-theatre trial by fire sort of put a humorous spin on the adventure. Besides, Friday promised to be a better day. The rain had stopped. After a pleasant breakfast at Angelo's on Sixth Avenue we explored the 59th Street, Fifth Avenue area. A quick walk through the Plaza Hotel where we had once stayed years ago brought back fond memories. This was followed by some casual shopping and a nice stroll through Central Park.

Early afternoon found us at the Neue Gallery to see the Gustav Klimt painting of Adele Block Bauer (The Woman in Gold) which had been confiscated by the Nazis shortly before World War II. Only after a lengthy legal battle was it returned to its rightful owners in 2006. That evening we enjoyed an outstanding meal at Estiatorio Milos, a Greek seafood restaurant on 55th Street which had been recommended by Scott Aumuller. But Saturday would be the big day; that's when we would visit my father's childhood home in Brooklyn.

After a quick breakfast at Dunkin' Donuts on 7th Avenue Saturday morning, we caught the metro at 53rd and 7th Avenue and got off at the last stop, the 1 WTC. We had last been at this site in December 2001, shortly after 9-11. At that time the mood was one of darkness and grief. Now the majestic Freedom Tower heroically rising 1,776 feet above the concrete at street level helped create a new atmosphere. It is difficult to view the mammoth octagonal structure of shining glass and steel dominating the skyline without garnering a feeling of pride and hope for our country's future. At the same time the somber memorial pools paid homage to the victims of its recent past. I was glad Becky and I included this tribute in our itinerary, but it was almost too much to grasp in a meaningful way. Instead of standing in line to ride the elevators to the top, we elected to move on to our next mission.

We hailed a taxi on West Street and informed the driver of our destination; 209 Greene Avenue. Meandering through lower Manhattan we passed the Old Town Hall (1812) and then crossed over the Brooklyn Bridge to enter New York's most populous borough. We turned onto Flatbush Avenue and briefly onto Fulton Street before finally turning onto Greene Avenue. When the driver stopped in the 200 block area we paid him and exited the car to explore my father's childhood home and neighborhood in Brooklyn.

There was nothing remarkable or startling about the area at first glance. The row houses were four story homes built in the late 1800s with light brown or grey bricks. Many of them showed signs of wear and deterioration of the window frames and doorways, but the overall buildings and roofs seemed to be in surprisingly good shape. The area was multicultural with whites, black, Hispanics and Asians all well represented. Dispersed throughout the block were small shops and restaurants and occasionally public schools. The Brooklyn Technical High School my father attended at age twelve was five or six blocks away by Fort Green Park.

We found the house number 209. I had Becky take several photos of me standing in front for the record. As described by my father in his biography the house was twenty feet wide and almost fifty feet deep. In addition to the four stories there was a full basement. All three upper floors had a full bath and two or three bedrooms. The kitchen and dining room were on the first floor. The main living area was on the second floor.

More difficult to describe was the mystical aura and emotional spell the surroundings induced. I had never seen this neighborhood before except as a small baby. But a distinct déjà vu feeling was undeniable. As a child we sang "Sidewalks of New York" in grammar school. It conjured up thoughts of my father's childhood. Perhaps I was just reconnecting with those feelings. Or perhaps my impressions as a baby somehow were etched in some remote corner of my brain waiting for the right stimuli to elicit the latent images.

I couldn't help but contrast these images with those of my own childhood home on Admiral Drive in Concord, Tennessee. To the north Admiral Drive slowly ascended a long hill to Sonja Drive which ran along the top of the ridge where many childhood friends lived. To the south the road ran down a short hill, crossed over Turkey Creek with a small wooden bridge and then rose again to meet Highway 11-70, also known as Kingston Pike. In between our house and the creek were pastures sometimes leased out to grow soy beans and other times for our three cows or my sister's horse.

So I was glad we visited the old Brooklyn neighborhood. I think it would make my father glad to know we did so. But it seemed to be missing something. Maybe a small plaque that said "Childhood home of William Barber Cottrell 1924-1988. Director of Nuclear Safety ORNL (Oak Ridge National Laboratory) 1959-1984." Nothing fancy; just a small bronze plaque would do.

Viewing my father's childhood home filled a void in my memory bank and helped me expunge the repressed angst that had been held captive these last twenty-seven years since his death. It seemed as if I was looking down from a perch where I could see his life in toto. But what did his brief life mean? What wisdom could I garner from this unique perspective?

In a nutshell he lived an uncomplicated life motivated by challenges of his career, the needs of his family and service to his church and community. If not for his excellent autobiography describing his run-in with the AEC on safety issues, I would not have known the details of this confrontation. But even without the specifics, I could sense he was a man of integrity and principles. Did I somehow inherit some of these traits? Or did I witness behavior patterns and subconsciously integrate them into my neuronal control center? Would my father's life help explain how I reacted and dealt with the numerous political and personal challenges in my career? I am unable to make that call. But I would be delighted if someone thought so.

Around 11:30 a.m. we ambled down Greene Avenue back toward Fulton and then Flatbush Avenue. Our destination: "Junior's", a famous Brooklyn deli-restaurant known for their cheesecake. I ordered a simple tuna melt and Becky a bowl of pea soup. But soon our table was loaded with bread, slaw, beets and other sides. The strawberry cheesecake was to die for. I am a lover of Southern cooking and soul food, Cracker Barrel and comfort food. Junior's has them all beat. This Brooklyn thing has a lot going on.

Saturday evening we opted to try Felidia's, a boutique Italian restaurant on 58th Street that Gerry had recommended. We weren't disappointed. The atmosphere and service exuded old world style and charm, and the whole affair from the Suave Classico to the *torta di carote* would have pleased even the most demanding epicure. We weren't surprised when we later learned that the head chef, Lidia Bastianich, was selected to prepare food for Pope Francis on his recent New York visit.

From 58th Street we took a cab to the Lincoln Center where we had tickets for "*The King and I*". Seeing this revival classic in the Beaumont Theatre was a double treat. So we finished off our New York trip in style. We couldn't have done any better.

Our return flight home to Charlotte was much better than the original leg to LaGuardia. Actually it was just the opposite. Instead of being three hours late; we arrived sufficiently early to catch the one p.m. rather than the originally planned 3 p.m. flight. Thus three hours late on the initial flight, and two hours early on the return journey. It didn't totally compensate for our initial tribulations. But it was certainly better than piling on.

Nothing brings reality home like a 4:35 a.m. alarm on a Monday morning; especially cruel after a brief vacation. I mechanically nuked my Eggo, blueberries and syrup, slurped down some coffee and cranked my Honda CRV at 5:20 a.m. to begin my twenty-five minute drive to Huntersville. Once I enter the doors I transition into work mode. Very little phases me. It's almost like I never left.

But the New York-Brooklyn trip had been worthwhile. It helped me bring closure to the repressed feelings of my father's premature death. It helped me appreciate his life and career. It also helped me find clarity and purpose in my own profession. No specific or concrete answers, but a feeling that my mistakes were not random, but had an underlying logic; and when it all ended, I could retire with a sense of satisfaction.

Speaking of retirement, my professional corporation, NAPS, had planned a party the very next Sunday after our trip. It was to be an all-purpose retirement party for both myself and Scott Aumuller, and also to honor Wes Hudson as he became a full partner after three years of service. The event was hosted at the gorgeous home of my partner, Sara Arnold, and her husband Dennis. After a brief swim and a nice meal of grilled hamburgers and sides, Bill Goglin presented Scott and I with retirement gifts. My gift was a package of ten golf lessons with the pro at the Cabarrus Country Club. Finally I would get technical support where I really needed it. It was certainly appreciated.

Nevertheless, Scott and I had both signed up to work through 2016; so full retirement was still an illusion. But the party was telling. It officially stamped Scott and I as "has beens," as if that designation was not already obvious. I had described myself to nurses as the "Ghost of Christmas Past" and as an "ol' timey" doctor for some time. They seemed to enjoy that. But I was still actively practicing with the young bloods. The trick was to profit from everything you saw in your rear-view mirror, without taking your eyes off the road ahead. I was fortunate the years had been kind to me, but I was fondly anticipating the closure of my career in an orderly step wise manner.

Around this time, the CHS system, including our small Huntersville facility, was blessed by a visit from JCAHO, also known as the "Joint Commission." This commission, founded in 1951 by a merger of committees from the American College of Surgeons, the American College of Physicians, The American Medical Association, the Canadian Medical Association and the American Hospital Association is the primary entity that accredits health care facilities, usually on a three year cycle. I had met with this agency many times in the past; three times with Dr. Swan as the Associate Director of Anesthesia and twice as the Director of Anesthesia in the early 90s. The trick was to anticipate what aspect of patient care they would be inspecting and be prepared to tell them what they wanted to hear.

I didn't worry much about these inspections anymore; I wasn't a director. Unfortunately, I was the only anesthesiologist available for the Huntersville Surgery Center when questions arose about our preoperative evaluations. I succinctly explained our system to the inspectors. Everyone seemed pleased with my answers. I was glad to help out. Later, however, I discovered that I was the cause of a minor demerit. Why? I had a face mask tied around my neck and dangling in front of me when I spoke with the committee. This is a broach of protocol. Face mask should be discarded after every case and a new one adorned when re-entering the OR. My bad. Despite this we scored well overall. I am happy this was my last JCAHO encounter.

The next item on my fall agenda following the JCAHO visit was a little more pleasant, my annual fall golf outing with my younger brother, Steve. Since his birthday was October 1, the contrived explanation for spouses was a birthday gift (green fees) for a brother. In addition it allowed an early peek at the fall colors. This year we would be joined by Steve's son, Lee, and our middle brother Scott. I got a T Time for four Cottrells at 9:30 a.m. on Saturday October 3 at the Gatlinburg course. I decided to come up a couple days early to enjoy the peace and tranquility of early fall in the Smokys.

It rained off and on all day Thursday and Thursday night. Friday was no better. This cast grave doubts on the fulfillment of our golfing plans. The problem was Tropical Storm Joaquin which was stalled over the Bahamas. We needed rain, but when would it stop?

Out of this dilemma a new plan was spawned. My cabin was about-ten minute drive from Gatlinburg, twenty minutes from Pigeon Forge and thirty minutes from Sevierville. Right outside of Sevierville on Chapman Highway the building where EMCO Williams had been was still standing. It was the synthetic marble factory where I had worked the summer of 1971 before entering medical school. Though the factory had long since relocated, I decided to visit the old site to reminisce about that summer.

After driving thirty minutes in the rain, I pulled into the parking lot of the building. After their business relocated years ago, it had housed a candle factory for about ten years. Now the sign read "Barkers Lounge." I watched as a six-year-old girl and her dad entered the front door ahead of me with a beautiful golden retriever. It was a dog motel. The business owner explained to me that she merely leased the building as had the previous occupants. She well remembered the marble factory which had relocated to Old Knoxville Highway. I was allowed to stroll the grounds and look around. I discovered the place where we used to mix the resin and the limestone in a large vat, and the door leading outside where we used to take our morning breaks. That was good enough for me. I took several pictures and then got back in my car to return to the cabin. This was not an earth-shattering adventure, but it unleashed a cascade of memories and feelings regarding my early years.

Doing hard manual labor for two dollars an hour right before medical school was both humbling and enlightening. It helped me appreciate what a major segment of our population must do to survive. It also provided a baseline barometer by which all future employment could be contrasted. By that standard even my $12,000 annual salary as a resident was generous.

Medical school had been quite a struggle for me initially, but eventually it got easier. It is curious to note how I drifted toward the specialty of anesthesia. My summer activities consisted of a job with the Blood Mobile of the American Red Cross '72, an ASA preceptorship in Birmingham Alabama '73, and a civilian clerkship with the army at Walter Reed '74. These jobs provided the ideal background for someone pursuing a career in anesthesiology. But I didn't actively seek out these particular jobs. They were left on my doorstep. It seems to me that the specialty chose me rather than vice versa. Was I subconsciously programmed to make these choices, or was it all just a series of improbable coincidences?

The excellent residency program at the University of Florida placed a strong emphasis on research and academic endeavors. Perhaps a more service-oriented, clinically-focused program would have made my transition to private practice smoother. But my residency program instilled in me a passion to understand the body's cardiovascular and respiratory physiology; this ultimately made me a better doctor. In addition, the experience in Gainesville also provided me with a wife and ultimately three healthy children.

Choosing Concord, North Carolina, for private practice over the other possibilities was obviously a critical decision. But it seemed to be pre-ordained. Both Bill Swan and I had grown up in Concord, Tennessee. How could I resist? Of course the hospital and community were both very desirable in their own right.

The early days of practice were idealistic and nostalgic. A time to finally put years of schooling and training to a practical use. A time to take a stand and find a niche in the community. A time to have babies and relive your childhood. It was a time for your professional career and personal life to thrive synergistically. It was a time for life in all its glories. And it was a time for promises of greater things yet to come.

For a while it seemed the 1980s would fulfill most of its promises. All three children were healthy, if not thriving. Heidi found some fulfillment teaching aerobics at the Sportscenter and riding her horse

"Missy" in addition to raising the children. My career seemed to be flourishing. Who can forget such dear patients as Mrs. Hockenberry and others. My plate was full.

Why then did things fall apart in the late eighties? When Dr. Swan retired abruptly in the spring of 1989, I inherited a well-run low cost anesthesia department. But it was somewhat behind many progressive departments in its scope of services. It was due an overhaul. This alone was a mammoth undertaking. And yet, at the same time I had accepted responsibility for coordinating the Medical Examiner (ME) schedule for Cabarrus County, serving as program chairman and then president of the Cabarrus County Medical Society and serving as chairman of the finance committee for Central United Methodist Church. My plate was more than full. Something had to give. Unfortunately it was my marriage.

At forty years old this was arguably the low point of my life. This domestic instability was certainly a hardship on my children. They lost the immediate companionship of a doting father. Perhaps they gained a role model of honor and perseverance. I can only hope so.

Ever optimistic I helped build a new department with all new physicians based on the practice of supervising CRNAs. Services expanded and the department grew steadily if not precipitously. My marriage to Becky in 1993 augmented this optimism and helped me re-invent my image and lifestyle. She helped provide a strong foundation on which to rebuild my life.

Nevertheless, instability and dysfunction, both inside and outside the department threatened the existence of our new anesthesia group by the mid-nineties. Whether due to my inexperience and innocence or to the aggressive actions of a lame duck administration is unanswerable. But things happen for a reason. So in 1997 we embraced our new group and watched in amazement as rapid growth continued under the leadership of Bill Goglin.

The late nineties is remembered as a time when all aspects of my life seemed to be flourishing: professionally, personally and financially, much like the mid-eighties. Nothing but blue skies from now on. How could we have known the new millennium would bring such sinister weather? The collapse of the tech bubble in 2000 not only zapped our retirement plans, but also our trust and confidence in the financial system. The 9-11 attacks wounded our pride and sense of security. Billy's problems which began in 2003 were very humbling and draining in many ways. If humility is good for the soul, mine must have been in hog heaven by 2004. Note to self: maybe try not to ride so high next time.

But we picked up the pieces collectively and individually and resolved to rebuild our future on solid ground. We slowly regained confidence and optimism. Even the collapse of the housing bubble couldn't stop us now. By 2010 I had much to look forward to; Billy's release from federal prison in 2011, cessation of call in 2012, the collective success of all my children and eventually retirement.

At the same time I enjoyed moderate success, I began to look for explanations and understanding for the paths I had chosen both personally and professionally. I found some clues by reviewing documents and correspondence with the hospital administration in the eighties and nineties. I also gained some insight by reviewing my father's autobiography and eventually visiting his childhood home in Brooklyn. There seemed to be some general parallels in our career challenges. Finding complete closure on one's life and career is an elusive goal. But at times I felt I was getting warm.

It was now 9 a.m. Saturday morning October 3 when Steve called me. It was still raining. In lieu of golf we decided to meet at the Mountain Lodge Restaurant on 321 right outside of Gatlinburg for a leisurely breakfast. He had been retired from the public school system several years now and was working part time for Uber. It was nice to catch up on family news about our siblings and extended family. All our children were currently in a good place. But we both had experience with a child who had strayed from the beaten path. They had to find a way on their own.

I am generally an advocate for taking the easiest path possible. Unfortunately, the easiest paths don't always lead to the highest summits. It is much more complicated than that. God bless all those who struggle off the beaten path; help them find their way. There is redemption for all those who struggle, but the payments come in unpredictable installments.

I paid the restaurant bill, my brother's birthday gift, and then backed my Honda out of the gravel parking lot and then headed east on 321 toward my cabin in Pittman Center. The rain showed no signs of stopping. The mountains were beautiful nevertheless; patches of red and yellow from dogwoods and maples on the mountainside promised an abundant expanse of brilliant colors would soon put on a dazzling show. It occurred to me that I was at peace with the world. Revisiting my father's life and death had helped me understand my own journey through this world. I can appreciate and admire how he dealt with adversity in his life and in his career. Now I wonder –what would he think about mine?

Epilogue

Reviewing my career of 38 years in medicine by writing my memoirs has been both a rewarding and humbling endeavor. I can see now, more than ever, that I was blessed to work with outstanding surgeons, anesthesiologist and other physicians and that I took for granted that advantage most of the time. Though a common shortcoming among professionals, it is a deplorable one none the less. I do not claim that all my decisions and actions were flawless or without controversy, but merely that they were made at the time according to my best judgment and with the ultimate goal of optimizing patient outcome. Undoubtedly I was not always the most user friendly colleague nor was I the most skilled negotiator, although I believe I improved somewhat in both categories as the years rolled by. My goal in writing my memoirs has been to illustrate the concerns that influenced me as a practicing anesthesiologist and to gain empathy for what it felt like to be in the midst of a busy and challenging practice. In no way am I judgmental of, or feel ill will toward those with whom I had disagreements; on the contrary I hold them in high esteem. Likewise I have found great satisfaction in serving and interacting with the citizens of Cabarrus and surrounding counties. Through them I have learned much about perseverance, self-reliance and personal integrity. My hope is that as a physician I met their expectations as a professional and that our relationships were mutually beneficial. In the final analysis, that is how I believe my medical career should be appraised.

Selected Bibliography

—∞∞∞—

BOOKS

Atwood,Tony. The Complete Guide to Asperger's Syndrome. London: Jessica Kingsley Publishers, 2007.

Chestnut, David H. Obstetric Anesthesia—Principles and Practice, Second Edition. St. Louis, Missouri : Mosby, Inc., 1999.

Collins, Vincent J. Principles of Anesthesia, Second Edition. London : Henry Kimpton Publishers, 1976.

Cottrell, James E. Anesthesia and Neurosurgery, Second Edition. St. Louis Missouri: C.V. Mosby Company, 1986.

Cottrell, Jeanette and William B. An American Family in the Twentieth Century. Self-Published, 1987.

Pendergast, Mark. Uncommon Grounds. New York : Basic Books, 1999.

Sykes, Keith. Anesthesia and the Practice of Medicine: Historical Perspectives. London: Holder and Stoughton Ltd, 2011.

Vanderburg, Timothy W. Cannon Mills and Kannapolis. Knoxville, Tennessee: The University Of Tennessee Press, 2013.

Zeitlin, Gerald. Laughing and Crying About Anesthesia: A Memoir of Risk and Safety. London, Allendale Publishers, 2011.

ARTICLES

Applebome, Peter. "Milltown Pensioners Pay for Wall Street Sins." *The New York Times* (July 30, 1991).

Avidan, Micheal S. "Anesthesia Awareness and Bispectral Index." *New England Journal of Medicine* (March 13, 2008).

Beecher, Henry K. "Study of the Death Associated with Anesthesia and Surgery: Based on a study of 599,548 Anesthetics in Ten Institutions 1948-1952 Inclusive." *Annals of Surgery* (July, 1954).

Cooper, Jeffry B. "Preventable Anesthesia Mishaps: A Study of Human Factors." *Anesthesiology* (December, 1978).

Dail, W. Clarence. "Glossopharyngeal Breathing by Paralyzed Patients." *California Medicine* (September 1951).

Devereaux, PJ. "Effects of Extended-release metoprolol succinate in patients undergoing non-cadiac surgery (POISE trail): a randomised controlled trial." *Lancet* (May 31, 2008).

Mclean, J. Duncan. "Dose-dependent Association between Intermediate-acting Neuromuscular-blocking Agents and Postoperative Respiratory Complications." *Anesthesiology* (June, 2015).

Mendelson, Curtis L. "The Aspiration of Stomach Contents into the Lungs During Obstetric Anesthesia." *Anesthesia Journal of Obstetrics and Gynecology* (August 1946).

Rimer, Sara. "Desparate Measures—A Special Report. Embattled Parents Seek Help at Any Cost." *The New York Times* (September 10, 2001).

Smith-Arrant, Gail. "NORTHEAST STAFF CHIEF IS LEAVING IN LETTER, DR. THOMAS TRAHEY CITES HIS LACK OF CONFIDENCE IN THE HOSPITAL'S VISION FOR FUTURE. CEOS TRY TO CALM STAFF CONCERNS OVER PENDING MERGER WITH CAROLINAS HEALTHCARE SYSTEM." *The Charlotte Observer, Cabarrus Neighbors* (March 8, 2007).

Stoelting, Robert K. "About APSF, APSF-Foundation History." www.apsf.org (website) (September 2010).

Bio

William Cottrell is an anesthesiologist who has been in private practice over 38 years in Concord, North Carolina. He has served in various capacities including president of Cabarrus County Medical Society, Chairman of the Department of Anesthesia and as a medical examiner for Cabarrus County. His medical practice is complimented by a love of writing, acoustic guitar, golf, community and family including five grandchildren.

Cottrell grew up in the area of Knoxville, Tennessee. He graduated from the University of Tennessee in 1971 with a B.S. in Chemistry with high honors. He received his MD degree at Emory in Atlanta, Georgia where he also served as student representative to the Southern Medical Association annual convention in 1973. He completed his residency in anesthesia at the University of Florida Teaching Hospitals in Gainesville, Florida in 1978.

71639877R10171

Made in the USA
Columbia, SC
01 June 2017